Life Is Always Smiling:
Stories from My Life

by Chen, Hui Xian

D1531370

This book is dedicated to all the lives
that I have touched
and to all the lives that have touched me.
But, most especially, my sincere thanks
goes to my dear grandparents
and my parents
who brought me forth
into this family of kindness.

Life Is Always Smiling: Stories from My Life
Copyright © 2014 by Chen, Hui Xian
Paperback Edition
Illustrated with Photographs. All Rights Reserved.
Front cover photograph by Chen, Yi
Back cover photograph by Phyllis Lefohn
* * *
Paperback design by Jim Sluga

Chen, Hui Xian's Family

It is a Chinese tradition to have a family's last name appear first. It is also a tradition that when all the brothers and sisters of the same family are given a two-character first name, they all share the first or second character of that first name. Our shared second character name, Xian, means "contribution". My father and mother wanted each of us to grow up to be an honorable person. To that end they gave us first-character names to inspire us. I've always said I am one of seventeen children. Actually, I am one of eleven. Some babies died in the womb and some died as infants.

Here is my family:

Father	Chen, Shao En	b. 10-26-1889
Mother	Lin, Guo Rui	b. 7-23-1894
Oldest Brother	Chen, Cheng (honesty) Xian	b. 9-08-1916
Second Brother	Chen, De (morality) Xian	b. 12-17-1917
Third Sister	Chen, Ai (love) Xian	b. 12-21-1919
Fourth Sister	Chen Yi (loyalty) Xian	b. 2-27-1921
Fifth Brother	Chen, Gong (respect) Xian	b. 5-07-1927
Sixth Sister	Chen, Mao (prosperity) Xian	b. 5-07-1928
Seventh Sister	Chen, Min (smartness) Xian	b. 5-06-1930
Little Brother	Chen, Yao (brightness) Xian	b. 8-9-1932
		d. 12-10-1941
Myself	Chen, Hui (wisdom) Xian	b. 8-01-1933
Ninth Brother	Chen, Gao (happiness) Xian	b. 8-16-1934
Tenth Brother	Chen, Kai (generosity) Xian	b. 10-17-1935

Map of Chen's China

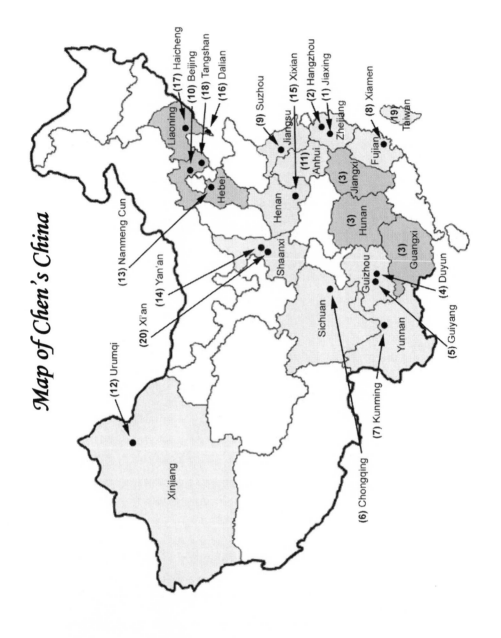

(17) Haicheng
(10) Beijing
(18) Tangshan
(16) Dalian
(9) Suzhou
(15) Xixian
(2) Hangzhou
(1) Jiaxing
(8) Xiamen
(19) Taiwan

Liaoning
Jiangsu
Anhui
(11)
Zhejiang
Fujian
Jiangxi
(3)
Hebei
Henan
Hunan
(3)
Guangxi
(3)
Guizhou
Duyun
(4)
Shaanxi
Guiyang
(5)
(13) Nanmeng Cun
(14) Yan'an
Sichuan
Yunnan
(20) Xi'an
Kunming
(7)
(12) Urumqi
Xinjiang
(6) Chongqing

iv

Legend for the Map of Chen's China

(1) Jiaxing, Zhejing Province – My birthplace and my home town

(2) Hangzhou, Zhejing Province – Where my family and hospital staff went when Jiaxing was threatened by the Japanese aggression

(3) Jiangxi Province, Hunan Province, Guangxi Province – My family was on the run as refugees through these provinces during the Anti-Japanese War.

(4) Duyun, Guizhou Province – Where my family settled in 1940

(5) Guiyang, Guizhou Province – Where Cheng Xian, De Xian, and Ai Xian studied Western medicine

(6) Chongqing – Alternate capital of China during the Anti-Japanese War and where I lived for a year

(7) Kunming, Yunnan Province – I lived there for a year.

(8) Xiamen, Fujian Provence – The front where Qian, Jiang was sent

(9) Suzhou, Jiangsu Province – I joined the revolution there.

(10) Beijing – The capital of China where I received my college education and worked as a translator and a teacher for many years

(11) Anhui Province – Xia, Kai Zhen our nanny was from there.

(12) Urumqi, Xinjiang – The marching girl I met at Tien An Men Square was from there.

(13) Nanmeng Cun, Hebei Province – I was sent there to remold my ideology after the Anti-Rightest Campaign.

(14) Yan'an, Shaanxi Province – The revolutionary base where I paid a visit during the cultural Revolution

(15) Xixian, Henan Province – Location of May 7th School

(16) Dalian, Liaoning Province – I was transferred there to work at the Liaoning Institute of Finance and Economics.

(17) Haicheng, Liaoning Province – Location of first earthquake on February 4, 1975

(18) Tangshan, Hebei Province – Location of second earthquake in July, 1976

(19) Taiwan – My fourth sister lives there.

(20) Xi'an, Shaanxi Province – Capital that served many dynasties throughout Chinese history

v

Table of Contents
Stories from My Life
Part I

Stories from My Life
Part I continued

Stories from My Life
Part II

Stories from My Life
Part II continued

A Poem

A human being is a part of a whole,
called by us the universe,
a part limited in time and space.
He experiences himself,
his thoughts and feelings,
as something separated from the rest—
a kind of optical delusion of his consciousness.
This delusion is a kind of prison for us,
restricting us to our personal desires
and to affection for a few persons nearest us.
Our task must be to free ourselves from this prison
by widening our circles of compassion
to embrace all living creatures
and the whole of nature in its beauty.

—*Albert Einstein*

Part I

My Parents Realize a Dream and Start a Family

My father Chen, Shao En, was a surgeon who dreamed of owning a hospital. His reputation was well-known due to his great skill and profound knowledge of medicine. He was even more cherished because of his beautiful heart and his selfless spirit of service.

Following Chinese tradition, a marriage was arranged for him to my mother, Lin, Guo Rui, a graduate from a normal school in Hangzhou.

My Parents (1944)

Soon after their wedding he sent his bride to study medicine in Shangyu with the hope that they could enjoy a working partnership and create ideal careers together. My mother was a very smart and gifted woman. Four years later when she graduated from medical school as a gynecologist, my parents both found jobs at a western hospital run by Americans.

My mother had been born into a very wealthy landlord's family. When she reached the age of seven, her family forced her to have her small feet bound. There was an old Chinese saying, "A pair of small feet, a jar of tears." It implied the enormous pain a girl had to suffer when her feet were bound for her toes were turned under in the bindings. This made the bones break which resulted in 3-4" long feet, which made movement very limited. Culturally, the small feet were considered beautiful. In fact, it was said that no man would marry a "big-footed" woman.

After her feet were bound she found the pain to be unbearable, so my mother climbed out of her bedroom window one evening. Crawling to a church nearby, she knocked at the door of the American priest with whom her mother was familiar. She cried bitterly and begged him to help her, "Priest, please tell my mom to set my feet free. They hurt so much I can't stand it." The foreign priest knew about the cruelty of this vile feudal practice. Of course, he was willing to help with such a personal appeal from the suffering little girl. He took her back home and kindly talked to her mother, reasoning with her to spare the girl. She obeyed and unbound her daughter's feet. Upon first hearing this story, I could not help but admire my mother's courage and intelligence.

During those days in China, it was uncommon for a woman to have such a fulfilling career. She was a rarity, as she loved her work. My mother was also a very fertile woman. She gave birth to fourteen children and had three miscarriages, yet never took time off work during her pregnancies. With so many births, she only breastfed her second son and provided a wet nurse for the other babies' nourishment. At the birth of each child, a nanny was also brought on to care for it, so we often had many people living at our home.

As there was only one hospital owned by Americans in Jiaxing, my parents wanted to build a hospital of their own to meet the needs of the local people. After saving money over several years, their wish came true. In 1932, my parents established their own hospital, the "Jiaxing Trinity Hospital" in Jiaxing of Zhejiang province. They also opened a nursing school, which was attached to the hospital. Their successful treatment of the ill and the enthusiasm shown to the hospital patients by all the doctors and nurses led to a thriving business. Like my father, my mother had an angelic heart and was always ready when help was needed. Sometimes, though, she was too softhearted and people took advantage of her. That said, the beautiful hearts of both my parents were bound together in a meaningful life. Guided by greatness, they did so much for so many people. As far back as I can remember, they were always working, working, working.

My father did not limit himself to one area of expertise; his interests varied from music to literature to religion, and even to sports. Every Saturday evening, my father, mother or older brothers would lead Bible study in the auditorium of the hospital. More and more people joined the group including doctors, nurses, in-patients and even our neighbors. This was my introduction to Christianity and the Bible. Usually after Bible study there were recreational activities. One of my aunties was a musician who taught piano at Shanghai Conservatory of Music, and was the personal accompanist of Madame Guan, the most famous singer in

China at that time. She often came from Shanghai to visit us on weekends. We would never let her go without requesting that she play some pieces of music for us. All of us brothers and sisters would often sing along with her beautiful performances.

To top it all off, my father would tell humorous stories while the whole group shared in the meal, which was usually laid out on a ping-pong table. One day, my second oldest brother, De Xian, asked my father a question, "Dad, we have never seen you quarrel with mom. How do you manage that?" It was an interesting question that caught everyone's attention. My father stood up and explained, "We made an agreement on our wedding day. I said to your mom, 'If rage crops up inside me, I will show it to you by smoothing my mustache and you will have to keep quiet right away. And if you are upset with me, please rearrange your skirt to warn me.' This practice has worked very well throughout our married life." He paused for a few seconds and said, "However, I was smoothing my mustache and she was rearranging her skirt all the time!" As he told the story he was vividly reenacting it as the whole auditorium roared with laughter. Everyone there was like our extended family; it was a wonderful and healthy atmosphere. Our happiness was reflected in our lives, because of such a harmonious environment.

While we enjoyed goodwill and harmony, the same was not true of the world. The Empire of Japan had long sought to dominate China politically and militarily. By 1937, everything began to change as the Japanese attacked Shanghai causing thousands of refugees to flee the city. As the last southbound train was about to leave Shanghai, hordes of people squeezed into the train and packed the cars like sardines. Hundreds of people even climbed onto the rooftops of the train or clung to the window frames in order to escape. But the Japanese planes did not spare them. They pursued the train, firing at the refugees and killing many people. When the crowded train passed through the platform bridge at the Jiaxing railway station, those who were not able to lower themselves quickly were knocked off the top of the train cars and died. Some even had parts of their bodies chopped off by the iron bridge structure.

Horror filled the air as people screamed crazily at the top of their lungs. The train stopped for emergency care in Jiaxing. Upon hearing the bad news, my father rushed to the station, bringing along all the hospital's doctors and nurses. They did everything they could to save lives as many of the victims were carried to his hospital for surgery. News of the free services from my father's hospital immediately became known throughout the city.

Soon, it was Jiaxing that was threatened by the Japanese aggression. Local governmental leaders advised my father to stay on. But my father was very determined. He stated, "My family and I would rather die than remain here to be slaves to a foreign power." Immediately, he arranged for all our family members and the hospital staff to leave for Hangzhou. He and a few doctors stayed behind to help as many refugees as they could. But, within three days of Jiaxing's total occupation by the Japanese army, my father had departed. Giving up everything, the hospital and all our homes, he joined us as we headed for southwest China. Like so many other Chinese people, we suffered unbearable hardships for many years.

I was only four years old when we left our Jiaxing home to flee Zhejiang Province. It was challenging to travel with the sixteen of us– fourteen children and our parents. The next three years of our lives were spent as refugees, constantly on the run, making our way through many different provinces. It wore us all down. Almost all of our money was given to the people who transported us from place to place. My parents did their best to take care of us but we did not have regular meals. As we traveled along, the local people would pay us with a little food or small amounts of money in exchange for the medical treatment my parents provided

Me at age 4 years

them. On one occasion we saw a young deer slip and fall from the top of a mountain. At first we kids were sad that it died, but then we were happy knowing that the dead deer meant that we would finally have meat to eat at mealtime. Our hardships were the greatest as we passed through Jiangxi, Hunan, and Guangxi Provinces. Mostly we kept on the move as we made our way along the river by rowboat or in trucks. There were no beds, so our only place to sleep was in the boat or the back of trucks as we traveled along.

I remember one day before lunch that our mother came to us as we fourteen children were sitting around a very low table on a boat sailing on the Zhujiang River. As she watched us sing a prayer to thank God for giving us food, she smiled lovingly and said, "A group of little pigs." After she left, my oldest brother suggested, "At the next meal when we sing the prayer, let's not sing the words. Instead, we will just do the melody while making sounds like little pigs." We all quickly agreed. Later, before dinner, we all sat down waiting for our mom to join us, and as soon as we began to sing our prayer, we all pouted our lips and made funny piggy sounds, "nu-nu-nu-nu", in tune with the melody. Mom could not help bursting into laughter, but we all kept making the funny pig sounds until the end of the melody. Even in hard times, we realized that we could have fun.

Sadly, during the years that we were on the run, three of my siblings died. In the countryside, there were no hospitals to provide medical treatment when my two older sisters got high fevers and became very ill. Even though my parents were both very experienced doctors, there was no way for them to get medicine. I can only imagine how my parents must have felt, having the knowledge but lacking the means to save their own children.

Home in Duyun

Finally in 1940, my family settled down in Duyun located in southwest China's Guizhou Province. My two oldest brothers, Cheng Xian and De Xian, and my third eldest sister, Ai Xian left us to continue

Cheng Xian & De Xian (1935)

their studies in Western medicine in Guiyang, the capital of Guizhou Province. That year I was school age, seven years old. Duyun was a small town surrounded by high mountains and big rivers. It had tall trees that kept green leaves all year round. But, the people there were very poor. In fact, there was a saying that was used to describe this area, "The weather is never sunny for three days; the ground is not flat even for three feet; and the people do not have three pennies." But, to my eye, it was a place full of beauty and mystery; my childhood was always a golden time for me. The house we lived in was made of wood and was located on the town's ringed road. It was a two-story home with a small, narrow attic on the top, which was my bedroom. The room had a window without glass, so we used paper made from bamboo for the windowpane. It served the purpose as the natural light could penetrate the paper to "brighten" the room and it could also protect the room from getting too cold in winter. In order to see the high mountains and broad sky from the attic, I often opened the window when the weather was mild. There were no electric lights in Duyun. I often lit a piece of Dengxincao (a special kind of grass, also an herb) soaked in vegetable oil in a small dish to get a dim light for the night so that I could read after dark. At bedtime, I liked to look out at the mountains with the stars twinkling across the sky. Almost every night, I could see "balls of fire" flying back and forth for a short distance in the mountains. I wondered what they were and got scared when a neighbor told me that they were ghost fires. But, I would keep watching them with curiosity, peeking over the quilt that almost covered my eyes.

An Adventure with the Miao People

China has fifty-six national minorities. In the mountainous area around Duyun, most inhabitants were Miao people. The Miao people loved to sing and dance, and they were very good at playing reed-pipe wind instruments. Their enchanting and mysterious melodies always touched my heart. Early morning before dawn, I would often wake to their music and be easily carried away with the dreamy sounds. Then, I would get up and lean out the window to watch the Miao people passing along the mountain paths on their way to the market. The beautiful melodies I had heard at dawn would linger in my head throughout the day.

One autumn day, a Miao boy told me that every year during the Moon Festival, they held a huge group wedding ceremony. The young Miao people would go to the Big Bridge where there was a spacious square at the river's edge. There, all the young people who would have already dated and agreed to marry would gather. He told me that family and friends would all attend this traditional Miao celebration. Before their group wedding, the boy said that the young men would stand in a big circle with their brides-to-be, dancing at its center. Each girl had a big ring fastened at the back of her waist. The young men would throw a hook attached to a long rope into their intended's ring. He told me that the girls would dance closer to their lovers for an easier catch, so that mistakes happened rarely. When they were all "hooked up", the Miao tribal head served as chief witness to the weddings. Afterward all the families and well-wishers would shout, sing, and dance to the special Moon-Festival music.

The night before the Moon Festival, I scarcely slept for I was eager to see the big event. At dawn, I heard group after group of people passing along the mountain path as they played their instruments. I hurriedly dressed and took my school bag that I had filled with food in preparation for the adventure. I tiptoed down from my attic without making a sound and quietly opened the back door. As soon as I stepped into the backyard, a huge flock of colorful little birds that had been sitting in a nearby willow tree got startled and flew away. What a sight! I had never seen so many beautiful birds all at once. It felt like I was in a fairytale. I ran to join the Miao people, who warmly welcomed me, a Han girl with a big smile. I was very excited and felt honored by their acceptance. One middle-aged Miao woman asked me what my name was and why I wanted to go with them. I responded to her in her own language, saying that I loved their music and I hoped to observe the wedding ceremony. She put her arm around my neck and we walked together enjoying the music as the fresh fragrance of the mountain trees filled the air.

After almost half a day of walking, we finally arrived at the Big Bridge. It was already decorated with wild flowers and ornaments that were made from bamboo and other local plants. A platform had been built and at its center stood a very big armchair and a long table that was piled high with a variety of fruit and other food. There were hundreds of Miao people at the square, all beautifully dressed. All the young people, their families and friends were there, readying for the big celebration.

I was so excited, because prior to that day I had often watched the young men and women sing to each other from atop two different hills. Their love songs were very touching and the melodies were pleasant to the ear. Every singer expressed their feelings through their own words as they "dated". On occasion, I had seen several young men singing to the same number of girls on a distant hill. I decided that it must be some kind of "group dating". It had been so much fun to watch and listen to their traditions. I learned that after they had found the right mates, they would eagerly await the next group wedding.

People came in groups–one family per group. When night fell, music echoed throughout the valleys. After the huge bright moon made its way from behind the mountains, the chief of the Miao people took his place in the square. The brides and grooms had long prepared for this exciting moment. When the Miao chief took his seat and announced the opening of the ceremony, more than fifty young girls began to dance gracefully in the center of the square.

The brides-to-be looked extremely beautiful, each with pretty silver adornments worn in their hair. They had all different kinds of silver necklaces and bracelets worn around their necks and wrists. I learned how to tell their age by the number of necklaces they had on, one for each year of age. Most girls had sixteen to eighteen necklaces. The brides had sewn and embroidered their wedding dresses themselves, which usually took years to complete.

Just as I had been told, the young grooms formed a big circle around the dancing girls and waited for the bride-to-be to come near to make it easier for the hook to land in the ring around his sweetheart's waist. To make an accurate throw-and-catch, the young men had to have honed their skills well. For according to the Miao custom, the young man had to marry whichever girl he hooked. As expected, the girls danced nearer and nearer to their loved ones. And I watched as each young man threw his hook with great care! When all the girls were "hooked" by their lovers, the Miao chief voiced his congratulations to all the young couples and their families. Everyone was elated to have gone through the ceremony successfully. Great joy and excitement filled the square as beautiful music echoed throughout the whole valley. People danced, sang, and drank until midnight. Then they said their good-byes to one another and headed home.

By the time we returned to where I had begun my journey, it was almost dawn. I waved good-bye to my Miao friends and rushed to my home. I found that the back door was locked, so I had to climb in through an open window. I quietly crept into my attic room without disturbing anyone else in the house. You could just imagine what punishment I received afterwards since I had been missing for a whole day. But, it was well worth it!

I Love Butterflies—But!

The following spring in my same attic room, I had an unforgettable experience. I found layer after layer of baby caterpillar worms everywhere on the walls and ceiling. I was scared and tried to use the mosquito net to protect myself. But my efforts were in vain, as they fell on my bed and all over my mosquito net. I could hardly get up out of my bed without them touching me.

It seemed that hardly any time passed before the caterpillars grew very big; they were nearly two inches long and had long black hair. A thick layer of black caterpillars coated the whole ceiling and the walls of my room. Their fuzzy black fur floated into the air. It got into my pores and caused irritation that was sometimes painful all day long. I had several sleepless nights and many uncomfortable days. It felt that I was living in hell!

We had no pesticides at that time, so my fourth sister, Yi Xian, tried to help me burn some hay inside my room to kill off the caterpillars. After we smoked up my room, most of them fell to the floor and we collected a few dustbins full of dead caterpillars. But, there were many survivors. Then in a few days, another layer of caterpillars appeared in the attic. There were so many that it was impossible to kill them all. The only solution for me to avoid the caterpillars was to move out and let the invaders take over my bedroom. And they must have had a happy time during their transformation, for weeks later, they all changed into big, black butterflies with white spots on their wings. They flew out of my window into the broad blue sky adding their beauty to nature. Even though I hated the caterpillars, I did enjoy seeing the big, beautiful, black and white butterflies flying freely in the air.

Later, I would come to realize that this happening had been wholly caused by me. During the spring, summer and autumn of the previous year, I had always left my bedroom window wide open. Whenever I saw butterflies coming into my room, I would get very happy and excited. I loved watching them sit still and rest on my walls and ceiling, or flutter their wings as they flew around my room. I had no clue what they were actually doing.

No one had ever told me that butterflies were the parents of caterpillars. I was only seven years old and I had not learned anything like that at school. I had allowed them to fly freely into my attic room, which provided them with the chance to lay eggs on the walls and the ceiling. But, I had given them too much freedom, which later brought disaster upon me! From then on, whenever I opened my widow to enjoy the view, I would take care that no butterfly stayed very long in my room. Instead I would chase it out of the attic after I had watched its wonderful dance. For the rest of my life, caterpillars have terrified me the most of any type of worm!

Punished by My Teacher

I began my studies at an old-style private school. My teacher was the owner of the school and he only taught one class. This teacher was an old man with a long beard. He wore thick glasses in round black frames over his sunken, gloomy eyes. I never saw the slightest sign of a smile on his face, so I thought maybe he had never learned how to smile. Every day, he would come into the classroom wearing a long black gong robe, pulling a long face as though we all owed him money. Without looking up, he would start us chanting with him the hundred surnames of Chinese families, "Zhao Qian Sun Li Zhou Wu Chen Wang…" It made no sense to me at all, so I eventually quit going to his school.

After that, my parents sent me to a public elementary school where we were taught Chinese, mathematics with an abacus, music, physical training, and drawing. I liked this school very much. I was active in the physical training class, I drew well, and I was a good singer. Attentive in class, I did my lessons well. As a result, all the teachers liked me and so did my classmates. I was even appointed to be the class monitor. Things went smoothly for the first year. Then one day during the second year, three boys in my class did not hand in their compositions. Our teacher was very angry with them and reprimanded them by striking their palms one by one with a long, thick bamboo ruler. The boys screamed at the top of their voices. I wept for them. This old Chinese teacher had a stern face and he was so strict with us. After he punished the boys, he announced in front of the class that if any of the students did not hand in the homework on time, I would be held responsible.

Not long afterward, I was on my way to school early one morning when the same three boys stopped me. They handed me some herbal grass and said, "Now, monitor, you are going to get hit by the teacher today because we have not done our homework. But we have collected this herb grass for you to rub your hands so that your palms will not hurt as much." I was astonished and puzzled at their behavior. Before I could say anything, they grabbed my right hand and violently rubbed my palm with the fresh grass until it became numb. Then they did the same to my left palm. I was totally at their mercy as we walked together in silence to the school.

When the school bell rang, I got so nervous that I almost forgot to call the class to stand at attention to greet our teacher. When he found out that the same boys had not done their homework again, our teacher flew into a rage. However, this time, instead of yelling at them, he demanded that I come to the front of the room and stretch out my right palm. He lifted up the bamboo ruler and hit me with all his strength. It hurt so much that tears rolled down my cheeks, but I refused to cry out. Instead, I bit my lip until blood dropped onto my blouse. The teacher was so unreasonable. I was very angry with him, but I decided to put up with it for the time being. All the rest of the day, I received so much love and compassion from my classmates, even from the three naughty boys. Yet, none of them voiced their complaints about the teacher's unfair treatment of me. For during those days in China, the students had to obey the teachers, no matter what. And although I remained silent for the whole day, my heart was filled with anger.

After I got home, I decided not to mention a word of it to anyone other than my little brother, Yao Xian. Only a year older than me, he attended the same school. Yao Xian was a very smart and understanding boy. Since we always shared what was on our minds, that night as I told him the whole story, he, too, became upset. Even though he was very sick and weak due to his sufferings from periodontitis, he encouraged me to stand up and fight back.

The next morning as I left home at the usual hour, I did not head for school. Instead I walked toward the big river a couple of miles from our home. I hid my school bag under a huge rock on the riverbank and sat down under a tall parasol tree. It was a warm morning and the air was clear and fresh. I felt so relaxed and free. Since I'd had a sleepless night, I immediately fell asleep on the sand. When I woke up, it was around noon and I felt hungry. So I picked up the seeds that had fallen from the parasol tree and ate them to soothe my stomach. I was determined that I would never go back to that class again. I simply did not understand why the teacher should have punished me, when the fault was that of the other students. It was unfair, absolutely unfair! I had heard stories about parents punishing their eldest child if the younger ones made a mistake. I found a similarity between that kind of punishment and the one I had suffered from our teacher. What was wrong with adults? Did they not have any sense? And why should the school allow teachers to hit the pupils? I was deep in thought while playing with the cobblestones, but I could not come up with any answers.

The weather was extremely hot that afternoon but the big tree provided me with good shade. There was no one around, only mountains, trees, and the big river. The air was filled with the noise of cicadas. Then suddenly, dark clouds gathered and it threatened to rain. I thought of going home, but it did not seem like the right time. I just felt that I had to wait a while. At that moment, the lightning flashed and a thunderstorm broke open as it began to pour down. I protected myself by leaning against the big tree. Luckily enough, I was not stuck by the lightning.

The river soon began to rise as the sky became even more cloudy and dark. It was frightening to be alone on that riverbank. I began to shiver with cold and fear. But within half an hour, the storm was over and I saw the silver linings appear around the dark clouds. Taking my school bag out from under the rock, I readied for my return home. Scarcely had I started down the muddy path, when I slipped and fell to the ground getting my shorts very dirty. I ran back to the water's edge, took off my shorts, and began washing them in the rapidly flowing river. Unexpectedly, I saw what looked like a fish swimming along the riverbank with its head above the water. When it swam closer to me, I reached out my arm to catch it. The creature was startled and flung its tail. Oh, my god! It was a long, thick water snake! I was more startled than the snake. Unconsciously, I threw my arms out and ran away. Moments later, I realized that in my fright I had thrown away the most important thing, my shorts!

How could I go home with my lower body naked? I rushed back to the edge of the river intending to get my shorts, but only found that the swift currents were carrying them further and further away. Since I was not a swimmer, I could only stand there and watch my shorts churning around and around in the big swirl of the deep, swift water. The only thing I could think of was to wait until dark. So, I hid myself behind a huge rock and hoped that no one would see me. Time never passed so slowly!

Finally, night fell and it was safe for me to go home. While walking home, I bent my body forward so that my blouse reached down farther to cover my front and I used my school bag to cover my butt. I entered the house through the back door hoping to avoid being seen. Unfortunately, my mother was in the kitchen. When she saw me in that state, she was astonished and really frightened. I will never forget the expression on her face at that moment. Immediately, I told her the whole story and begged her not to send me back to the school again. After hearing this, my mother was angry both with the teacher and with me, since I had skipped school instead of revealing the truth to her earlier.

The next morning, my mother accompanied me to the school and had a talk with the schoolmaster about this matter. As a result, I was put into another class of the same grade. Even so, I kept wondering when the awful corporal punishment would be abolished at the school?

An Early Loss

A few months later that year, my little brother, Yao Xian died during the night as we slept. He was only nine years old, one year older than I, and was my closest friend. I loved him dearly. He was smart, nice, and cared about me. Unfortunately, he had gotten a disease called periodontitis and as there was no proper medication available for this disease during wartime, Yao Xian suffered immensely despite trying several folk remedies.

We shared the same quilt and slept on opposite ends of the same bed. His illness had worsened during the winter and I found that his feet were very cold during the night, so I held them close to my chest hoping that he could feel warmer. One morning, I found his feet icy cold. I held them tighter for a while. Then I suddenly realized something wasn't right. So, I sat up quickly and leaned over to look into his face. His eyes were tightly closed. As a child of eight, I did not know what death was, so I shook him but he did not move. He had stopped breathing during the night.

He was only nine years old; he died so young! I cried for many days over his death. I lost my dear brother and my best friend. For many days I did not talk much, I just cried whenever I thought of him. I had no interest in playing with my younger brothers either, because in my eyes, they were just babies who knew nothing but silly games. They were six and seven years old, respectively, and often made too much noise in the house. I missed my brother, my confidant, and my favorite playmate. Somehow, I thought that if it were not for the war, he would still be alive.

Once Again—Wrongly Punished

Late one afternoon, my two naughty younger brothers broke a very expensive, beautiful glass as they were wrestling for fun in the sitting room. The glass was from my mother's favorite set of glassware. Now, one of them was shattered. As they quickly picked up the broken shards of glass, they whispered worriedly to each other.

When my mother came home from work, she was in a very bad mood. She found a small piece of glass on the floor and asked who had broken a glass. The boys replied in unison that I had done it. I was so astonished to hear their lie that I began to yell at them. Then my mom asked me if it was true. I was so upset that I shouted at her, "No! They fought and broke it!" My rude attitude angered my mother further, and she said, "This language to me?! Why weren't you watching your brothers?"

I continued to talk back to her loudly, "I am only one year older. How can I take care of them? They are so naughty!" My mother took up the broom and hit me really hard. Crying bitterly, I ran up to my little room in the attic. Another unfair punishment. At that moment I missed my dear brother Yao Xian even more and felt so lonely. As I went to bed without dinner, I tearfully made up my mind to run away from home.

The next morning, I walked aimlessly toward the mountains behind our house. Without a destination in mind, I just decided to climb up the mountain. Eventually, I reached the two big caves that I had often seen from my attic window. There were many legends about these two caves. Some said that a long, long time ago two black dragons lived in the caves. It was said that there was still a chest containing treasure at the deepest end of one of the caves. Legend also had it that there were big snakes that lived in the caves. The more I thought about all of that, the more fear gathered in my mind until I wondered if I still had the nerve to pass by. But, there was only one path leading to the top of the mountain, so I plucked up my courage and with my eyes nearly closed, I ran past the entrances of the two caves. Nothing happened! But, what I did experience when I ran by the openings of the caves was the echo of my own footsteps. I felt so relieved!

Then, I continued to climb up the mountainside. When I reached the summit, I looked afar to the other side of the mountain. Off in the distance, I could see one mountain after another. Having decided to go so far away that not even my mom could find me, I descended from the mountain. Half way down, I found a small stream that ran very swiftly. Since there was no mountain path, I followed the stream. As I stepped carefully downstream, I was showered with tiny splashes from the stream's cool, clear water. I bent over to have some sips of water; it was icy cold and tasted a bit sweet.

As I moved downward with the blue sky overhead, I felt embraced by the morning sunrays. A spring breeze brought me comfort and I felt fantastic. The mountain was dotted with colorful wild flowers and the valley was filled with the thrilling songs of different birds. I was in a wonderland! I began imitating the birds' sounds, especially the kuku bird. Entranced, I totally forgot why I was there.

I followed the twists and bends in the stream and at one turning point it flattened out. There, the water had shaped a small pond that was the size of a bathing basin. The sun's light went through the clear water to highlight colorful sparkles that immediately caught my eye. I rushed to the pond and saw dozens of transparent stones in the shallow water that were within my reach. So I stretched an arm into the water and took out a handful. They were so pretty! I had never seen such beautiful stones in a stream before. They reminded me of the precious stones I saw on rich ladies' rings. Without any pockets on my blouse or my pants, I wasn't able to take any with me. So, I put the sparkling stones back into the pond and planned to come back to get them.

I kept walking on the mountain without any idea of where to go. I continued over another mountain and then another, even though I was both hungry and tired. Finally, I sat down under a big tree and fell asleep. When I woke up, the sun was moving toward the west and I realized that I was in the middle of nowhere. I began to worry about what would happen if I could not get out of the mountains before dark.

As I stood and looked around, I was greatly surprised to see that down to my right there was a little hut on top of a small hill, not too far away. I was overjoyed and quickly walked toward it. When I approached the hut, I saw a little Miao girl about five years old standing in the door staring at me. I smiled at her and she immediately ran back into the hut. In a moment, the girl came out with her mother, a very pretty Miao woman. She came up to me and with a warm smile questioned me, "What is your name? Why did you come here? How did you find your way?" Her sweet manner calmed me down.

I told her my story and how I had run away from home. She told me it was not right to do that and that my mom must be terribly worried. She led me into her home and offered me some rice, which I ate like a hungry wolf. The Miao woman asked me to spend the night in their hut, since it was too late to go far away to my home.

Early the next morning, she baked some sticky rice cakes for breakfast. Then she used a carrying pole, putting me on one side in a basket and her daughter in the other basket. I told her that I was too heavy to be carried. She replied that she often took one hundred *jin*[1] of rice to the market, besides her daughter was not able to walk so far. That was the first time in my life that I had been carried in a basket. It was quite an adventure. The woman sang folk songs all the way down the hill, as she followed the long river toward the town where I lived.

We arrived at my home some hours later. The woman knocked at our door and my mother came out. She looked very pale. It was obvious that she had not slept for the whole night. I lowered my head, feeling guilty for having run away from home. Murmuring "Mom!" as tears rolled down my cheeks, I entered the house without saying anything more. The Miao woman explained everything to my Mom. Then my mother welcomed her and her little girl into our house for tea. She even offered the woman money but she graciously refused. Later on, Mom always ordered our rice from the Miao woman so I saw them frequently.

Following that experience, my Mom never hit me again. She knew that I was an honest girl, but one filled with a fighting spirit! But, it always seemed such a pity that I never got my precious stones from that little pond.

---

[1] Equal to 1.1 lbs

She Escaped from Apes!

There was a small town named Dushan that was only a few hundred *li*[2] away from the town of Duyun. Many girls from surrounding towns, like Dushan, would arrange to be married in Duyun. Usually, the brides had to be carried from their hometown along mountain paths into Duyun in a wedding carriage. Legend had it that once in a while, a group of apes would come out of the mountains and kill the carriage bearers in order to grab a bride for their "Ape King".

One summer morning, I saw a large crowd of local people standing around a woman who was dressed in rags. They listened to her tell an extraordinary and terrifying story that occurred months earlier. She said that she was in her wedding carriage headed for our town, Duyun. In accordance with the old tradition, it was a wooden carriage that was held aloft on men's shoulders. The carriers, as well as other townspeople accompanied her, playing drums and trumpets. A family's wealth could be determined by size of the wedding parade. The simplest and cheapest way was with two people, one to carry the front and one behind. Those with more money hired at least 4 carriers, each holding a pole, and many others accompanied them and made beautiful music. The bride's face and the carriage were covered with cloth, silk if they were rich.

During this bride's ride, she heard a loud noise. Apes had surprised her small wedding party and her coach, which was abandoned by the panicked men who had carried it. They were so frightened that they ran away. Scarcely had she realized what was happening, when a huge ape tore the curtain away. As it reached in and grabbed her into his long arms, she had fainted away.

When she came back to consciousness, she found herself lying on a thick layer of banana leaves in a big, dark cave. She was wearing her bright red wedding *gong* (dress), but the beautiful flowers in her hair had been lost in the struggle. The "Ape King" sat nearby and watched her. Even though she had screamed loudly at him, she said that the ape had remained still, making no movements. She rushed to the opening of the cave, but found more apes standing guard there. She soon realized she could not escape from them. But she was a smart girl and had made a

---

[2] Equal to 1/3 of a mile

plan. She calmed down and ate whatever fruit the apes gave her. She obeyed the "Ape King" because he obviously liked her and treated her well. For about a month, she was captive in the cave, both day and night. It seemed that the "Ape King" had begun to trust her because he would leave the cave sometimes unguarded. She had even been able to go out to sun herself without the other apes at their post.

Since the apes would often climb tall trees and pick fruit, she learned to follow them up to get food. All the apes seemed to like her and she got along with them very well. In order to keep up with the apes along the mountain paths, the woman ran fast and became familiar with all of the routes. Several months passed quickly. One morning before dawn, as the "Ape King" slept soundly, she quietly left the cave. Fleeing for her life, she rushed down the mountain path as fast as she could. She believed that if the apes caught her, they would tear her to pieces. As day broke, she realized that she was close to Duyun. When she saw the first human, she breathlessly asked for his help. The apes never came into the town because they were afraid of the people. As she spoke, more and more people encircled her, listening to her story. The news spread very fast throughout town.

The poor man who had lost her as his bride came to take her to his home where he fed her. Then he sent for her parents in Dushan, requesting that they come to take her back to their home. In a few days, they arrived and everyone cried miserably. Her parents had been broken-hearted, for they thought they would never see their daughter again.

This smart and brave young woman went back to Dushan with her parents. It was a shame but everyone knew that no man would ever marry her after such a horrible incident. But, in my heart, she was a heroine; I admired her wits and courage. In the old Chinese society of the 1940's, such a wonderful girl would stay single all her life and likely suffer humiliation from others. It truly seemed unfair.

Why Was She Murdered?

Behind our house in Duyun, there was a little hut built of hay. In it lived a widow and her only son who was about 20 years old. Together, they farmed their own land, which encircled the hut. To us, the widow seemed a bit odd, but the son was nice and very friendly.

One day the young man was to be married to a pretty girl of eighteen, who was from a poor farming family. Dozens of farmers came for their wedding ceremony, and our family was happy to attend, too. I was very excited to go to the wedding because I knew the young man. Since his family was also poor, they could only serve their guests cakes made of fresh corn and homemade rice wine. I had never tasted such a delicious kind of fresh cake before. (And to this day, I still long to have a bite of corn cakes like that!)

A few months after their wedding, the young man was taken away to serve as a soldier in the Kuomintang Army. His bride was left alone on the farm with her mother-in-law who did not treat her very well. A long time passed and she did not hear from her husband. Finally, the family was informed that the young man had been killed in the war. Both the mother and the young woman cried bitterly for many days.

The pretty wife had become a widow at the age of nineteen. Everyone had such pity for her. But according to the old Chinese tradition, she could not marry another man unless the mother-in-law allowed her to do so. As time passed, fewer and fewer smiles were seen on her cute face. Seldom did she talk to anyone and she looked very sad nearly all the time. Her mother-in-law took no pity on her, for everyday she was made to work long hours like a slave in the fields.

A year later, I noticed that her body was changing. It became evident that she was pregnant, and I was so happy for her. At that time, I was too naïve to know that it could be a disaster if a woman got pregnant without having a husband. Whenever I was home, I would frequently hear cursing from that little hut. I could tell that the cursing was from the old widow. And while I could not figure out what the curses were about, I felt that the old woman was very angry with her daughter-in-law.

Months later during the middle of the night, my family and all the neighbors were aroused by terrible screams that came from the hut. We thought it must be the young woman crying out during labor, so no one went over to the hut. Everyone assumed that the young woman would be attended to by her mother-in-law, or by other helpers while birthing. But following the terrible screams, there were no cries of a baby as we had expected. There was only silence.

Early the next morning before going to school, two neighbor girls came by and asked me to go to visit the young mother with the newborn baby. We all had pity for that young woman so we hurriedly went to the hut. We knocked at the door but nobody answered. We thought that she must be tired after giving birth to the baby. But after repeated knocking, it seemed strange that no one came to the door at all. Where was her mother-in-law? Finally we pressed our ears to the window but only heard the very weak cry of a baby. So we decided to ask some adults to find out what had happened inside the hut. Two women were able to come and they pushed open the hut's door. Oh! What a terrible sight!

The young mother lay dead in a huge pool of blood on a long table, her face pale in terrified expression. Her upper body was bound to the table with thick ropes, and her lower body was bare. Blood was still dripping from the table to the earthen floor. A long, iron fire-tong protruded out from her vagina. On the ground lay a baby boy, half-dead; he was very feeble and making a whimpering sound. The umbilical cord had not been cut off from the placenta. The two women cut the baby's cord and handed him to us three girls as they immediately rushed from the hut to get the local government officials. Wanting to take good care of him, we wrapped the baby in a piece of old cloth we found in the hut and took him to the door of my house.

We sat at the threshold of the door and looked at the baby very closely. The three of us did not really know what to do, as he was so weak that he breathed with great difficulty. With tears in our eyes, our gaze never left his pale face. A half an hour or so later, we saw people go into the hut after which no one was allowed entry. Very soon, a government official came to take the baby boy from us and said that he would be sent to an orphanage.

The three of us went on to school together. All we could talk about was the young mother and her baby, but we were so puzzled. What had really happened to the young mother? For the whole day, my mind was not on school. I made thousands of guesses, but I would learn that none of them even came close to the truth.

When the school day was finally over, I rushed home in one breath and was told about the horrible murder. The young woman had gotten pregnant by her boyfriend that she had grown up with since childhood. She had been killed in the cruelest way imaginable. The mother-in-law and her sister had bound the young woman to the long table after deceiving her into thinking that it would be easier to deliver her baby that way. Once the baby was born, the two sisters had thrust a hot fire-tong into her vagina that killed her. They had planned this terrible murder ever since they found out that she was expecting a child. When the young woman screamed out during her labor, they were confident that none of the neighbors would come to rescue her because everyone knew when she was due. And screams were natural and common during labor and delivery at home. After they murdered her, the two sisters had fled. But they had not run very far when they were arrested and confessed to their crime.

There were so many questions on my mind. Why had the young woman been killed just because she got pregnant with her boyfriend? Why had her mother-in-law not allowed her to leave after her husband died in the war? How could her mother-in-law kill her in such a brutal way? She was so young. I strongly felt that she should have had the right to remarry and enjoy the rest of her life! Those old traditions had to be changed! For a long time, I thought deeply about these issues but got no resolve.

The Two Men Were Beasts!

One afternoon I was headed home after school and I saw a group of strange people. Two middle-aged men were beating on a big metal gong to attract the public's attention. A group of people gathered as one of them yelled, "Come, come to see the wonderful show of the big-headed dwarfs who come from a dwarf country. Look at them, they are in their twenties but they are so short. They can show you all kinds of tricks!"

I turned to stare at the dwarfs who were standing behind the two men. They really looked odd to me. In all, there were seven dwarfs, three females and four males. Their heads were the size of an adult's with mature faces, but their bodies were only about two to three feet high and they had very short arms and legs. I had never seen humans that small and strange looking. Curious, I watched their shows. They sang and danced and spoke to the audience just like normal people. The females wore make up and had very colorful skirts. The on-lookers were amused as they laughed and applauded them.

One of the two masters began to collect money from the crowd. As more people gathered to watch, more money was taken in. Then, a person who had sat behind them, stepped into the center of the circle. This man was of normal height but his head was small, the size of a large pear. He was referred to as "Pear-Head Man". As he spoke, I could not understand a word he said. He tried to sing, but his voice sounded weird because he always poked his chin upward when he tried to talk or sing. His eyes could barely open.

After the show, they turned and left. Watching those strange people from behind as they walked away, my heart was filled with very uncomfortable feelings. I found myself wondering about these poor people and questioned, "Is there really a dwarf country in the world as described in the fairy tales?"

Later that evening, many people were sitting or standing in front of their houses taking in the cool air. People were still talking about the strange performances. I overheard one conversation between two neighbors. "They cheat people. Actually, they kidnapped two or three year-old kids and put them into jars to limit their physical growth. For some, the whole body was kept in the jar, leaving only the head out. So their heads are usually bigger, more normal size, but their bodies are very short. And they were never allowed to sleep on their backs, so they had to stand in the jars all the time during the years of growth. For the "Pear-Head Man", they used a small jar that limited the growth of his head, so his brain did not develop well."

When I heard all this, my heart broke and I cried bitterly for those kidnapped kids. I wanted to beat those two slave masters! I waited for them to come back, but they never showed up again in Duyun. This unbearable information bothered me for many years. So strong was my desire that those cruel men be arrested and punished, and then no more children would suffer a similar fate. But, I had no way to do that.

A Terrible Disease

In Duyun, the only path for me to take to school was a very narrow one that led to the big road and my destination. Along the narrow path, there was a huge fruit tree that was named "chicken feet tree" by the local people. In autumn, the tree bore lots of chicken feet shaped fruit that we picked up off the ground for our after school snack.

One autumn afternoon, while three of us pupils were walking on our way home, we saw several people lying on the ground near the big "chicken feet tree". We thought they were napping under the tree after having enjoyed the sweet, juicy fruit. But, as we came up closer to them, we realized that they were dead.

All poorly dressed, we thought they must be the inhabitants of the dozen or so huts that had been built behind this big tree. We turned around in hopes of seeing some adults but all we saw was more dead people on the ground close by. We were so scared that we rushed home and told our families about it. They all rushed up to the scene. One of the adults became very aware of something and told us all to leave the spot as quickly as possible. Later, the whole vicinity was blocked off and no one was allowed to go near it, or to the dead bodies.

Later, we were informed that all those people had died of acute malaria that had passed through the area very fast as people were stricken with high fevers and constant diarrhea. As people died, their bodies lay exposed to hundreds of flies, which would sit on them and then pass the disease onto other people. The next day, that forbidden area was set on fire. All of the huts and the big tree were burned to the ground. I was afraid that there might have been other infected people who were burned to death as well.

Months later, whenever I walked by that tree which was reduced to black charcoal, I would think of the poor people who died so suddenly because of the terrible disease. The whole small village had just vanished! Who had cared about them?

Sharing My Tenth Birthday Dinner

During the war with the Japanese, Chinese people's lives were miserable. The Japanese armies, who committed unbelievably horrid acts toward the Chinese people, occupied most of our territory. They burned people's houses; they raped women and even young girls; they used Chinese people as living subjects on which to do their so-called "scientific experiments". Many people died from this "scientific research" or had their bodies destroyed in the process. Many patriotic Chinese people were buried alive. Even pregnant women's bellies were cut open as the Japanese soldiers took out the fetuses and placed them on the knife points of their rifles. Some babies were placed under millstones and died as they were ground to mash.

We Chinese, men and women, old and young, were furious over the cruelties carried out by the Japanese armies. As children, we were organized to do whatever we could to support our own army in the fight against the Japanese. We collected money for the front by selling dolls that we made ourselves and from polishing people's shoes. At school, we learned anti-Japanese songs and went to the streets to share them with the local people. Participating in parades, we shouted slogans and sang the anti-Japanese songs. My fourth eldest sister, Yi Xian, was our music teacher at the elementary school. During the weekends, she sometimes took us–her younger brothers and sisters–to the mountains and taught us more anti-Japanese songs. They were very inspiring. We sang them while we sold handicrafts that we had made in our effort to collect donations for the soldiers who were fighting against the Japanese.

By 1943, it was already the sixth year of the Anti-Japanese War. The Chinese people had suffered so much and everyone was anticipating an end to the war. But instead, the Japanese armies became more and more aggressive. When they changed the tactics of approach, our family had to run for our lives once again! That year, the Japanese troops began launching an attack from the rear in southwest China, intending to occupy that region. At that time, Chongqing was the capital of China. The Japanese air force bombed many of the cities in Guangxi and Guizhou provinces. Not a single day passed without the blare of the air raid sirens.

At the edge of Duyun where we lived, there was a very high mountain called the East Mountain. The local government set up an air raid station with a very tall pole at the mountaintop. As soon as they received information from the front that the Japanese air force was headed in our direction, they would put a big red lantern on top of the pole and blast the siren. If the enemy planes flew into our area, they would add a second red lantern on the pole. That meant everyone had to run for safety into the air raid shelters. As the planes came closer, one or two more red lanterns would be added and the siren rang out faster and louder.

During those moments, the town itself became quiet. No one was in the street or left at home. In the shelters, people dared not make any noise. If a baby started to cry, the mother had to do something to stop it. Once, in our shelter, a baby cried just as the Japanese planes were flying overhead. The mother tried in every way to stop the wailing of her baby but it only cried louder and louder. Finally she had to use a towel to muffle the baby's cries. A few seconds later after the planes passed on, the mother discovered that her baby was dead. She had smothered the baby accidentally. The poor mother stamped her feet on the ground, screamed crazily, and hit her head repeatedly against the wall of the cave. Her head and face became stained with her blood as her life was in danger. But, people had to wait for the siren to stop before they could be released from the shelter and take her to the hospital.

During another air raid not long after that, the Japanese planes flew in very fast toward our area. People panicked and ran to one of the nearest shelters and it was soon over-filled with people. The shelter guard locked the cave's gate from the outside as he was supposed to do when there was no more room for people. Without enough oxygen in the shelter, the people tried to move forward to the gate in order to get air. But those who were not strong enough to go through the crowd had to remain where they were. People in the front banged on the gate and begged the guard to open it, but he yelled back that he was not allowed to open the gate while the enemy planes were flying overhead. Screams and cries filled the cave. After the siren signaled the air raid was over, the guard opened the gate. It was a terrible and miserable sight. Hundreds of people had died in the shelter due to the lack of oxygen. Only the very few people who had stood closest to the gate had survived.

During those days, we saw group after group of refugees pass through our town as they headed toward Sichuan province. Most came from Guangxi province, which was almost completely occupied by

Japanese troops. Many of the people in Duyun were ready to move on to other areas as well. Our family was preparing to go to Chongqing, China's temporary capital during the Anti-Japanese War.

It was mid-summer and I was excited that my birthday was approaching. According to the Chinese tradition, the tenth birthday was very important for a child. Even though life was difficult at that time, my sister, Yi Xian still planned to cook something special for our family at my birthday celebration. So, my sister made a big pot of noodles and put some sliced meat in every bowl. Since the weather was hot, we were going to have my birthday dinner outside in front of the house just as most families did in summertime.

No sooner had the whole family sat down for dinner, when along came a group of refugees. As they approached us, we could see that they were shabbily dressed. It seemed that they were a family and each one carried an empty broken bowl in one hand and a walking stick in the other. All looked very hungry. The eldest woman came to our table and asked for food. Immediately all my sisters and brothers stood up from their seats while my sister Yi Xian and I invited the refugees to sit down and eat the noodles. They ate so frantically that it seemed they had dumped the noodles right into their stomachs. When they found out that it was my tenth birthday celebration, they expressed their gratitude with tears in their eyes. Their birthday wish for me was for good health and longevity. And although my family had not eaten, we were all very happy to celebrate my birthday in this way.

Our Family Splits-Off in Different Directions

My Grandparents with me on the far right

As the Japanese armies advanced ever closer to Duyun, our whole family planned to leave for Chongqing. However, in order to make enough money to support the entire family, my father left us to take a job as the president of an army hospital in Kunming. My mother also went to work at that hospital. They left us younger children in the care of our fourth sister, Yi Xian, and her husband, Yao, Yi Fu, who was an official in the army. It was a heavy responsibility for a young couple to shoulder, but they took very good care of us four younger ones. Only years later did I come to realize just how greatly Yi Xian had influenced my childhood.

Life was very difficult in Duyun. Often we only had a hot pot on the stove with clear water, a piece of rock salt and some Chinese cabbage for dinner. Yi Xian was only in her early twenties when she took responsibility as "mom" to her four younger brothers and sisters, plus her own son. Fortunately, she was not only gifted at running the house but was also good at storytelling. Having read us almost all the fairy tales by Hans Christian Andersen, her gift in making up fantastic stories came forth. Yi Xian truly enjoyed being surrounded by us at night as we listened to her stories. All those beautiful fairy tales became deeply imprinted in my mind. Having a mind filled with mythology, my interest in exploring the mysteries of life expanded as I was growing up.

Good Training

Our fifth brother, Gong Xian, and my sixth sister, Mao Xian, had already gone to study at a boarding high school in Guiyang. They had been pretty independent, and during the winter and summer vacations they had come to spend time with us.

The visits by my fifth brother, Gong Xian brought about many family events that made lasting impressions. During my childhood, he had a great impact on me. A very intelligent young man, he was especially good at mathematics. If he could not solve a math problem during the daytime, he was sure to get an answer from his dreams. He was considered by my parents to be the smartest child of the family. Gong Xian was always full of energy and had a strong will to be a natural leader. Whenever he came back home for summer vacations, he would always create a new "project" for us to work on.

One day, he gathered us four younger brothers and sisters and claimed that he was going to train us to be brave. He commanded us to jump from the balcony of the second story down to the ground while holding a big paper umbrella painted with tung oil, as the parachute. By nature, I liked adventures so without any fear I performed accordingly. I dropped down like a rock without getting any assistance from the "parachute" for the umbrella turned inside out as I jumped down. Luckily enough I did not break my legs. But my bottom hit on the rough ground so hard that a sharp pain persisted for about a week. My two younger brothers, Gao Xian and Kai Xian, fearlessly did the same and hurt their bottoms as well. However, none of us complained to Yi Xian. We were praised by our "leader", which made us all feel proud of our bravery. It was my seventh sister, Min Xian, who was three years older than I, who hesitated when her turn came because she was old enough to know the danger. Recognizing this, Gong Xian yelled at her, "You are a coward!" She felt so embarrassed that she cried.

Another day when Yi Xian was out shopping, Gong Xian instructed us to play a new game. He asked us to climb up a ladder one-by-one to the indoor beam of the house and jump down from there. The beam was at least thirty feet above the ground. While one was up on the beam, the rest of us were holding three corners of a quilt waiting eagerly to catch the jumper. Gao Xian and Kai Xian tried one after the other and were successfully caught in the quilt. They found it so much fun that they did it again and again and were highly praised by "Commander Gong Xian."

I could not wait for my turn to come. So I climbed up the ladder to the beam very quickly and jumped. With a loud thud, I fell off the edge of the quilt onto the ground because I had not jumped right into the center of the quilt. I suffered one more week's pain. But this exercise was less dangerous than jumping to the ground from the balcony of the second floor with a paper umbrella. I felt fortunate to have been trained by brother Gong Xian in my childhood; it toughened me up. Later, I was considered quite a brave woman in every respect. I owe all credit to him.

Bombed Out of Duyun

Emergency air-raid warnings were an everyday occurrence. One afternoon in Duyun, the air-raid sirens blared continuously. The bombs kept exploding in the area where we lived. But before people could get into the designated shelters, countless Japanese bomber planes suddenly filled the skies of our town. The sunlight was gone as bombs went off simultaneously. Through the horrifying sounds of constant explosions, panicked screams and cries of the townspeople could be heard. Finally, the planes blew up even the air raid shelters.

My fourth sister, Yi Xian and her husband made a decision that our family should not delay any longer. Along with their son, they quickly led my sister and two youngest brothers out of the house. As the dreadful bombing continued, we all ran as fast as we could to save our lives. About twenty minutes after we had rushed out of our house, we heard an explosion behind us. A bomb had hit our house and from a distance we saw the fire engulf it as it burned to the ground. Now we were truly homeless.

That night, we hid ourselves in an air-raid shelter, trembling with fear and cold. When we came out of the shelter the next morning, we saw hundreds of corpses lying by the roadside, in the ditches and in the fields. On the electrical wires strung out between the poles, we saw arms, legs, and human body parts hanging down from the wires still dripping with blood. It was all our people! I could not help crying. It was the first time in my life that I witnessed the horrible crimes committed by the Japanese troops.

Yi Xian and Yao, Yi Fu knew we needed to escape from Duyun immediately, so we hurried on to Chongqing. They stopped as many of the passing transport trucks as they could in an effort to get us a lift. But, we could not afford the drivers' fees for they wanted to charge us a fortune. Finally, around noontime, the driver of a truck carrying dozens of bombs agreed to take us to Zhungyi on the condition that we would run the risk of sitting on the unevenly packed bombs. While he assured us that it was not dangerous to sit on the bombs, he still requested a lot of money.

Altogether there were about fifteen "passengers" sitting atop the load. I was sitting on a bomb in the left front side of the truck, holding my youngest brother on my lap. A biting north wind blew hard through a hole, about the size of my hand, in the tarp just beside me; it made for a very cold draft. My eight-year-old brother kept crying because he was freezing. I moved a bit to press my back against the hole in an effort to stop the draft. As we headed toward Zhungyi, the truck had to pass along rough mountain roads full of turns and twists. Despite this, after a few hours, everyone fell into a deep sleep.

All of a sudden, there was a loud crushing sound and the truck leaned to the right and came to a stop. The driver yelled loudly, "Get out of the truck! Quickly! Quickly!" Without time to think, we all jumped out of the truck. The driver had been holding the steering wheel very tightly with his foot pressed hard against the brake. After all the passengers were out of his truck, the driver leaped out of the cab. As soon as he let go of the steering wheel, the truck's delicate balance gave way as it rolled over a cliff all the way down into the Wujiang River. With a big splash, it sank into the water, unexploded bombs and all. The dark waters of the river ran deep and swift. That's why it was named Wujiang[3].

The driver looked at us and breathed a sigh of relief. He explained that there had been an oncoming truck from the opposite direction. The road was too narrow at the curve for two trucks to go through at the same time. However, the other driver did not see our truck and almost hit us. How dangerous it had been! We all thanked the driver for saving our lives.

There was still a long distance to Zhungyi, so we had to continue our journey on foot. It was a long and difficult journey, but there was no other way. Night was approaching and we were all hungry and exhausted. Eventually, we saw some electrical lights off in the distance. It turned out to be a small town. We couldn't find any place to spend the night except for a stable. Since there was no food available, we had to go hungry that night. The stable was dirty and wet. Horse manure was everywhere and the smell was unbearable. There was not an inch of dry space for us to sit, so we squatted by leaning our backs against the icy cold walls and waited for the day to break.

Morning finally came. My brother-in-law asked Min Xian and me to follow him to get food for the family. We saw a shabby hut in the middle of the fields and approached it. When we knocked at the door, a woman answered. He asked her to sell us some food, but she refused. Even after

---

[3] *Wu* means black; *jiang* means river.

handing over money to her, she still refused, so he had to force her to give us food. Putting his hand in his pocket, he said, "I have a gun." The woman got scared and immediately took out a large basket of yams from the back room.

My brother-in-law thanked her again and paid her even more. This time she smiled as she took the money. We carried the yams to the rice field to wash them before eating them. In the field, we saw a farmer working. As we got closer, I was shocked to see that both of his legs were covered with leeches that were sucking his blood. When he saw us, he stopped working to hit his legs very hard with a branch of a tree. Then, to disengage the leeches, he pulled them off as quickly as possible. His legs were bleeding where the leeches had been. Oh, my God! What a miserable life the farmers were living!

After we ate we continued walking until we got to Zhungyi. That night we had some rice and vegetables for dinner at a small restaurant and we had a sound sleep at an inn. Later, we found another truck to carry us on our journey to Chongqing, the capital of China during the Anti-Japanese War.

A Poor Boy Never Forgotten

We arrived at a hot springs area called Nan Wen Quan. It was a small town that had a lot of springs with hot bubbling water coming up from the ground. We temporarily rented a small shabby house and lived there for several months. The house was close to a hot spring pond, where everyone went to wash clothes or take a bath. It was winter, so the weather was damp and very chilly.

At that time, I was not able to go to school, so I stayed home to help with the housework. Every morning the air was cold, which made the pond look like a big boiling pot with steam coming out. Usually, when I went to the pond to wash clothes, the steam was so thick that it was hard to see the people through it.

Out of curiosity, one day I walked to the opposite side of the pond to see what it looked like. There I found a boy about my age sitting on the steps of the pond, soaking his legs in the warm water. When I walked up near him, he lowered his head, but continued to hit the water with a branch in his right hand. As I looked at him closely, I saw that he wore an old torn cotton-padded jacket with short pants. His eyes were big but very dim, and he actually looked quite sad.

One evening, I went deliberately to see if he was there. In the twilight, I vaguely saw someone on the steps of the pond. I approached him quietly and asked why he had not gone home. He lifted his head and looked at me without saying a word. Since it was late, I returned home. But I stayed awake almost all night.

As soon as day broke the next morning, I took some food and a basket of dirty clothes to the pond. Instead of going to the usual washing spot, I went around the pond to where the boy sat on the steps. I had decided that he did not have a home to go to at night. As I handed him the food I brought, I started talking to him. From the very few words he spoke, I learned that he was a homeless child. He spent most of his time, especially in winter, here so that he would not freeze to death. From that day on, every morning, I would take some food from our kitchen and offer it to him. Other kind people also gave him food to eat. Very soon, we became friends and a smile would appear on his face when he saw me.

One sunny day, I sat beside him and washed clothes. When I finished and prepared to go home, the boy asked me if I would like to visit another hot spring pond close by. As soon as I said, "Yes", he suddenly stood up in the water. Oh, my God. I was shocked to see that his legs were almost as thick as his waist. They had swollen from being soaked all the time in the water. I felt so sad because I could not do more for him. All I could do was give him some food and talk to him every day. Life went on like this for several months. Then my family moved to downtown Chongqing. When I said good-bye to the boy, I cried and he did, too.

During that war, there were so many kids who similarly suffered such miserable lives. My heart was heavy for a long time. Even to this day, his image will appear in my mind, although if he lived, he would be in his seventies.

In the chaos of the war, there was a time when our family scattered into several groups and we could not get in touch with each other for a couple of years. Life was very difficult, especially for some of the younger ones, including myself. One can only imagine how much pain our parents suffered with their children missing from their daily lives.

Living Through Hardships

Later, after we arrived in Chongqing, with its mountains, we had to live in a wet and dirty deserted air-raid shelter in the Liziba district. It was so bad that I got rashes all over my body that itched so much I could hardly sleep at night. We could not afford any effective ointment so I suffered a lot. And for a period of time, my seventh sister and I tried to make a little money by boiling up "big bowl tea" for the passing rickshaw men.

In Chongqing, we met up with our two elder brothers, Cheng Xian and De Xian, and our third sister, Ai Xian. They all came to Chongqing from different places in China. Yet, at this time none of us children had any idea where our parents were. In order to give our fourth sister, Yi Xian a break, our brother Cheng Xian and his nice new bride took responsibility for the care of my youngest brothers, Gao Xian and Kai Xian. Our third sister Ai Xian willingly took on the responsibility for my seventh sister Min Xian and me. A few months later, the two boys, Gao Xian and Kai Xian, moved with our oldest brother to Xi An where he found a job.

Our sister, Ai Xian, was serving in a Kuomintang army hospital as a nurse at that time. Since her pay was too low to support the three of us,

My third eldest sister, Ai Xian (1940)

she found a cleaning job as a maid at the hospital for my fourteen-year-old sister, Min Xian. Too young to work, I stayed at home to cook for Min Xian and myself. Actually, the two of us lived under the staircase in an office building at the army hospital. We had no bed, so we slept under our blanket on the floor that we covered with some dried grass. It was a small and dark place, so small that we could not even stand up straight. It was a place they had used to store brooms, mops and pans. Min Xian went out to work every day and I was all alone at "home". Outside at the back of the building, I made a stove out of three broken bricks. I collected dried branches for fuel to cook our very simple meals. Since Ai Xian lived in the nurses' dormitory, she had her meals at the army cafeteria. When she could have extra food, she would bring it to us.

Min Xian received a monthly payment, which was only one sack of unhusked rice. The two of us would carry the heavy bag to the other side of the mountain where there was a mill. The owner of the mill did not charge us for grinding the grain, as he kept the hulls as payment for his work. The sack was so heavy that it was hard for us to make it up such a long and steep path as we climbed over the big mountain.

We had to stop often and rest along the way. It was so quiet on the mountain as though there were no other people on the path. The only sound we heard came from the electrical wires atop the poles. All the while as we ascended and descended the mountain there was a ringing in my ears. It sounded like a woman sobbing, which gave me a very sad and lonely feeling. Later, throughout my life, whenever I heard a similar sound, that memory of carrying the heavy sacks immediately returns to me.

There was no money for us to buy vegetables, to say nothing of meat. Therefore, my major task was to find wild vegetables in the nearby fields. One day we had completely run out of rice. I had to find more wild vegetables so we would have something for dinner. As I came to the open fields, I saw rows of cornstalks. In checking an ear, I found that the corn was ripe. I loved corn and could not resist the temptation. Pulling up my worn skirt to hold them, I picked some ears of corn. Just as I was ready to go back home, I heard an old woman yell at me, "Give back the corn or I will beat you!"

As I turned my head, I saw the old woman running toward me. I was so frightened that I immediately started to run. As she chased me, she shouted, "Stop! Stop!" I just kept running as fast as I could. Then, I threw one ear of corn to the ground. The old woman stopped, bent over, and picked up the corn. I quickly figured out that it had bought me time so I could get farther away from her. So I threw down another ear so she would stop to pick it up, and then another, until I was out of her sight. I knew in my heart that stealing was wrong, but I was so hungry! Up to this day, whenever I have thought of this, I still feel ashamed. If ever I meet her, I will apologize–but that is truly impossible, now.

This way of life lasted for half a year until Ai Xian found a boarding school where we could live and have plenty to eat. Because it was located at the top of South Mountain in Chongqing, it was named South

Mountain Elementary School. One might expect that since an American Catholic Church ran it, there would be a number of American nuns taking care of the school. And there were nuns.

It was 1945, I was in the fourth grade and Min Xian was in the sixth grade. Most of the other children there were from rich families. The two of us were allowed to attend even though we had no money for our tuition. Instead, we had to work at the school. Every morning, we were the first to get up as we started our assigned cleaning jobs at six o'clock. We swept the classrooms, cleaned the windows, mopped the floors and wiped off all railings along the corridors of the second floor. I especially liked the rail-cleaning because I would climb over the railings and hang there to wipe the bars from the outside. Quite adventurous, I thought!

One morning, two American nuns happened to walk by and saw me dangling outside the railings. Astonished, they told me not to clean the bars from outside of the railings and said, "If you fall down, you will get killed." I obeyed and climbed back onto the steps, but I thought they were too fussy.

Somehow, the nuns liked me a lot and would often talk to me. One morning as I saw them coming my way, I stopped them so we could talk. "Good morning, nuns. I have something important to tell you. Last night I had a very strange dream. In fact, I dreamed of the death of the great president of your country, Roosevelt. And I saw the American citizens crying about his death." The nuns stared at me and said, "Are you crazy? Stop talking such nonsense!" But I insisted, "Truly, I dreamed of the death of the president of the United States." Then they warned me not to talk about it anymore and hurried on their way. Later that afternoon, news came that, indeed, President Roosevelt of the United States had died. Why had I dreamt about his death? I was only a child of 12 and did not know anything about politics. I did not even know where the United States of America was located.

On an early summer day that same year, I had a chance to go into downtown Chongqing. A big city, the streets were filled with so many people. Through the crowd, I saw the back of a thin, tall man who wore a long dark blue gong. He was walking very fast as he carried a medicine bag. My heart leaped as I thought it was my father. So I ran to catch up with him and called out, "Dad! Dad!" But the man kept walking as if he did not hear me. As I reached him, I pulled at his sleeve. He stopped and looked down at me with a stern face. It was a stranger! I was so disappointed that I cried right there in the middle of the street. We had not heard anything from our parents for more than one year. Min Xian and I felt like orphans. Ai Xian had to work such long hours in the army hospital that she had no free time to be with us. We longed so much to see our parents.

On August 15, 1945, after eight horrible years, news of Japan's surrender was announced. Our boarding school was filled with cheers as we hailed the victory over the Japanese invaders. The Chinese people would suffer no further tortures from the war. I was so happy that day! The terrible war had finally ended and the long nightmare was over. There was finally hope for us to find our parents and all of our other brothers and sisters.

After the victory, Min Xian and I stayed on at the school. Our third sister, Ai Xian, left the army hospital and set out to find our family. With the help of her friends, she discovered that our parents were in Kunming, and left to join them.

A few weeks after Ai Xian left for Kunming, a friend of hers came to our school to inform me that she had indeed found our parents there and she gave me a plane ticket to travel by myself to join our family in Kunming. Min Xian had to stay a little longer so she could graduate from the South Mountain Elementary School. The American nuns and teachers at the boarding school were happy for me and even held a farewell party. I sang a solo at the party, a lullaby. It was the first time in my life that I performed in front of such a large group.

The following day, Ai Xian's friend took me to the airport. She had told me not to bring anything except my school bag. It would truly be very light travel. As a farewell gift, she had gotten me a box of Chinese checkers that would easily fit in to my bag. Encouraging me not to worry, she said that my family would meet me at the airport in Kunming.

A Huge Change

The victory over the Japanese invaders ended my life of misery. To begin with, I was on an airplane. In those days, only rich people had money to ride in a plane. I did not look like a rich girl. I was in shorts with a faded blue sleeveless top. The shoes I wore were homemade and clearly worn out. My hair was long and dry and I looked quite pale. So, when I boarded the plane, nearly all the passengers stared at me with curiosity.

Some rich, heavy-set ladies looked at me out of the corner of their eyes. As I stared back at them, I was thinking that they looked very ugly. Dressed up, they were adorned with gold earrings, thick gold necklaces and diamond rings. Their faces were "painted" white as walls and to me their lips looked 'bloody', just like animals that had finished eating their prey! Dumbfounded, I sat back in my seat.

Then the woman sitting next to me asked, "Where are you going?" I answered, "I am going to Kunming to be with my parents." As she asked me more questions about myself, my answers quickened. This woman seemed to be friendly enough, so I took out the Chinese checker set that Ai Xian's friend had given me. I asked her if she wanted to play with me, to which she agreed. Since it was a game that needed three players, another woman who had been listening joined in. We played several times and each time I was the winner. They said, "This girl is very smart!" To which I smiled proudly.

It was nearly dark when the plane landed at the Kunming airport. But as soon as I walked down the airplane steps, I saw several familiar faces. My family had come. Waiting for me were my father, my mother, my second and fifth elder brothers, and my third elder sister, Ai Xian. Yet, I was not all that excited. On the contrary, I felt like I didn't belong to this family. They looked so rich. All the men were wearing suits. Dressed up, the ladies had on lots of jewelry, both necklaces and rings. Even my mother's lips were coated with that red lipstick. It was awful! They all came to me with smiles on their faces. However, I could only muster a soft voice to greet them by name, one-by-one.

The drive back home was in fancy cars. I had never before experienced that. When we got there, my sister took me into the kitchen. An old nanny, called Yang Ma, fixed me fried rice with eggs. It was so delicious! I sat on a small stool until I had finished eating it all. Yang

Ma, our old kitchen nanny, looked at me curiously and asked me if I had had enough food. She spoke in the Yunnan dialect, which I understood because I knew the Sichuan dialect that was quite similar. Yang Ma seemed surprised as she realized that I had understood what she meant.

As soon as I had finished eating, Ai Xian came back into the kitchen carrying some gasoline. She washed my hair with warm water, and rinsed it in the gasoline to rid me of any lice. Then she wrapped my head in a big towel. But she was not done yet. Placing me in a big wooden tub, she scrubbed me all over and finished by wrapping me in a bath towel. All of the clothes I had been wearing were left in the kitchen and my sister told the old nanny to throw them away. Obviously, my sister did not want me to go to sleep in my bedroom with lice in my hair or clothes.

After my sister led me upstairs, she opened the door of a room and said, "This is your bedroom." The brightly lit room cheered me up immediately. It was beautifully decorated. There was a single bed with pink sheets and a quilt, a desk with a chair, and a dresser. On the walls were some colorful cartoon pictures. And a large pretty doll sat on the desk smiling at me in the light of the lamp. Everything looked so clean and neat. I felt that I had mistakenly been led into the bedroom of a princess. It was the first time in my life that I had such a well-furnished bedroom.

As my sister put me to bed, she said, "Do not get up tomorrow morning until I come in for you." Turning off the lamp, she left me alone in my own room. The bright moonlight from the night's full moon lit up the room. I covered my naked body with the new quilt and laid my towel-covered head on the comfortable pillow. I was too excited to fall asleep. I kept wondering if everything in front of my eyes was real. It had only been a few short hours since I looked like a beggar girl carrying a worn out school bag. Here I was sleeping in such a beautiful bedroom within such a big house. I turned my head left and right as I looked at the room in the moonlight.

I am not certain how quickly I fell asleep, but by the time I woke up, the sun was high and the room was filled with sunshine. I wanted so much to get up but I had no clothes to wear. So I had to wait for my sister as she had instructed.

Around ten o'clock in the morning, my sister opened the door and came in with several shopping bags full of clothes. As she opened up the bags, she asked me to choose what I wanted to wear. I was amazed to see so many pretty dresses all at once. Finally, I picked a light yellow dress with a striped pattern. I particularly liked the ribbons across the top on the front of the dress. It was a good thing I waited for her to take the towel off my head. For when she took it off, there were lots of dead lice and eggs in it from my hair. In the kitchen, my sister washed my hair again, and I was fed a quick breakfast.

Then we were off to a hairdresser, which was on the seventh floor of a tall hotel building. It did not take long before I had a new haircut. My sister smiled at me approvingly, as if my hairstyle finally went with the new dress. Next, she was scheduled to have her own hair done, so she asked me to wait for her on the same floor.

I left the hairdresser's room to seek an adventure. I visited many rooms on the same floor but found nothing fun to do. Then to my joy, I

Having arrived in Kunming (1945)

found a great spiral staircase. It had a handrail made of bronze. The railing was shiny, and it looked very smooth and inviting. Without a second thought, I mounted the handrail on my stomach and slid from the seventh floor all the way down to the lounge. It was so much fun! But, as soon as I began to climb the stairs to repeat the slide, I was shocked to see that there was a thick dark line right down the middle of my new dress from sliding on the bronze. What could I do? It was too late for regret. Had I known ahead of time what would happen to my new dress, I would not have played that game. I actually did not care so much about the new dress, I was more afraid that my sister would yell at me.

Terrified, I dared not go up to the seventh floor again. I squatted down, leaned my back against one of the thick round pillars in the lounge, and waited for the impending punishment. About an hour later, I heard my sister's voice. She had been looking for me on the seventh floor when someone told her I was down in the lounge. As she walked down the stairs in her high-heeled shoes, she was smoothing her hair with her hand, looking very happy. When she saw me, she apologized that she had kept me waiting for so long. I was unwilling to stand up lest she see the dark mark on my dress. Of course, her face changed as soon as she saw the dirty streak and she quizzed me on what had happened. I said, "I did not know it would make a dark mark on my dress." My sister condemned me, "Don't you know you could be killed when you slide down so far like that?!" This was a much better response from her than I had expected; I felt her love for me. Yet I would never forget that beautiful yellow-striped dress that I had only worn for a few hours.

After several weeks of living in my new home, I came home from school one day for lunch. There was no one at home except Yang Ma. She was in her sixties and was always cheerful. That day, while I was eating my lunch, she looked at me with amusement and said in her Yunnan dialect, "Do you know when you first came home that night, I thought you were a maid bought by Mrs. Chen, your mom, to help me with the housework. It turns out that you are Miss Number 8. Hah! Hah! Hah! Hah!" She laughed so much that saliva ran out of her toothless mouth. I was not used to being addressed as Miss Number 8. But from that day on, the title followed me right up until the Communist Party took over.

Life was so luxurious during our time in Kunming. My parents opened a clinic and enjoyed a high reputation in the city. Owing to my parents' social position, the people we were in contact with were all high-ranking officials or popular intellectuals. I was taken to the best restaurants, to rich families' homes for parties, and even to see Hollywood movies. Years later, during the Communist political movement, whenever I needed to self-criticize and root out my bourgeois thoughts, I always thought back to this period in my life, because by nature, I loved to be with poor people.

My Grandfather Chen, An Fen

In the summer of 1946, a year after the end of the Anti-Japanese War, my grandfather and I flew back to his hometown, Hangzhou, from Kunming. I was only thirteen and my grandpa was already in his early

My Grandfather (1946)

seventies. We resided in his old dwelling on the edge of the city after an eight-year absence. It was a big house with a huge backyard and thick bamboo bushes at the rear. There was a well in the middle of the yard. Beside it, there was a date tree that gave a lot of shade when the sun was high.

To keep him company and perhaps for my safety, we shared one big room leaving empty all the other dusty rooms. The weather was extremely hot and humid. Since there was no shower in the house, grandpa used to wash his upper body with warm water before bedtime. I frequently offered to scrub his back and found that his muscles were solidly built like a young man. One evening out of curiosity while rubbing his back, I asked, "Grandpa, you are old but how come you are so muscular?"

He turned to look at my naïve face with a mysterious smile and said, "Don't you know that I used to practice martial arts? At the age of five when I began to learn, I had a great master who taught me not only martial arts, but also how to read and write. Later when I was eighteen, I was hired as a bodyguard for an American minister. The minister took me along when he traveled over the Pacific Ocean, the Atlantic Ocean, and the Mediterranean Sea. I had a lot of adventures."

My interest was aroused. In the past I had never spent much time alone with my grandpa. In a big family like mine, the grandchildren never had a chance to ask about the personal stories of the older generations. Now that I lived all alone with grandpa, I had the privilege of learning all about him. So I said, "Grandpa, what I know about you is that you once owned a cow farm."

"Yes, but that was much later,"

I quickly finished scrubbing his back and urged him to sit on a bamboo couch in the courtyard. After making him a cup of tea, I hurriedly pulled up a small stool close to his knees. Then I sat down and began to cool him with a big cattail-leaf fan, waiting for him to tell his stories.

His eyes shone in the moonlight. Grandpa stroked his long white beard and slowly began, "After I married your grandma at the age of twenty, I quit my job as a bodyguard and made a living doing carpentry work. We were both Christians, and life was happy even though we were often short of money. Then we had two sons; the older is your Dad.

"On a gloomy afternoon about six years later, I went to visit a friend of mine who owned a cow farm. As soon as I entered the gate of the cattle pen, a calf rushed directly towards me. The calf knelt down before me with large teardrops running down its face. I was shocked and asked my friend what had happened to this calf. He told me that he had decided to kill its mother because she was too old to keep as a milk cow, so he had isolated her in the slaughterhouse that day. The calf stayed kneeling on the ground before me, crying. I had never seen an animal crying. And I could not bear seeing the baby suffer from the pain of losing its mother. Even an animal could love its mom like that. So, without a second thought, I bought both the mother cow and her calf and took them home.

"When your grandma learned the story she thanked God for giving us the two animals. She immediately emptied the room where we kept firewood and carpeted the floor with dry hay. We looked at our contented rescued animals with much satisfaction even though we were not sure how to make ends meet in the days to come. Your father and your uncle were happy to have two new members in the family. Every day after school, they would lead the cow and her calf to the neighboring grassland to feed them. It was a "game" the boys enjoyed the most. In just a few days, we found that the mother cow's udder was full. We began to milk her and she gave large quantities of milk every day. Our family could not consume so much milk, so we shared it with our neighbors. Some of them wanted to pay for the milk. Later, the calf grew to maturity and gave a lot of milk as well. After a couple of years, we bought more cows and more cows until we could depend on the farm for a living. Our dairy business went very well. Over the years, we had nine children in all, six sons and three daughters. We had enough money to send them all to college or technical schools where they received a good education."

As I listened, my young heart was filled with gratitude to both my grandfather and the calf. Grandpa was an extremely compassionate man. Though he seldom talked, whenever he did, his words carried weight. Grandpa's life experiences proved true the old saying, "Everything that goes around comes around." That's an unforgettable spiritual lesson my grandpa taught me.

Grandpa paused for a sip of his tea and became quiet. He closed his eyes as if deep in thought. "Grandpa," I said waking him up, "can you tell me what you saw during your voyages? I have never been to the sea. It must be a great experience to sail in a boat over the vast oceans!" As I looked at grandpa with eyes shining in wonder, I anticipated him telling me more miraculous stories about his life.

He said, "When I was young, I was full of energy and enthusiasm. Yet I was overwhelmed by the news that the American minister wanted to take me along to travel the seas. There was not a big crew on the ship but all of us were strong and capable. During the two years that we traveled, I saw many strange things, both at sea and on shore. There were many sea lions and we saw big sea snakes swimming along the bottom of the transparent waters. And once, a huge sea turtle almost overturned our ship. Everywhere we went whales and dolphins were our frequent visitors. We landed on many islands during our travels. We often saw native people dancing, and when we felt welcome, we joined in their ritual ceremonies. Sometimes the minister had to pay for permission to enter their territory. Most of the crewmembers were Chinese, and the minister spoke pretty good Chinese as well. But he also had the ability to communicate with many different tribes. He would preach wherever he went and he cured peoples' diseases with his medicines, so we did not encounter much trouble with the natives. We set foot in tropical jungles where we saw beautiful flowers and strange plants. Once we came upon a cactus-like plant that would wrap people up in its big leaves and eat them if they mistakenly stood too close underneath."

"How could the plant eat people? Did it have teeth?" I interrupted. He replied, "No, it just sucked the blood and dissolved the flesh. After the plant released its victim, only the bones were left." I shivered as I pictured the man-eating plant like a terrifying demon. However, my curiosity kept growing. "Did you ever see a marine man?" I was imagining what a man who lived in the sea would look like. Grandpa shook his head and replied, "No, we did not have the luck to see one." As I sat at grandpa's knee, I fixed my eyes on his lips, drinking in every word he uttered as vivid pictures emerged one after another in my mind's eye.

That evening and ever since, I would consider grandpa to be the wellspring of my already wildly imaginative mind. He was not merely my grandpa; he was my hero, my teacher, my inspiration. We spent many nights like this as he told me stories about my father's childhood. He expressed how dutiful and nice my grandmother had been. And how sad he was that she had died during a fall while trying to escape the bombing during a Japanese air raid. He also related many stories from the Bible.

A Wonderful Composition

Early one winter morning when I was living in Hangzhou with my grandfather, I went to the kitchen to prepare our breakfast. As soon as I opened the kitchen door, I saw a cat catch two mice at the same time. The two mice had been fighting over a piece of meat and the cat caught them in the act. Both became victims and neither of them got the meat because the cat took that as well. It was not a happy scene.

Afterward, I thought a lot about this incident. At that time, the Kuomintang and the Communist Party were having a civil war. As a child, I was told they were fighting for the power to govern China. I thought they were both wrong. I remembered how I had observed the cat eating the mice and even the piece of meat that they had been fighting over. I naturally related it to the political situation in China.

That same week, our Chinese teacher asked us to write a composition choosing whatever topic we would like. I was already in the sixth grade, nearly ready to graduate from elementary school. I really liked composition class. So I sat at my desk holding my ink brush as I thought about the story of the cat and the mice. Deciding it would be interesting to write about, I composed, in detail, what I had seen that morning. At the end of the composition, I wrote, "The two mice are just like the Kuomintang and the Communist Party, both fighting over the territory of China. If they go on like this, they will be equally

Me at age 14 (1947)

exhausted and some outsider, a stronger country, may come and beat both of the parties and occupy China. The Chinese people suffered a lot during the Anti-Japanese War. China has just freed itself from the occupation of the Japanese invaders. I do not want to see the re-occurrence of that terrible history."

A few days later, my Chinese teacher came to the classroom with a big stack of composition exercise books. After putting them down on his desk, he came up to me with a big smile. He handed me my composition exercise book and returned to the front of the room. Then he spoke to the class, "Chen Hui Xian wrote a wonderful composition last week and I want her to read it out loud." I got a bit nervous at having to read it to everyone. The whole class was very quiet, but at the end of my recitation, they gave me a big round of applause. The teacher said, "When you write a composition, use your brain and speak out your point of view. I like her composition because she expressed her viewpoint clearly."

Later, the teacher asked the class monitor to post my composition on the back wall of the classroom. Soon, many students from other classes came to read my article and I became the center of attention for a while. How naïve I was at that time. Just how naïve I would learn much later in life.

High School in Jiaxing

Throughout 1946, all my family members returned to Jiaxing one-by-one from different parts of China. My father was the last to come back from Kunming because something unexpected occurred.

On the appointed day, as he was about to board the plane, he was called back to work because the governor of Yunnan Province, Long Yun, needed emergency care. My father had to forego the flight and head

The whole family in Jiaxing;
I'm on the far left (1948)

back from the airport. Within ten minutes after the plane took off, thick smoke poured out of the plane, then it suddenly exploded in mid-air. All of the passengers were killed, including two of my cousins and one auntie. Two days later, my father took another plane and flew to Shanghai. Everybody remarked on how very lucky he was to have been called from the airport to treat the governor. It saved his life and changed the lives of the many others he would come to impact in later years.

Near the end of 1946, my parents began to rebuild their Trinity Hospital in Jiaxing. During the disastrous eight years of war, the hospital was brutally damaged and there was almost nothing left, so my parents had to put all their savings into rebuilding it. On New Year's Day in 1947, Jiaxing Trinity Hospital reopened its service to the public. The local people were very happy. In addition to the hospital, my parents also opened a medical school to train physicians to serve in the countryside.

The time came for me to go to high school in Jiaxing where my parents and all my brothers and sisters lived, so I sadly left my dear grandpa. It was a pity that I had only one year to spend alone with him.

After successfully passing the entrance examination, I was admitted to the area's best private high school. Xiuzhou High School was an old Christian school of high quality that enjoyed a very good reputation. Many students traveled from Shanghai and Hangzhou to study there.

The school's tuition was very expensive. What was unusual was that my tuition was paid in rice, not in cash. Following the end of the Anti-Japanese War, the value of Chinese money was in flux. Effected by inflation, cash might decrease its value overnight. In order to guarantee the value of the tuition, the school only accepted rice, no Chinese currency. Before I was allowed to register, my father had a servant carry one *dan*[4] of white rice to the school. Their temporary registration office was set up in a big classroom, one corner of which was filled with heaps of rice. Several men kept busy receiving the tuition while the students and their parents stood in long lines, waiting to register. The scene was more like a market place than a school.

It was truly a good school. The teachers were responsible and taught well. The classrooms were big and bright. We had a large classroom where music classes were held. I liked singing so I joined the school chorus and we often practiced there. The school's auditorium was huge and often school meetings were held there, as well as concerts and other performances. The gymnasium was very big and well out-fitted. There were even several types of gymnastic apparatus and on occasion we had gymnastic exhibitions. The high school students played basketball, and we all enjoyed the basketball games.

In the gym, we took physical training classes. Our Physical Education teacher was strict, but a very nice person. All the students liked him. In the late afternoons, I always hung out in the gym before going home. It was always full of activity and happy noises.

Xiuzhou High School provided its students with many great opportunities to learn. We often had famous musicians coming from big cities to play music for us. There were also wonderful lectures given by well-known speakers. On occasional trips, our teachers took us to Hangzhou or Shanghai to visit museums or to enjoy the beauty of nature. Many graduates from my school went for further studies in the United States and became famous scholars.

During the three years in Xiuzhou High School, my school life and family life were full of unforgettable happy times. At school, I was an excellent student. I was not only good at all of my studies, but I also participated in physical and recreational activities. I got along with the teachers and my schoolmates very well. Mother announced to all of us

---

[4] Equal to 50 kilos

children who were still studying at school, that whoever came out in the top three of their class, she would award with a pure-gold ring. For three years, including six terms, I won six gold rings. My success brought great joy to my father and he promised to send me to Yanjing University for a college education and he said that I should plan to study diplomacy in the future.

My mother rarely seemed to have the time to check our homework except for one day when I was in junior high. After school that day, I went into her room to say hello to my parents. She stopped me short and asked me to recite a text from my English book. Luckily that day I had reviewed just enough to be able to recite "The Selfish Giant" which our teacher had just assigned. I recited the English fluently, which pleased my mom, but surprised me because I never knew my mother's English was so good.

My mom would never miss any opportunity to educate us. One noontime, we four youngest kids came home from school for lunch. Instead of a table full of delicious dishes, there was only a broken bamboo basket covered with a dirty cotton cloth. Mother lifted the cover and we saw some buns. "This is your lunch today," she told us. "I traded with a countrywoman. She was penniless but begged me to save her sick child's life. I admitted her child to the hospital and I requested this basket of food from her in return. You should eat the buns and remember there are still many

With my five youngest siblings; I'm on the left (1948)

people suffering. And you should study hard so that you can serve them when you grow up." The buns were made of wild vegetables and chaff and they tasted as bad as they looked. Silently, we ate them and went back to school. That memorable lesson remains fresh in my mind to this day.

A Gift Is Required to See Him

While living in Jiaxing, our parents made friends with lots of Americans; many were ministers and doctors. They were often guests in our home and we saw them at church nearly every Sunday. Our whole family usually attended church on Sunday mornings. After attending Sunday school, I would always go to the adult church service and sit by my parents. They would listen with great interest to the minister talk and sing the Christian psalms.

Singing was also common in our church. I particularly loved the Christmas carols. On Christmas Eve, I would join the group as they sang Christmas carols door-to-door for the Christian families. In return, the families gave us gifts and candy. Some of them even came out to join in the caroling. So, we gathered more and more people as we went along. For me, that was the most exciting experience of the year and I often stayed up all night. In my father's Trinity Hospital, Christmas was a big event. We put on short plays, sang songs and had big parties. I often played the part of an angel with big feathered wings. While I did not know about religion, I soon grew to love and respect Jesus for all that he had done to save people in the world.

One day before Christmas, on my way home from school for lunch, I saw a group of doctors and nurses surrounding an American minister in a big conference room of my father's hospital. It was obvious that he was showing them something. As soon as he saw me approaching, he held up a picture about the size of a book and asked me, "What's in the picture?" I immediately answered, "It's Jesus!" Everyone was so surprised at my answer. "Why, I only see clouds," one of the doctors said and all the others murmured in agreement. Then the minister said, "Hui Xian is right. Another American minister took this picture when he was traveling through the desert in Africa. It was a hot day and he was riding on the back of a camel when he heard his name called from the sky. He looked up and saw Jesus in the clouds and immediately took a picture of him. The minister had shown this picture to many people, but very few could actually see the face of Jesus. Most people only saw clouds. "You see" said our minister, "One needs a gift to see him."

56

Heroic Efforts by My Father

One day in 1948, something unexpected happened. Around noontime, three wounded people–a mother and her two sons–were carried into the hospital for emergency care. That very morning, the family was digging sweet potatoes in their field when the older son found a ball-like iron object. Not knowing what it really was, he wanted to show it to his mother and younger brother. So he tossed it over to them. The loud explosion shocked many other farmers nearby. When they ran to the spot, they found the three unconscious and covered in blood. It was an abandoned land mine that had exploded!

The Japanese army had buried the mine before they retreated. What a vicious crime, I thought. The wounded family members were carried into surgery. To save three people at the same time required many hands. I was asked to help even though I was only fifteen and untrained.

My father and two other surgeons treated their life-threatening wounds. The mother's right leg had to be amputated because it had been shattered. The younger boy's face was badly damaged from the blast and the older boy's internal organs were exposed. It was a horrible sight! Everybody was busy in the operating room. The surgeries were very demanding and difficult. The whole medical team worked until midnight without food. But they were only able to save two lives. The older boy died late that afternoon. It was another nightmare caused by the Japanese even though they had long been driven out of China.

My father fainted after the long hours of extremely intensive work. He became very ill and never regained his strength.

During his illness, my mother worked as the substitute director of the hospital. Several of my older brothers and sisters assisted her because they had all majored in Western medicine and worked at the hospital. This lasted for more than a year. It was the same year that the People's Liberation Army liberated Jiaxing.

The Liberation of My Hometown

By May of 1949, the town of Jiaxing was in utter chaos. Kuomintang troops were retreating, but gunshots were heard all day and night and schools had to be closed for several days.

嘉興秀州中學思藝級畢業同學旅杭留影 1949.11.5.

Me (circled) on a trip to Hangzhou with my class

One morning, while I was in my second floor room at home, I heard the roar of a plane. I wondered what was going on, so I went out onto the balcony. Suddenly, I saw a plane descending at high speed until I could see the pilot clearly. He was firing at something on the ground and the fire shooting out of the plane seemed so close to me that I became paralyzed with fear and my feet could barely support my body. The pilot wore the Kuomintang army uniform, and I could easily make out his features, as his airplane flew by. It then became obvious to me that he was firing at the Communist troops.

The battle was over very soon. The People's Liberation Army soldiers appeared everywhere in Jiaxing. Many workers, students and ordinary people were celebrating the liberation of our town. We were called back to school and taught two very popular dances: the "waist drum dance" where we played drums that hung on a strap around the waist and the *Lian Xiang*, a folk dance from the liberated area that used a bamboo stick with coins in it.

Without knowing exactly what was going on, we children excitedly joined in the activities. In the streets we sang, danced and joined in the shouting of slogans, "Celebrate the liberation of Jiaxing!" "Long live the

People's Liberation Army!" and "Long live the Communist Party!" Even though I did not really understand what all this meant to our country or to me, personally, I was still happy. Longing for a change in our country, I pinned great hope on the new government. Soon after the celebration, everything returned to normal. As school resumed, I continued in the second year of junior high school.

My First Love

In my class, there was a very bright boy who was a year younger than me. His name was Qian, Jiang. Like me, he had escaped to the southwest of China during the Anti-Japanese War. While living there, he had learned many dialects as he had traveled to many provinces. His cousin, Qian, Xue was a gifted girl in art and was a very good friend of mine. Qian, Jiang's father was a famous artist and his mother was an actress who had died during the war.

He was good at music, art and acting. He had even played one of the major characters in the most famous Chinese children's movie "San Mao Street Urchin" written and drawn by his uncle, Zhang, Le Ping, a famous Chinese cartoonist. Qian, Jiang, Qian, Xue and I were all in the same class in school. But, at school, I seldom talked to Qian, Jiang lest our classmates gossip about us. Often we chatted and did homework together after school. Either he came to my home with his cousin or I went to one of their homes. Over time, I became very familiar with his three brothers. His eldest brother was a music student and the second eldest studied art. His younger brother was still in elementary school. We would often recount our own stories from the war and exchange ideas on our likes and dislikes. We enjoyed each other's company very much.

My first boyfriend Qian, Jiang

On Christmas Eve in 1948, Qian, Jiang came to the backdoor of my home to give me a bag of candies and peanuts with a beautiful Christmas card he had painted. He shyly asked me in a low voice, "Do you want it?" I nodded and thanked him. It was the first time in my life that I had accepted a gift from a boy. We both knew that we liked each other, but we had never expressed our feelings for one another before then.

Several months after the liberation of Jiaxing, it was a Monday evening before dinner and our family was gathered together talking in the dining room. My fifth brother took a letter from his pocket, tore it open and read it aloud. The letter was addressed to me from Qian, Jiang. It said, "I have joined the art troupe of the People's Liberation Army and I am leaving for Fujian and the front soon. I wish to see you before I leave. Please meet me at the entrance of the East playground at 7 o'clock this Friday evening." My fifth brother started to laugh and said, "Sister 8 is now dating! Sixteen years of age is the best time!" Then the whole family began to tease me. I was so upset and embarrassed that I cried and left the dining room without eating my meal.

For the rest of the week, Qian, Jiang did not show up in class. I missed him so much. When Friday came, I wondered if I should go to meet him that evening. Too timid and shy, I did not go. On Saturday morning, I was in chemistry class doing experiments in the lab with the door open and I felt somebody watching me. I turned and saw Qian, Jiang standing at the door with his bright eyes fixed upon me. I stared at him for a while as if to say goodbye to him. He was in a brand new army uniform, looking so handsome and radiating with vigor! Then he saluted to me and quickly left. My heart sank and I dropped the glass beaker from my hand. My classmates heard the sound of breaking glass; they all rushed to help me. I immediately squatted down to wipe up the solution, while tears nearly ran down my cheeks. I thought I would never see him again. I knew Qian, Jiang's uncle Zhang, Le Ping was a very progressive artist. He must have had a great influence on his nephew, but, I had never expected that Qian, Jiang would have made such a quick decision to join the Communist army.

Later, his brother told me that the troops were heading down to the south of China. Weeks later, I received a letter from Qian, Jiang. He was already in Xiamen in Fujian province. He told me that his art troupe was busy performing operas for the local folks and the soldiers and that he was learning how to act. He seemed to love his new life. He also mailed me a picture of him in his army uniform. I was so impressed! He asked me to mail him a photograph of me so that he could attach it to the first page of his diary. At the end of the letter, he asked me to wait for him.

I felt relieved and realized how much I loved him. Later, we communicated with each other through letters, though not frequently because his art troupe traveled constantly. He told me he studied many things in the army such as politics, Mandarin, and he had begun to play the violin and *erhu*[5]. He also encouraged me to join the revolution. The Korean War started and news arrived that Qian, Jiang's art troupe had been sent to the front in North Korea. We lost contact.

---

[5] A Chinese stringed instrument

Moving on to Senior High School

As I graduated from junior high school, plans were discussed concerning my senior high school education. My parents wanted me to be able to study at Yanjing University (today known as Beijing University). My father hoped I would major in diplomacy, as he had often told me that he considered me the most promising intellect among all his daughters.

Plans were made for me to study at Jinghai Girls' High School in Suzhou, located in Jiangsu province. It was a famous Catholic girl's school. On September 1, 1950, I entered Jinghai Girl's High School, which was located across the street from a private university, Dong Wu University. There was also a first class Catholic hospital located next to our school. The area's environment was beautiful and quiet, so it was given the name, Tianci Zhuang, which means "a manor that was a gift from heaven".

Our school's garden was huge, with green lawns and a rich variety of flowers. What impressed me most were the sweet-scented osmanthus trees, and there were dozens of them on campus. From outside the school wall, one could smell the fragrance of the osmanthus flowers. It blossoms in autumn and when the fragrant blossoms dropped from the trees, the lawns would be a yellow carpet of osmanthus flowers. Girls from our school would lie down on the grass and bury their noses in the flowers to enjoy the wonderful fragrance. We also collected osmanthus flowers, took them home and dried them. In the south of China, people use osmanthus flowers to add flavor to their famous desserts.

Our dormitory was big and kept very neat and clean. The nuns were very strict with us. No one was allowed to leave the dorm without making the bed. Soon after starting the term, I made new friends at school. But, there were four older girls in the third year of senior high that lived in our dorm. I did not like them much. Instead of studying hard, they sneaked away from the school at night to meet their boyfriends. Sometimes they returned to the dorm very late.

One day, I happened to be sick and had to be absent from class to rest in bed. The four girls, having spent most of the night playing outside the school, pretended to be sick and stayed in bed, too. Two of the nuns came into the dorm room with thermometers in hand and walked straight towards them. They gave each of the four girls a thermometer to test their temperature. The sisters were surprised to find that all of them were running a high fever yet they did not look very sick. Then the nuns lifted their blankets and found warm, roasted sweet potatoes on their beds. What a trick! They had used the potatoes to heat up the thermometers. I could not help laughing quietly under my blanket.

The sisters got them up out of bed and sent them off to class. I thought the nuns might also come to my bed and take my temperature. But, they simply told me to get a good rest, smiling as they left the room.

During that term, I often went home to see my father, as he was still very ill. Once when I was washing his feet, I found some pamphlets beside his pillow. They were all Mao, Ze Dong's works. Father had read them all. From his understanding, he told me, the Communist ideas were similar to his. "They serve the people," he said. "So do I."

Finally—Cruel Men Are Punished

Another day, I heard that there was a strange patient admitted to the hospital next to our school. It was an odd-looking woman with a head that looked like that of a pig, yet she had a human body. Many students went to look at her. She could not talk but only make noises like a pig. This immediately reminded me of the pear-headed man and the group of dwarfs that I had seen in my childhood. With compassion and curiosity, I went to the hospital and found the room where she was staying. I peeked in from the window and saw her sitting on her bed with her head lowered.

The story was that she had been kidnapped when she was three years old. Some cruel men had beaten her head and face until every inch of her head was bleeding. At the same time, they had stripped off the skin from a live pig's face and stuck it on to the girl's face. Ever since then, the girl had looked like a pig. Those cruel men used her to make money in the same way I had previously seen men do when I was a child.

My heart sank as I heard the story. But this time, the new government arrested and punished those men. I learned that they had been executed. The woman was sent to the hospital for surgery to remove the pigskin and for plastic surgery to restore her human face.

I remembered how upset I was when I heard the stories about pear-head, pig-head and those dwarfs. I was full of hatred for those evil people who made them look like that. I wanted to believe that the evil men from my childhood had been arrested and punished in the same way. I could hardly imagine how people could be so cruel. The Communist Party would never allow such things to happen again; I began to admire the new government.

A Life-Changing Year

School life was good and peaceful and my transition from junior high, to high school went smoothly. However, in November, I got a long-distance phone call from my aunty telling me the terrible news of my dear father's death. The grievous news came like a lightning bolt from the sky.

My father had always worked too hard and he had never taken the time to rest following the strenuous surgeries on the family that had been injured by the landmine. Treated for tuberculosis, my father stayed at a hospital in Shanghai for over a year. The results were not good so he returned to Jiaxing. He resumed work as head of the hospital although he had been bedridden for about two years and had lost considerable weight.

A cure was never found for my father. Before his heart stopped beating on November 25, 1950, he suddenly opened his eyes wide and looked up at the corner of the wall above the door. "Do not cry," he told the family members gathered around his bed. "Look, angels are here to take me back to God. They are blowing trumpets." Then, with a faint smile on his face, he closed his eyes. He died a peaceful death. All the family members were by his deathbed except for me. My heart broke when I heard the news. Traveling by bus, I rushed back home in tears; I felt that I was drowning in a sea of darkness.

I arrived in Jiaxing to see my father lying on his deathbed, his sacred body in a pure white robe with a big embroidered red cross on his chest. Our tears of sadness had wet his deathbed. My father was only sixty years old, but he had lived his life to the fullest. His was a life full of enthusiasm, and a life that was dedicated to saving so many other people's lives. Most importantly, he had served as a role model for all his children.

Before his death, my father wrote an Ethic Will. It has been a document I have tried to live by all my life. He wrote:

> *May we give our strength to the weak people;*
> *May we give our compassion to the sufferers;*
> *May we give our wealth to the poor people;*
> *May we give our heart and soul to almighty God.*

The day we held the funeral procession on the main road of Jiaxing, hundreds of people lined up along the roadside watching, many of them weeping. As one of the youngest children, I walked near the end of the family group behind our father's coffin. I turned my head and saw more and more people join us at the rear of the procession. When we got to the cemetery, countless people from Jiaxing were already standing there waiting for us. My father had lived a worthy life and so many people loved him.

According to my father's last will, my mother donated all the properties and facilities of the Trinity Hospital to the local government. Trinity Hospital had accomplished its mission. Two years later in December 1952, the government celebrated the gift with a big ceremony to accept the donation. My mother, my brothers and sisters, together with all the doctors and nurses in the hospital were greatly honored by the gathering. At that time, I was studying at the Beijing Institute of Foreign Languages and was unable to attend. Later, the government changed the name of my parents' hospital to Jiaxing Hospital of Gynecology and Obstetrics. In the years that followed, all of my brothers and sisters who had worked at the Trinity Hospital, moved on and found jobs in other public hospitals.

I Join the Army

When I returned to school after father's funeral, everything had changed. The government was calling upon the youth of China to support the war to "Resist U.S. Aggression and Aid Korea". School was cancelled. In every corner of the campus, students and teachers were talking and debating with excitement. My enthusiasm was aroused and I began to draw cartoons to propagate the political movement, while my best friend Liang, Xin Zhi wrote poem after poem to go along with the cartoons. Having suffered so much personally and having witnessed the bitter life of the Chinese people during the Anti-Japanese War, I was determined to join the army and support the cause.

Soon, I became the target of a group of Christian students from Dong Wu University. The leader of the group condemned me saying, "You are a Christian. If you want to join the army, you'll have to get permission from God. Don't you know that the American armies are

Me at bottom left before joining the military cadre school (1951)

from Heaven? They have come to save China." I fought back saying, "No! They are not. Any army from any country that invades another country is an invader, not an army from Heaven." This group of university students was mostly young men. They were so angry with me that they trapped me in a music room and ordered me to pray all night for God's response. Staying alone in that tiny room, I was both hungry and cold. But I was not sad; I wanted to fight!

When day broke, the leader of the group came and asked me, "Did you get an answer from God?" I said in a very loud and angry voice, "No, I did not even pray." He raised the bible over my head and said in a trembling voice, "You are a sinner!" At just that time, our political teacher, Comrade Hao showed up with some girls from our school. He said to the young man, "Go back to your own school. This girl has the

68

right to decide what she wants to do. You should not force your ideas on her." Defeated, the young man left without saying another word.

That afternoon, the political teacher organized a debate. One side was a supportive group formed from progressive students of our school and the other side held opposite opinions. The opposing group was basically students who were very much influenced by a female minister named Long, Xiang Yun. This woman had been giving lectures at almost every church in Suzhou, warning people not to support the "War to Resist U.S. Aggression and Aid Korea". The argument that afternoon was heated and exciting. It was no surprise to me that the former won and the latter lost. After listening to and participating in the argument, I was even more determined in my motivation to join the army. I knew that my country would not be able to stand up to another invasion. Everyone's suffering and misery had only just ceased with the end of the Japanese war. We needed peace to heal our wounds and improve our life.

In light of my commitment to join the army, I became the center of attention. Newspaper reporters even came to interview me. They wanted to write an article about my determination to join the army. It was published in the Suzhou Daily. Very soon, my seventh sister, Min Xian came from Jiaxing intending to advise me not to leave home to join the army. She told me that my mother wanted to fulfill my father's promise and send me to study at the Yanjing University after I graduated from senior high school. But my sister and my mother misunderstood. My decision to join the army was not because of my father's death. It was my support of the new government. I explained everything to my sister and convinced her to make a speech in support of my decision. She was easily persuaded and gave a wonderfully supportive talk at a school meeting. She was honored as a "Glorious Sister!"

First, I applied to join the navy, but was rejected due to my age; I was a year too young for the consignment. Soon after, I was admitted to the Military Carder School to study foreign languages. The atmosphere was inspiring. From morning until night, the whole city echoed with the Soviet revolutionary song, "Song of the Youth League Member". People sang, *"Listen! There sounds the warning of the bugle. Put on your army uniform and take up your arms. The Youth League members gather together! March to defend our country with one heart. Let's say good-bye, dear Mama. Please kiss your son to say good-bye. Good-bye, Mama. Don't be sad. Don't feel miserable. Bless us a safe trip. Good-*

bye, dear hometown. The victorious star will shine upon us. Good-bye, Mama. Don't be sad. Don't feel miserable. Bless us for a safe trip!"

Without going back to Jiaxing, I called my mother to say good-bye. I left the school in a wagon along with some other students. It was the first time in my life to ride in a wagon. As the horses pulled the cart quickly along the stone-paved road, the rhythm of their hoof beats sounded like music to my ears. I felt so comfortable and my heart was filled with joy and excitement. The next morning, the prospective military students from all of Suzhou's different high schools and universities gathered to board a train headed for Beijing.

College Life in Beijing

Right after New Year's Day in 1951, we were on our way to Beijing. It was a long trip from the south to northern China. After two days of travel by train, we finally reached our destination. Coming out of the old Beijing railway station in Qianmen district, what first caught my eye was a wedding carriage held upon the shoulders of four men professionally dressed in old-fashioned costumes.

At the front of the whole procession were two men—one beating a gong and one blowing a trumpet. The group was passing the Qianmen Gate, its brick walls covered with thick bushes of messy weeds. The ceremony did not seem to be that of a rich family, but it was still quite impressive. For me, it seemed a bit too old-fashioned for a city like Beijing. At that time, in our southern part of China, only people from the countryside practiced such old traditional ways of marriage.

Once the carriage was out of sight, I looked around at the people walking in the streets. All of them were poorly dressed, mostly clothed in dark blue or gray. I was disappointed. Beijing was not the modern city that I had expected; it looked old and shabby.

After we passengers got off the train, trucks took all of us language students to the Beijing Foreign Language School (which would later be renamed the Beijing Institute of Foreign Languages). Our school was located next to the Summer Palace at the original military camp of Ci Xi, the dowager empress of the Qing Dynasty. The dorms were big and old with gray walls: Each dorm held about 30 to 40 students who shared double beds in one large room.

That year the winter was extremely cold with temperatures about 20 degrees centigrade below zero. It was snowing heavily and the ground was covered with at least a foot of pure white snow. Most of the students were from southern China, so it was their first time to see snow. We were all excited but we were also freezing. However, with our revolutionary spirits, we were prepared to endure any hardship, including severe cold.

That very first evening, we were given our uniforms. Instead of being the green color of the military, ours were black. And each of us got a thick padded coat and a pair of pants. I was short; therefore, I had to roll up my sleeves and trouser legs in order to look proper. The lining of the uniform was made of white cotton cloth and it formed a sharp contrast against the black material of the outside. I had my long braids cut off and I had to bind my short unevenly trimmed hair with a ribbon before I put on my new uniform. I was confident that I looked very much like a revolutionary. But, as I stepped out in front of my comrades, they all burst into laughter, so I laughed, too.

There was a big iron stove in the dormitory and after dinner it continued to put out enough warmth for us to get to sleep. But scarcely enough time passed for dreaming before the bugle would loudly call us to wake just before daybreak. We would quickly line up in front of the dorm for our morning jog. It was terribly cold and we had to wear our caps pulled down over our ears so they would not freeze off our heads. But, no one complained. In the darkness, our running steps could be heard through the cutting north wind as the military

Four close schoolmates (L to R)
Ai Qing, Lu Po, Hui Xian, De Zi

training instructor yelled, *"Yi, er, san, si* (One, two, three, four)." As we jogged, the students echoed back, *"Yi, er, san, si"*, in loud voices full of youthful vigor.

After our morning run, we would all rush to wash our faces and brush our teeth at the big cement pond built between the two dormitories. The water of the pond was always frozen over. Some of the boys would break up the ice with rocks so we could get to the water beneath. Steam rose up out of the openings as if the water were warm. Of course, it was simply because the air temperature was colder than the water below the ice.

We made quite a scene with so many of us dressed in black uniforms during the morning ritual around the pond. The hardest part was brushing our teeth, for the toothbrush quickly froze solid. In the cold air, if you did not wash quickly enough, both your wet towel and the toothbrush would freeze. Gradually, we all learned to finish the whole routine in just a couple of minutes.

Our school, the Beijing Foreign Language School, was established in Yan'an at the location of the revolutionary base during the Anti-Japanese War. While we were there, the language departments taught

English, Russian, and French. In our English Department, the professors were: Ms. Bertha Hinton from America, Mr. David Crook and his wife from Canada, and Ms. Margaret Turner from England. There were also many Chinese professors bursting with knowledge: Xu, Guo Zhang; Zhou, Jue Liang; Wang, Zuo Liang and many other well-known scholars of English.

With Professor Margaret Turner and classmates (1953)

After a general testing of our English abilities, we were put into different classes of study. The better students made up the top-level class, including my life-long friend, Wu, Qian Zhi (Charles Wu). He was the most outstanding student in the school even though he was only 16 years old.

Our teachers were highly competent and very friendly. I was in Margaret Turner's class for two years. She was the best teacher I ever had in my life for her classes were always lively and interesting. As students presented their oral compositions, she would record everything we said in shorthand, then type them out and return them to us the next day. Underscoring all the good sentences, she also noted the mistakes, and even the slips of the tongue or stammers each student had made.

Margaret was a great singer, too. She taught us quite a few old English songs, including "Three Gypsies". Whenever we put on shows in English, she would open up her personal suitcases and allow us to use her beautiful dresses for costumes. Her enthusiasm for her work could be felt in everything she did and every word she said. She truly was a model teacher.

My school life was very happy and I believe others would have agreed. Every morning we all would practice singing on the playground. Our phonetics professor Zhang, Zheng Xian taught us to do "Dog's Pant" to help with our breathing along with other basic singing skills. He said, "Your voice should be clear and resonant. When you translate for the deputies of our country, your voice should reach the end of the conference hall of the United Nations without a microphone."

Our morning vocal practice made it sound more like a music school than a language school. But the singing practice helped us overall. Not only did we speak and do our readings in loud voices, but most of the students loved to sing. We even had a school chorus in which both Charles Wu and I sang. I also made many good friends, such as De Zi, Bei Bei, Ming Qiu and Ai Qing, among others.

During weekends, there were often wonderful shows performed by singing and dancing troupes from the Soviet Union and New Democratic countries. A ballroom dance party was a regular Saturday activity. And on Sundays, we often went to have picnics at the Summer Palace since it was within walking distance of the school. The old evergreen trees at the Summer Palace gave us so much cool shade in summer that we would nap under the trees. Boating was our favorite sport and we would sing to our heart's content while rowing the boats. Our mixed vocal group regularly sang all kinds of folk songs from the Soviet Union, Poland, Bulgaria, Yugoslavia, etc.

During those years very few people visited the Summer Palace, so it was very quiet. One summer afternoon, two of my classmates were reviewing their lessons in the Long Corridor when Premier Zhou, En Lai walked by and leaned over their shoulders to peer into their books. The students lifted their heads up and were very surprised to see Premier Zhou! Premier Zhou smiled and said, "You are students of English. Good. Study hard and you will be useful to the country." They soon realized that about ten feet away stood Chairman Mao, Ze Dong with his two children, viewing the beautiful scenery of Kunming Lake.

As soon as Chairman Mao, his children, and Premier Zhou walked away, the two students ran as quickly as they could back to the classroom. Breathlessly, and in loud voices, they said, "Go see. Chairman Mao and Premier Zhou are at the Summer Palace. Be quick!" Our whole class jumped from their seats and rushed to the Summer Palace. Near the end of the Long Bridge of Seventeen Arches, we found them standing by the bronze bull. Chairman Mao seemed to be explaining to his children about the importance of the bronze bull. At a distance, we followed and watched them until they left the Summer Palace. What an exciting moment!

On a Saturday afternoon, our Youth League General Secretary had all the girls of the school summoned together. He said, "Tonight, we have invited many high-ranking military officials to participate in our dance party. They want to learn ballroom dancing. Please have patience in teaching them." After dinner, dozens of high-ranking uniformed military officials came. They were all in their forties or fifties, and some of them were quite over weight. As the party began, each girl was assigned to instruct one particular military official. Truly, it was difficult to teach them to dance. Their bodies were a bit stiff and their legs were not flexible enough for ballroom dancing. And while the officials were attentive, it was very tiring to teach them. We girls had a tendency to giggle, but we dared not do so in front of them, for it was our political duty to teach them.

After the party when we all returned to our dorm, instead of going to bed, we jokingly made fun of our male dance partners. We laughed a lot. Some girls complained about the pain in their tiny bruised toes from the heavily built military men stepping on them. Others were describing the unbearably bad breath of the garlic lovers. One skinny girl said, "My guy held my hand so tight he almost broke my fingers." Unfortunately, one girl from our dorm reported our misbehavior to the school leader. The next day, we were all criticized for being disrespectful to these important revolutionary leaders.

Despite this behavior, a strong political atmosphere prevailed at the school. Apart from regular studies in politics, we had at least one lecture every week on different topics, such as current international situations which were given by governmental leaders or personal experience lectures given by combat heroes. This greatly influenced me and, as I learned more, I began to change my thinking and to depart from the old concepts. I respected the revolutionary heroes and was determined to learn as much as I could from them. I began to work very hard to change myself so that I could become a true revolutionary. In fact, I had sent in an application to join the Youth League. But acceptance was difficult for me because of my family background. Since my father had owned a hospital, he was considered a capitalist. Even though my mother had already donated the hospital to the government following my father's death, I could not change my family's bourgeois background.

Yet, it was clear that as long as I behaved well politically, I could still be considered progressive and revolutionary. So, I took part in all kinds of political activities. Within the school's kitchen, I taught the cooks to sing revolutionary songs and helped them with their own political studies. In the countryside, I helped the peasants do farm work and I was chosen to speak about how I had struggled against the counter-revolutionary influence and what led me to finally join the revolution.

In 1952, during my second year at the language school, the government began a movement against the "Five Evils". The five evils were: bribery, tax evasion, theft of state property, cheating on government contracts, and theft of economic information by the owners of private industrial and commercial enterprises. The government was determined to dig out all the evils, which had brought much harm to the country. University students were called upon to participate in this nation-wide political movement. I was appointed to be the group leader of five other girls in my school. Our assignment was to persuade the wife of a grafter to reveal where she and her husband had hidden the money that they had received from bribes.

According to the government's information, this merchant had made a huge amount of money by providing inferior medical cotton and gauze to military hospitals during the Korean War. As a result, many wounded Chinese People's Volunteers and Korean army soldiers died of infections caused by the inferior medical supplies that had not been properly sterilized. What a crime! This merchant had made a large amount of money at the sacrifice of many lives. And while he had already been arrested, he would not confess to his crime.

In order to solve the case, the government sent the six of us girls to stay in the merchant's home and persuade his wife to confess her knowledge of the crime. In the beginning, she insisted that she knew nothing about what her husband had done. We explained the government's policy to her and told her the stories of the medical difficulties and deaths of the soldiers from the Chinese People's Volunteers. Very often, she was touched to tears by the sad tales of the heroes. But, still, she would not reveal where they had hidden the bribe money.

We then told her that if she told us the truth, the government would lessen the punishment and her husband could come back home after serving his sentence. The woman had three little children and of course she was afraid to lose her husband. We were very good to her and treated her family like our own. For the whole week, we cleaned her house and courtyard, cooked for them, and did their laundry. Finally, one morning, she told me that she realized that her husband had committed a terrible crime and she was now willing to hand over all that her husband had hidden.

First, she led us to the open courtyard and asked us to take the pomegranate trees out of two big pots. At the bottom of each pot, were two bags full of gold bars that were about one inch wide and 6 to 7 inches long. Next, she led us to the kitchen and asked us to remove a pile of coal from the corner. Then, out of the ground, we dug two big jars full of gold ingots. We took out piece after piece of gold in different sizes from the jars and piled them up on the dining room table. Then the wife said, "I have given you everything that we have hidden. Truly there is no more!" It was hard to comprehend the massive stacks of ingots and bars of gold that sat on the table. None of us had ever seen so much gold in our lives.

That day, I was running a high fever from a severe cold and was feeling very ill, but I was so happy to have accomplished our task. We sat down and I told the girls to count how many pieces there were altogether. The woman was standing near the table holding her one-year old baby boy in her arms. No one even noticed that the baby had grabbed a small piece of gold, which he held tightly in his little hand. As we counted, the woman told me that she needed to go to the market to buy some vegetables. So I said with a smile, "Okay!" Half an hour passed, and she came back with a basket of vegetables. As I lifted my head, I saw that the baby boy was holding a small gold ingot. I was astonished. He must have held it the whole time that his mother had shopped without her even realizing it.

It was nearly dark when we finished counting the gold. We had kept a very clear account of all the gold pieces and had separated them into different boxes according to their shape and size. Still seated around the table, we began to eat our dinner, when suddenly there was a terribly loud banging at the front gate. We immediately got nervous since it was well past dark.

As the woman and I opened the gate, six men rushed inside past us. One of them yelled, "Who is the leader of this group?" "Me," I answered. Then he said, "Why did you not report what you had done today to the local police station? The whole district now knows that you have found gold in this house. You are really lucky that we were informed of the facts soon enough and that we could come to protect you. You students have no experience and know nothing about this complicated society. What if gangsters had found out? They would have robbed and killed all of you." I was dumbfounded and stood there in shock, totally at a loss to speak.

That night, after all the gold had been removed and locked up at the police station, we slept in the house with dozens of plainclothes policemen surrounding the whole property. But, it was a quiet night and nothing happened. The next morning, all the policemen left. We six girls said good-bye to the woman and her children and returned to our school. We had done a wonderful job and were praised by the school leaders for our heroic deed. A month later, I was admitted to the Youth League based on my excellent behavior.

During my years in the language school, I developed several diseases due to the hard life and bad weather. Winters were extremely cold in Beijing. Having lived in a moderate southern climate, I was not used to such cold so all of my joints hurt. The school required that all students pass the physical training test, which had been adopted from the Soviet Union. I did very well with the first level but could never pass the second level because I could not accomplish the long distance running test. I tried many times, but always failed. As an alternative, we were allowed to do speed skating so I began to learn to ice skate. The first time that I attempted to stand on the ice (actually a frozen rice field) I fell down several times. I tried to stand up straight, but I still fell down. Each time I struggled to stand up, I fell down again and again. I simply could not balance my body while on skates. However, learning to skate was the only way for me to pass the second level of that Soviet system. No matter how difficult, I had to keep trying.

Finally, the persistence of practicing improved my skating skills tremendously. I even played ice ball with the boys' team, and often I was mistaken for a boy while playing with them. I even surprised myself with my own bravery and quick reflexes. During New Year's Eve of 1952, we skated until the bell of the Kremlin rang out. Together with my teammates, we hailed in the New Year while playing out in the snow.

I had so much fun during those days. But by the next spring I had developed arthritis and my knees hurt so much that I could not walk. I also suffered from migraine headaches. My classmates showed so much concern for me that they often carried me from our dorm to the classroom. During class, the teacher gave me special permission to answer questions while seated–instead of standing respectfully–since it was so painful for me to stand. I received acupuncture treatments from our school clinic for my pain, which provided much relief from the pain.

I seldom went into downtown Beijing. The transportation from the Summer Palace to Xi Zhi Men took four hours of travel one way on a small tractor-like vehicle powered by firewood. During weekends, we often went to play at the Summer Palace or in the countryside. I had a friend with whom I would skate whose name was Ji En. He was a very smart young man and studied very hard. He was younger than most of his schoolmates and therefore was nicknamed "Little Ghost". He and I often talked about what we had read, especially the novels. Frequently, we went to the harvested rice fields and climbed up the heaps of chaff, then rolled down from the top. We laughed a lot; we were like brother and sister.

During my university years, quite a few young men were interested in me and sought to start up a relationship. But, I already had my first love, Jiang, in my heart, so it was hard for me to really fall in love with anyone else. I talked a lot about my first love to my best friend Ji En and he understood about my feelings. Even though we were always together reading in the library, skating on the ice, or spending sunny days in the countryside, we never entered into a relationship.

In July of 1954, I was among 120 students that graduated from the Beijing Foreign Language School. The school arranged a camping outing in the woods for all the graduates. We hiked the mountains, and delightedly sang and danced away the evenings. One morning, we found a stream and soaked in it. The girls even washed their hair in the water. As our hair dried in the sun, we teased each other, laughing light-heartedly, because the sodium in the water had made us all look like "White Haired Girls".

In the end, it was very hard to leave our school and say good-bye to our dear schoolmates. Some of the graduates were sent abroad directly from the language school to work in the embassies of different foreign countries. Everyone was in tears when we went to see people off from the Beijing railway station. Friendships that formed between the students were so special and close, that we all felt like we were brothers and sisters.

An Exciting Career

After graduation, my assignment was to be a translator for the China National Import and Export Corporation. It was the only national

Me at 21 years old

corporation dealing in the business of imports and exports between China and the capitalist countries of the world. It was a good job, but with no understanding of business, I was worried about how I would do. And to be a businesswoman was not my dream, so I was not very happy. Yet, I worked hard at calming myself down and it helped me to read a novel about a Soviet woman who contributed tremendously to her country through the field of business.

In the beginning, while lacking knowledge of international business, I made many laughable mistakes in translation. For instance in one business meeting, I translated "charter party" from English into Chinese as the "British Constitution" which puzzled the negotiator on the Chinese side. Later, as I continued to learn more, the quality of my translation became much better and gradually, I began to love my job.

During vacations while in high school, I often visited my grandpa with great excitement. He always enjoyed good health because he regularly practiced his martial arts. Whenever he saw me, he was very happy and offered me good food to eat. Upon starting my college studies in Beijing, I seldom was able to go home, but I kept him informed about my school life through letters. With my new job in Beijing following graduation, I mailed a quarter of my first monthly salary to my grandpa. My auntie told me later he valued it so much that he kept the money under his pillow and never spent it. He told everybody in the family, "Hui Xian is a filial girl!"

Not only did I develop a love for my job, my love for music also flourished. I joined a choral group organized by the China Musicians Association. We had a great conductor who frequently directed us as we performed. Many of the friends I made were from professional art troupes. Full of enthusiasm, I also volunteered to translate letters that Chinese young people had received from other youths from English-speaking countries. I usually spent at least five to six hours a week translating their letters. Life was busy, but still eventful.

As a professional translator, I had many opportunities to work at important conferences and banquets sponsored by the government. One in particular was when Premier Zhou, En Lai received trade delegations from Singapore and Malaysia. There were forty representatives within the group. A banquet was held in the big ballroom in Beijing's Xin Qiao Hotel. As Premier Zhou entered the hall, there was great applause and all the representatives lined up to shake hands with him. My job was to accompany Premier Zhou and translate for him.

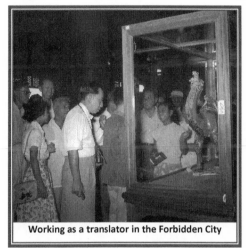
Working as a translator in the Forbidden City

About twenty minutes later as it neared the scheduled time for him to begin his opening speech, more than half of the guests were still waiting to shake his hand. The man responsible for our translators' team came to tell me that I should remind Premier Zhou of the time so he could promptly begin his speech. When I passed the message on to the Premier, he looked at me saying, "Don't you think that I should finish shaking hands with all of them?" I felt so ashamed, and I regretted following the advice of my group leader. The Premier was right; the schedule would have to be flexible.

Premier Zhou, En Lai actually began his opening speech with another English translator. He extended a warm welcome to all of the guests. The translation into English was, "On behalf of the Chinese government, I welcome you, the Singaporean-Malaysian trade delegation." But Premier Zhou immediately corrected the translator, "Singaporean *and* Malaysian delegations. Two delegations!" As he spoke, he held up two fingers to emphasize his point. With this, the whole hall began clapping in appreciation of the Premier's demonstrated respect for both countries.

Then, Premier Zhou asked the English translator if there was anyone at the event that spoke Malaysian. Actually, it turned out there was one, a Malaysian Chinese man who was working in the back room. When he was called out, he looked very nervous. He was not at all prepared for such an occasion. With a big smile, Premier Zhou, En Lai reached out his hand to grab the man's hand and asked him to translate for him. In an attempt to calm him down the Premier said, "I will speak slowly. You can translate well." This man was not trained to do oral translation, but he tried his best. Eventually he finished translating the Premier's welcome speech with many staggers and stammers. Premier Zhou thanked him and shook hands with him again. At that moment, all the guests stood up from their seats and applauded for a long time. Premier Zhou, En Lai was truly a great politician.

At another banquet in 1956, I was assigned to translate for Premier Zhou, En Lai again. As I was standing by the Premier before the banquet began, he asked me how many foreign languages I had learned. I answered, "Only English." He encouraged me to learn more foreign

I was Premier Zhou's Interpreter at this banquet

languages. He said, "Whenever I talk at the national banquets, before I say the second sentence, I have to wait for all the translators to finish translating my first sentence into different languages. I hope that someday I will need only one translator for all my guests from different countries." I was very much inspired.

Close to the end of 1957, Premier Zhou came to the Ministry of Foreign Trade to receive a big delegation from England. I was assigned to be his translator that day. He looked around as if expecting someone else. Then he asked me where the translator was who often translated for him when he came to the ministry, addressing him by name. I was surprised that the Premier had such a good memory and that he cared about the people who worked for him. I was required to tell Premier Zhou that he had another commitment. But, in fact, that translator would never translate again for him because he had been labeled a "Rightist" in the Anti-Rightist Movement early that year.

During the six years that I worked as a translator, I traveled all over the country translating for many leaders from provincial governments. Not every leader could speak Mandarin; rather they spoke their local dialects. When I was younger, during the Anti-Japanese War, I easily learned many dialects, so I was very effective at this job. I truly benefited from my life experiences from my childhood years.

I fully trusted the Communist Party and answered the calls of the government, yet I too, was nearly labeled a Rightist for my bold and honest opinions about the Party. At the beginning of the movement in 1957, there was a free airing of views. The head of our department mobilized us to voice whatever opinions we had about the Party or the Party leaders. The purpose was to help them improve in their work or behavior. Since I loved the Party, I thought it was a very good thing to do.

Receiving a Sudanese women's delegation (1956)

With a sincere heart, I hung a poster with big characters telling some of the stories I had heard from the women who came to Beijing from the countryside looking for their husbands. Back in 1951, when I was studying at the language school, there was a Central Government Cadre School located close by where many high-ranking cadres studied. There were many times that I saw countrywomen sitting along the roadside crying. After talking to them, I learned that their husbands had forced divorce upon them. Those cadres served in the army during the Liberation War and their wives supported them in many ways. They had supplied the army with food and made shoes for the soldiers. The women had raised their children through hardships without their husbands' help. Then, their husbands became leaders and lived in the big city, abandoning their country wives so that they could marry city girls. After listening to the stories I became very angry, but I could do nothing to help these heart-broken women.

The Party had asked us to voice whatever was buried in our hearts. So I poured out my opinions about this injustice. I finished my poster by writing, *"If the upper beam is not straight, the lower ones will go aslant—when those above behave unworthily, those below will do the same."* I was really aiming these words at Chairman Mao, Ze Dong. My poster was like breaking news! Many people crowded up front to read it and some of them said, "This young girl has a lot of nerve." I felt very proud of myself for acting so bravely, especially because I thought I was helping the Party to change for the better.

A few days later, the head of our department, Comrade Yang, called me in for a talk where he informed me that the Rightists in society were intending to overthrow the Communist Party. He said that from the next day forward, we would launch an attack politically on those Rightists. He said, "You must stand firm on the Communist Party's side to fight against the Rightists." At first, I did not understand what was happening. It was my understanding that all the people who spoke out were actually helping the Communist Party. After listening to Comrade Yang, I promised to take an active part in the Anti-Rightist Movement; I followed through as I had promised. During the whole movement, I did not sense there was anything wrong with my actions. With honesty and sincerity, I felt that I did everything according to what I was told to do by my department head.

Performing Soviet "Five Daughters"

I was so naïve. I never expected that I would be labeled "a problem person" and later be kicked out of a job I had been successful at for six years. My career totally changed and all because of my loyalty to the Communist Party. It seemed really ridiculous.

Marriage in My Future

A few months after our college graduation, my close friend Ji En was sent by the Ministry of Foreign Affairs to work in France. Before he left, he told me that he would like to "develop our friendship". In those days, use of that phrase meant to start a relationship. We really liked each other and had been close friends for three years. I knew I could be his girlfriend, but deep in my heart, I had more affection for my first love, Jiang, though I had not heard from him for several years.

Ever since I had joined the revolution and gone to Beijing, we had lost contact because Jiang had been moving from one place to another with the army. But what often came into my mind was that last tearful look he gave me from the door at the school's lab. All those years I missed him but I could not find him. Whenever I saw an army soldier on the street, I wished it were Jiang. Often I would dream of him and wake up in tears. As time passed, I was almost without hope, for I wondered if he would ever appear in my life again. Still, listening to Ji En express his affection for me made me so happy that I told him I would be loyal to him.

But an unexpected and dramatic event occurred at that point in my life. Only one month after Ji En left for France, I received a letter from my hometown. While the letter was addressed to me, it had been forwarded to me by an old nanny from the Jiaxing Trinity Hospital. The envelope was tattered and nearly torn apart from its long postal journey. The letter was from Jiang! My hands trembled as I opened his letter. He wrote,

> *Dear Hui Xian,*
>
> *For the past few years, I have been traveling China, from the south to the north and from coast to coast, but you have been always in my heart. I placed your picture on the first page of my journal and I look at it every day when I write in my diary. Before being promoted to a company commander, army regulations forbid any one to date, even though communication. Unfortunately, I have had to suppress my feelings for you. But now that I have been promoted to company commander, I have the freedom to express my feelings for you. And, I need to tell you that I think of you every single day.*

Where are you now? Are you at college or in the army? I do not know if this letter will ever reach you because there have been so many changes since Liberation. I can only send this letter to your old home address and hope you will eventually receive it. If ever you get this letter, please let me know everything that has happened with you. I miss you, and I love you.

In tears, I read the letter again and again. My heart was pounding and my mind turned over in turmoil. While I did not really know what to do, I immediately answered his letter and mailed him a few pictures of different stages of my life during our separation. I told him the truth about my feelings. I said how much I missed him and how hard I had been trying to find him, all in vain. It was difficult but I knew that I had to explain to him about my promise to be Ji En's girlfriend.

A few days later in the morning mail, I got a letter from Jiang that included many pictures of his life in the army. He truly had grown into a very strong and handsome young man. In this letter, he sounded very calm. He said he felt sad that he had lost me and that it was entirely his fault.

But, that very afternoon, I received another letter from him further describing his troubled feelings. He said he loved me so much that he did not want to give me up, even though he would feel guilty in trying to take me away from Ji En. After reading my letter, he said that he had rushed to the seashore where he cried bitterly. He knew it was immoral to ask me to be with him, but emotionally he could not help himself.

After reading this letter, I had several sleepless nights and had no idea how to deal with such a matter. My heart was truly broken! As a Communist Youth League member, I turned to my League organization for help. During those years, we were taught to depend on our leaders for advice if we had any problems. All the leaders in the League branch said that I should keep my promise to Ji En and that it was morally wrong to break up with him. They pointed out that Jiang had been absent such a long time and that he may have changed. The leaders said that I had been young and really did not know him very well, that we might not get along if we came together, and that it had only been a "child's love"!

More importantly, they emphasized that I should place my work as translator above everything else. If I married Jiang, I would have to go to the coastal city where Jiang was working. Such a job change might ruin my career. The alternative, they said, would be difficult–for Jiang to come and work in Beijing. Their opinions had a big impact on me and I could only trust that they were right. So, finally I wrote to Jiang and explained everything. His reply followed soon that I was correct in making this decision. As a revolutionary army soldier, he said he should not do anything morally wrong. We were both bound by the revolutionary principles and had to change our minds by holding our true feelings back. Though my pure love for him was strong, I had to restrain myself.

Several months later, Ji En came back to Beijing from Paris. The evening after his return he came to see me with gifts in hand that he had brought from France. We were happy to see one another. Under the dim light of the street lamps, I took out the letters from Jiang and told him what had happened during his absence. He took the letters and remained very quiet as he began to read them. He hugged me after finishing all the letters and said that he was touched by my decision to keep the promised relationship with him.

To my great surprise, Ji En did not call me at all during the next week. When I called him, he did not answer the phone so I could not help but wonder what was going on. The following Saturday, I received a letter from him saying that he had been filled with pain all week, so he had made a decision to end our relationship. He said he could not compete, for Jiang was gifted in music, he was intelligent and he was handsome. Ji En also said, "You two have been in love for such a long time. I know you refused him because of me. And I know your heart would always be with him even if we were to get married someday. I do love you but my love for you is not as deep and strong as Jiang's love for you. It would be wise for me to retreat, now, instead of regretting it in future."

With his refusal, I fell into a severe depression. I did not have the courage to tell Jiang what had happened, so I did not write to him. For a whole year, I lived with a deep sadness. During that time, there were no more letters from Jiang. We both needed time to bury our heart's true love deep within.

In my office, there was a Russian translator named Li. He acted interested in me, but I was very reluctant, trying mostly to ignore him. Constantly, he expressed his love for me and tried in every way to please me. Finally, I thought being with him would be a way to get out of my depression and start a new life. I agreed to go out with him. From the perspective of superficial conditions, he was okay. He was a League member and had joined the revolution at the age of 14. Sent to study Russian at the Foreign Trade Institute, he had graduated in the same year that I did. He was a good writer and he was handsome. I really did not know much about life then and I think that at that time, as young people, we were simple-minded. As long as one was politically sound and had a good job, he or she could be chosen as one's life partner.

Although I did not feel true affection for him, as I had for Jiang and Ji En, I had reached the age of marriage. For at that time, Chinese women usually got married around 25 years of age. And if a woman had not married by then, she would have been thought to be abnormal. Over time, I found that I was not happy about his behavior and most of the time we spent together was full of upset and quarrels. However, I still married him in 1957. Culturally, it was considered shameful to break up a relationship and those around would look down upon you. In looking back, it seemed to me that I lived for others' approval, instead of my own. That was such a big mistake on my part!

It was also a mistake for him to marry me; it turned out I was part of a "bet" he had made. He told me a year later, that one-day in 1955 after work, he and some single young friends were standing across the road from the office building where I worked. They were talking about finding girlfriends. At that moment, I just happened to walk down from the front gate of the building on my way to an important banquet that evening. Noting that I was all dressed up looking very pretty, he said that all their eyes fell upon me. One of them said, "This girl is getting extremely popular now. She is smart and cute. Who is going to get her?" Li said, "None of you will get her, but I will bet you that I can. I swear she will be mine!" So, he used me to show those fellows that he was more capable in pursuit than any one of them. With this as our foundation, our marriage was very shaky. There was no true love between us.

Reformed in the Countryside

A few months after our wedding, we answered Chairman Mao's call, along with many others from the same foreign trade company. Together, we went to the countryside to do manual labor in order to remold our bourgeois way of thinking. When we arrived at Nanmeng Cun, a village in Hebei Province, the local people treated us as if we were criminals. Adults looked at us with hatred in their eyes and the children threw small stones at us as we did manual labor in their fields. We were puzzled over why they mistook us for villains.

Me (circled) working in the countryside, Ling County, Hebei Province

Upon our departure from Beijing, all of us were presented with big red flowers to honor us. We received praise from our leaders that we were, in fact, the most active participants in the political movement. The Anti-rightist Movement was over and none of this group was labeled "Rightist". Why, then, did the people of Nanmeng Cun treat us in this manner? We felt both humiliated and annoyed. After a few days, though, the village head apologized for not having clearly explained the meaning of this political movement to the peasants. What followed was a change in attitude of the peasants, both old and young.

In the beginning, we found it very hard to adapt to the new environment of the countryside. Instead of our normal meals of rice, flour products and delicious dishes, we had only cornbread or sweet potatoes. There were very few fresh vegetables to go with our food. We were frequently hungry, as we did manual labor at least eight hours a day, outside in all kinds of weather. Our leaders in Beijing never said anything about our return to the city, and we feared that we would have to live in the countryside forever.

In the huts where we lived, there were countless numbers of frightening house lizards. We had to use mosquito nets over our beds, even during the cold weather. Even so, every morning I would find several dead lizards under my pillow. It reminded me of the days during the Anti-Japanese War when my room in Guizhou was filled with caterpillars. Through the difficulties, I reminded myself of our purpose in going to the countryside, which was to temper our revolutionary will. I tried my best to overcome the hardships and work as hard as I could to learn about modesty from the peasants. During my spare time, I taught the children to sing songs, washed their faces and hands, and trimmed their fingernails. Overall, I got along very well with the peasants.

In 1958 while we were still in the countryside, Chairman Mao promoted the "Three Red Banners". They represented: General Line, Great Leap Forward, and People's Commune. The whole country followed Mao's latest call with great enthusiasm. In an effort to catch up with the industrialized countries in the world, Mao requested that the peasants temper steel.

Throughout the countryside, peasants built earthen "furnaces" along the side of the roads or on hillsides. The village heads called upon the peasants to donate every single object made of iron from their homes, which was then thrown into the "furnaces" to make steel. The local folks brought iron pots and ladles from their kitchens, locks and other pieces of iron to the village office. In order to stoke the fires, the "steel workers" needed rooster feathers for the bellows. All the roosters in the villages were killed for their feathers. The slogan often was repeated, "Surpass the steel output of England within five years." All the young men stopped working in the fields, and instead, labored at the earthen ovens day and night. But, what was produced from their tireless efforts at the "steel furnaces" was not steel, just big lumps of melted iron.

After listening to the General Line propaganda of the government, the peasants thought that China's Communism would be realized in no time. They were excited that the People's Commune provided three free meals a day to all peasants. But, I frequently witnessed many people take more food than they actually needed from the Commune's cafeteria to feed to their pigs and dogs. In the past, the peasants had been very careful with their food. Never would they have fed their pig's cornbread or sweet potatoes. Instead, they gave them wild vegetables cooked in water that had been used to wash the dishes and pots. However, as food was provided free, they threw it away carelessly.

During these days, the newspapers were filled with articles about "bumper harvests" of rice and wheat. It was reported that different counties had recently produced ten times more rice or wheat than the previous year. Pictures of people standing on the piles of harvested rice and wheat from those "bumper harvests" were published in the papers. In actuality, people had gathered freshly cut rice or wheat stalks and bundled them together so that they were thick enough to stand on. It was a big trick! *The People's Daily*, the voice of the Central Government, carried these pictures to show how great Chairman Mao was and how well his "Three Red Banners" had worked. In order to show the brilliance of their leadership, the different provincial leaders competed with one another as their lies grew bigger and bolder.

When it was time to harvest the cotton produced at our village, there was not a single young or middle-aged man at home. They were all at the furnace tempering "steel". There were only old men, women and children left in the village. I was appointed the team leader of our village at cotton-harvest time. There were miles and miles of cotton fields. With the cotton ready to be picked–even though we did not have enough hands–I mobilized all the people in the village to collect as much as possible. We worked days and nights. But, it was just too much!

One morning, there rose-up a strong wind which blew the cotton off the plants and into the sky. Large pieces of cotton flew about in the autumn blue sky like snowflakes. An old peasant looked at the flying cotton crying, "It's a sin! What a great loss!" Had I had a camera, I would have taken pictures of that scene. For many years later, in my mind there often appeared the snowflake-like cotton drifting up into the sky.

As I was the team leader, I had to be a role model for all the villagers. For many days and nights, I did not eat much and did not have much time to sleep. Then my head began to swim when I was working in the fields. I felt there was something in my throat choking me so that I could hardly breathe and I was running a high fever. Finally, one

Working in the countryside
(1958)

morning while I was working in the fields I blacked out. When I regained consciousness, I was aboard a train heading for Beijing.

In Beijing, I was carried into the emergency room of a hospital. The doctor asked me to open my mouth. My throat hurt so much I could hardly do it. The doctor looked at my throat and said, "Oh, my Heavens! You are in danger!" He touched my throat with a medical instrument and two tonsils fell out. They were totally rotten. The doctor gave me an injection of anesthetic, cleaned my throat and stitched up the openings. I was hospitalized for a week and was sent to my brother's home for recovery because at that time I had no home in Beijing.

A few days rest helped me a lot and I had my energy back when I went to the doctor to have the stitches taken out. I did not feel pain at the beginning of the procedure, but when the doctor was trying to take out the last stitch on the left side of my throat, I felt he was pulling out my muscles. I screamed each time when he touched that part. So, finally the doctor gave up and said, "I am not going to take it out. The stitch will get dissolved in the years to come since it is sewed with a catgut suture. Leave it alone!" Later, the stitch did not bother me at all and I totally forgot about it. In another month I returned to the countryside.

Things had changed while I was gone. The Commune's cafeteria had closed, the "steel workers" came back to the village after many failures making steel in their furnaces, and what struck me most was that people had very little to eat. Winter came and only small amounts of corn and sweet potatoes were distributed to the peasants. The village head announced that it was all he could do, because the harvest that year had been very poor. Large amounts of various grains had been ruined in the rain because there were not enough hands in the village to harvest the crops.

Very soon, the trees in the village were stripped bare as people ate the bark. Some people even consumed the chaff out of their pillows. Others stuffed their stomachs with white clay. People were starving! For each meal, I was given a bowl of thin millet soup with a few slices of carrot. Like many others I, too, had terrible stomachaches from severe hunger.

An order came from Beijing that we should return to the city, immediately. We had to leave the starving peasants. All of us were in tears. But, what could we do to help? Terrible news kept coming from everywhere. People were short of food and many died of starvation.

I witnessed the terrible effects of the policies implemented by Mao. When he promoted his "Three Red Banners", he did not listen to opposing opinions from other government leaders. On the contrary, he criticized them for sabotaging his plan. As a result, millions of people died and tons of materials were wasted. But, no one dared to say a word against him. There was no freedom of speech. And having seen the punishment inflicted on the "Rightists", everyone was cautious with their words.

My Child Is Born into Famine

In 1959, I went back to work at the same company in Beijing, but I was transferred to the research department. No longer was I a translator. I did not feel upset because I thought whatever I was assigned to do, was revolutionary work.

That year, I got pregnant. As my husband, Li, did not really love me, he tried to talk me into having an abortion. He said, "I do not want a baby. If you give birth to a child, you will get old very quickly." I was not surprised to hear that coming from him. So I said, "I can feed the child all by myself." I already knew he would not be a responsible father.

By the end of 1959, life was extremely difficult. Food was scarce throughout all of China. Everyone was given a specific amount of food coupons to survive on. And each month, every household was given other types of coupons for daily needs, such as coupons for grain, sugar, vegetables, cloth, thread, etc. The coupons were used to limit purchases. It gave me headaches to sort out and arrange all those coupons and carefully plan how to use them so that they would last for whole month. There was almost no meat supply except at the New Year.

On January 25, 1960, my baby girl was born three weeks ahead of the expected date. She was so small that she had to be given special care in the hospital. The women in my ward began to gossip about me, "Maybe she is not married yet." "It has been three days and the father has never shown up." I did not care what they said. On the fourth day, Li came to see me. The first thing he told me was not to breast feed the baby. "You will get old very soon if you breastfeed." I cried and said, "The baby is pre-mature and she has to be breast fed." I did not listen to him and gave all my love and care to the newborn baby.

When I got home from the hospital a week later, my husband moved to the men's dormitory because he was afraid that the baby would disturb his sleep. I hired a nanny from Anhui to take care of the baby and me. Xia, Kai Zhen was a very nice woman; she took good care of the baby and of me and I was happy even though Li seldom came home to see us.

I named our baby Sha Sha, which was the name of the nurse who took care of Lenin, Russia's revolutionary leader. My baby girl was very lovely and healthy with my breastfeeding her. As for me, there was really nothing available for postnatal recovery except a dozen eggs the government provided for each woman with a newborn child. When the nanny bought back the 12 eggs and cracked open the first egg, a very bad odor filled the room. She said, "Oh, it is a bad egg." Then she cracked another. Again, it was bad. She cracked another and another. Out of the

My first daughter, Sha Sha
at 6 months old (1960)

12 eggs, there were only two that were edible. That was all the nutrition I got as I tried to recover my health.

Our nanny had come to Beijing from Anhui because her whole family was starving. She had six children, aged 6 to 16. The only way to save her children's lives was to work in a big city to make money. She told me the true situation in her home village. People had run out of grain and were living on wild vegetables. I gave her some rice coupons to buy food for her children. We all were living on the coupons the government provided for my baby and me. So we had to eat rice porridge in order to make the grain go farther. I encouraged her to go to the market and get whatever food she could mail back to her children. She bought popcorn and pop-rice that did not require coupons. I gave her some old clothes and pants to wrap the food in for mailing. She pressed everything flat so that more could be stuffed into the trousers. Parcel after parcel she sent back to keep her family alive.

One day, a man from the countryside came to tell her about her husband's death. He had been very sick, owing to hunger and the fact that the village heads had forced him to work in the fields where he died. My nanny ran into the street, crying over his death, telling anyone who passed by how he had died. Someone came to tell me about her actions. I rushed out of my room into the snow and dragged her back home immediately. I tried to calm her down. I explained that she could not cry in the streets and publicly reveal the truth about her husband's death. I said, "You are in Beijing. You are not supposed to act like that. You cry at home. Do you understand?" She was an innocent woman; she could not understand how dangerous it would be, politically, if she kept exposing the cause of her husband's death out in public.

From Translator to English Teacher

When my baby was six months old, I was transferred to teach English at the Institute of Foreign Trade. I never asked why I was given a new job. The leader only told me that I was needed in the school. And I never suspected others' motives, especially my leaders'. But, one of my colleagues said to me, "Don't you think your change-of-job is punishment? You must have made a mistake during the Anti-Rightist Movement." I was not aware of anything like that at all. I knew it was good to be a teacher and I loved teaching. So, I happily began my teaching career in 1960.

I became an English teacher (1960)

Long before the bell rang for my first class, I had entered the classroom. It was the first class of the first day of school. All the students were new and did not know each other. I was chatting with a girl student when the bell rang for class. The girl said to me, "Classmate, you'd better go to your seat quickly. It's time for class." I stood up and walked slowly onto the platform. I looked at the girl with a big smile and she stuck out her tongue at me. Obviously, I looked too young to be a teacher with my two long braids and red blouse and black skirt. I was actually 26, but I looked more like a college freshman.

The year 1960 brought even more disaster. People still had very little to eat. When winter came, the school cafeteria served only cornbread, as there were no vegetables to be found. Soup could only be made with chemical soy sauce. One piece of cornbread weighed two ounces. For the meal, male students were given four ounces of cornbread while girls received only three ounces. Women teachers usually bought three pieces of cornbread to have for both lunch and dinner. Taking them back to our office, we cut one of them very precisely into halves, one half for lunch and the other half for dinner.

Much of the time following lunch, we women teachers would put our dinner portion of cornbread on the big iron stove in our office. Afternoons were either for correcting students' papers or for political studies. One day, while everybody was quietly working in the office, a young male teacher broke the silence. "My aunties, (a humorous way to address older women), would you please remove your cornbread from the stove? I am so very hungry. The smell of that baked cornbread is almost killing me!" The whole office burst into laughter but, at the same time, tears of sadness ran down our cheeks.

In front of the school building (1965)

During those days, many people got sick from lack of nutrition. People suffered from edema and hepatitis, while many women and girls stopped menstruating altogether. While the government continued to speak of its success, the reality was that it could not satisfy its own people's needs.

At our institute, there were dozens of foreign students from rich African families. The government had to provide the foreign students with enough to eat. They had a separate dining room where they got potatoes–we ate the potato skins. This was true for cabbage, too, as we ate the outside leaves and they were fed the inner leaves. And even with insufficient food, the Chinese students studied hard and overcame these difficulties.

An Innocent Young Mother

In the fall of 1960, the government ordered the institute to send teachers and students back to the countryside to do farm work again. At that time, my baby was only eight months old and I was so torn about leaving her at home. On the one hand, I knew I had to go with the students and on the other hand, I did not know what consequences it would bring to my child and me if I took her along.

It was very difficult to leave her at home and to stop breastfeeding her so abruptly. Our nanny stayed to care for her and began to feed her the limited milk and porridge we received from the government. When I stopped feeding the baby, I developed mastitis, which gave me much pain day and night.

In the countryside, I was assigned responsibility for the kitchen work but we were given insufficient grain for making meals. The only things we could serve from the kitchen were wild vegetables and cornbread. The students complained of hunger and I tried to tell the

cooks to improve the food. The cooks were so angry with me and yelled at me, "Even a good daughter-in-law cannot cook something out of nothing. How can we improve the food without any supplies?" I just stood in the kitchen, crying.

New mother

We were working with the peasants in the mountains where there were countless apricot trees. One day someone came up with the idea of picking apricot leaves and mixing them in with the cornmeal so that the students could have a bit more to fill their stomachs. So, we used long sticks to beat the leaves off the trees that were nearly bare of apricots. While working, we saw apricots rolling down the mountainside but none of us dared to pick any up. All the teachers and students followed the rule that no one was allowed to take anything from the peasants. Eating the leaves was the only solution to help relieve the students' constant hunger. Life was very difficult during those days. We worked in the mountains for a whole month before being allowed to return home.

The day I returned and opened the door of my home, I saw my little daughter lying in bed. Her face was very pale and she was very thin.

When I held her up, she looked at me vaguely as if she did not recognize me. As I watched her, I was filled with a great sadness and tears rolled down my cheeks.

I soon learned that right after I had left for the countryside, her father sent her to a nursery and fired the nanny. I could hardly imagine how our baby passed those miserable days at a nursery. For the whole month, she had been fed cow's milk with other things added to it. It seemed that she could not digest milk as her feces looked like milk, too. With great care and feeding, it took me a long time to get her health back. I have never forgotten what the nanny said when I left the baby with her to go to the countryside. She sighed and said, "Barbarous!" But, who could refuse what the Party told us to do? I dared not even think of an excuse not to go with the students. The political pressure at that time was very intense. If someone did something against the current policy, they would be in trouble. They would either be humiliated as a backward-thinking person or be criticized by the leaders.

A Nightmare of a Marriage

Life was so hard in the early 1960's for a teacher and a mom. Food remained scarce and we were often short of money. In order to do my work well, I had to hire a nanny, which cost me half of my salary. Often close to the end of a month, I would sell my nice clothes and shoes–that I had worn when I was a translator–to provide more money. I was busy all the time and had no energy after work. But, I still had to care for my baby at night.

My husband would go dancing or see a movie on Sundays. I stayed at home with my baby while he went out to play. We had less and less communication with each other. Later, I got to know that he was dating a ballerina. She was an English student whom I was teaching privately during my spare time. Obviously Li had no love for me.

After I had married, Qian, Jiang and I occasionally wrote to each other but we never discussed our personal lives. He thought I had married Ji En, because I never told him that I had married another man. One Sunday, I was holding my lovely two-year-old daughter when I felt very lonely and sad. My tears dropped onto her face. She looked up at me with her big bright eyes and said, "Mom, don't cry!"

I knew that I needed to express my feelings to someone who could understand me. So I wrote a long letter to Qian, Jiang telling him the whole truth about my life. A few days later, he answered my letter saying that there were tremendous changes in his life as well. He told me of his thoughts about why I refused to be his girlfriend; he feared it was because he did not have a university education. So, he persisted in asking his authority to let him resign from the army and go to Beijing to study. But, he was refused again and again.

He was so upset and angry that he wrote in his diary that he felt like a headless fly almost bumping himself to death trying to get out through the windowpane. During the Movement of Anti-Rightists, everyone in his army unit was required to turn in everything he/she had written–even words written privately in their diaries. Clearly the descriptive passage he had written was considered anti-Party and he was labeled a Rightist. As a result, he was kicked out of the army art troupe and was sent to a geological prospecting team to remold his ideology. He suffered a lot of hardships during those years. He told me he was still deeply in love with me and he wrote at the end of his letter, "Come to me with your angel."

100

It was as if a volcano erupted in my heart as my love for him was rekindled! But, divorce was a big thing at that time so I did not take any action. I put Jiang's letter in my drawer.

A few weeks later, my husband showed me a letter addressed to him from Qian, Jiang. It was a lengthy letter. Li said he had written to him asking questions about this deep love he had for me. Evidently, Li promised Jiang that if truly convinced, he would divorce me and let the two of us realize our dream. I read the letter.

In the letter Jiang told Li that we had gotten to know each other when we were teenagers. He told him that he lost his mother during the Anti-Japanese War. He said that I had given him a lot of love and care; that I was kind-hearted and sweet, smart and brave, etc. He was so naïve that he even thanked Li for his generosity and promised that he would treat the child and me very well. After I finished the letter, Li grabbed it from my hand and said, "Now, I am going to accuse him of destroying our marriage! He is a Rightist and should be punished for that!"

From then on there was no peace in our home. My husband threatened me every day by saying that my name would be ruined because I had reconnected with my old boyfriend. Shortly thereafter, the top leader of his company called me into the office. The leader asked me about the truth and I answered honestly. To my great surprise, he did not criticize me. Instead, he advised me to try my best to improve the marriage relationship and solve the problem of Jiang, later.

As I said before, the foundation of my marriage was very shaky. I had finally agreed to marry Li because I was totally disappointed by love affairs. So, I simply remembered an old Chinese adage, "Follow the man you marry, be he fowl or cur". I knew Li was not the right man for me to be with, but I did not take marriage seriously. It's my own fault and in the end, I had to eat my own bitter fruit.

I Long for a New Life

Life became even more miserable. The ballerina continued to enchant my husband and I was always busy with work and our child; it was no way to live. I was longing for a divorce and wished that I could marry the man I truly loved. Each day was filled with sorrow and quarrels.

During the summer vacation of 1963, Jiang wrote that he had been transferred to my hometown, Jiaxing, to work as a conductor of an art troupe. At Jiang's invitation, I went back to my hometown with my three-year old daughter.

Me holding Sha Sha with the whole family (1962)

My mother was very supportive of me and met us at the Shanghai railway station along with Jiang. After 14 years' separation, we might not have recognized each other had my mom not been there. He had turned into a mature, handsome man. He smiled shyly and greeted me, "Hui Xian, how are you?" Looking at my daughter affectionately, he said, "Sha Sha is very cute!" Mom arranged for us to sit in a pedi-cab while we headed to her friend's home. We talked as we went through the busy city of Shanghai. That night, neither of us slept at all. In the sitting room, we talked and talked as we had so much to share. We barely noticed the bell of the grandfather clock striking on the half hour from evening to dawn. That was the happiest night I had ever had in my life.

The next morning, we all took the train to our hometown, Jiaxing. All the beautiful old memories came flooding back. We did not talk much on the train but kept smiling to each other as if we knew what the other person was thinking. I had never been so happy and lighthearted.

During the two-hour ride home, I expected that I would begin my new life soon.

We actually went to my second eldest brother's home. As soon as we entered the house, Jiang started to help my mom with the housework. He swept the courtyard and carried fresh water from the well. He was so strong and diligent. After dinner, he played the *erhu*[6]. He had learned the violin when he was a child and received advanced training in Nanjing at a music school while he was in the army art troupe. He so loved playing the *erhu* and had acquired great skill. The melody he played was so thrilling that it touched my heart.

The next day, his two brothers came to see me. One of them was an artist and the other a singer. We used to be playmates back in our teens. After lunch, we stood around the piano and sang many of our favorite foreign classical songs to the accompaniment of Jiang's brother, Ning. After listening for a while, my mother asked us to sing some of her favorite Christian hymns. She said, "The serenade you were singing sounded like crying to me!" Her words made the whole room laugh. It was the first time I understood what the term "generation gap" meant. It was such a harmonious gathering. Life seemed to have turned a new page for me.

Then something unexpected happened. In the afternoon of the third day, my husband, Li, arrived. We were all shocked at his sudden appearance. I asked him, "Why did you come?" With a cunning smile, he said, "I came here for political capital." I could tell that his mind was full of schemes. In order to hide the truth that he was dating the ballerina, he wanted to shift the blame of our divorce totally onto me. That's why he had made this trip.

In the evening, he talked to Jiang saying, "If you write down that you are the one who destroyed our marriage, I will immediately divorce Hui Xian." Jiang said, "I do love her but I cannot say anything that is not true. Li, you do not love her and you want a divorce, but you want to blame me for that. I am already in a very difficult political position. If I write down what you want me to write, I will be punished severely. I cannot do that."

The next morning, Li said that he was going to the market to buy something for Sha Sha and he took her with him. But, he did not return

---

[6] See page 62

and neither did our child. The whole family guessed that he must have left with Sha Sha. The next evening, I called Beijing and found out that he had gone back to our home with our child. In this way, he forced me to return to Beijing to take care of my daughter. But before I left Jiaxing, I talked to Jiang who said that he would wait for me unless Li did not want a divorce.

When I returned to Beijing, I was told that the ballerina had broken up with Li. Her leaders found out that she was having a relationship with a married man so she was transferred to work in Harbin as a way to solve the problem.

Later, I mostly lived in the dorm of the university. Li was seldom at home and when we saw each other there was no peace. During those days, he was chasing other girls. He said to me, "I am not ready to divorce you. But, some day when I am ready to marry another woman, I will divorce you immediately. For now, you are still useful to me because you can make money to support the family." To me, Li was worthless! I despised him!

With this situation, it was almost impossible for me to have a new life. And my workload was very heavy which led to my health being very bad, too. Even though I loved him so, I thought it would be very cruel to Jiang to have him wait for what seemed a hopeless future. So, I advised him to find another woman to marry. I would later learn that after three years, he married an elementary school teacher in our hometown of Jiaxing.

The class that I was teaching required all my time and energy; I simply had no time for a divorce. Besides, in those days, it was still very difficult to get divorced in China. So, I dragged along day after day, feeling sad, fatigued and sick.

The "Little Red Flower" Class

In the summer of 1964, I was appointed to aid a more experienced teacher in developing a model class in the university's English Department. As her assistant, I taught reading and oral English, corrected papers and coached the students. This class was made up of twenty top students who were selected from the senior high school affiliated with our university. The best facilities were provided to guarantee their successful language studies. Even the university president gave special attention to this class.

Very soon, our class became the role model for the whole university and the president called upon the entire student body to learn from it. Everyone knew that these students had been carefully chosen and that they already had a very good foundation in English. No matter who would have taught the class, the results would have been good. But, in order to single this class out, the president used every possible way to publicize it not only within the school but also in the higher education community throughout China. That's why there arose a strong aversion in the university. The class was nicknamed "Little Red Flower". People said, "The Little Red Flower is blossoming within the walls, but getting popular outside the walls."

While the other teacher taught articles from *Selected Works of Mao Ze Dong* as the major texts in the open classes, I taught selected material from the English classics in the afternoon when no visitors were present. However, the president and the other teacher told the public that the students only studied Mao's works. That's why their English was so good. It was a big lie! No one knew the true story except the students and me,

I coached the students with their oral compositions, directed short plays in English, and prepared them for the open classes every day. We had groups of visitors coming from different schools. On many occasions, the visitors outnumbered the students. Since our classroom was too small to hold so many people, we held our open classes in the auditorium.

First-Hand Experience of the Cultural Revolution

Chairman Mao, Ze Dong called to the people of China to criticize the Communist Party in an effort to discover where the government could improve. Scholars at some universities actually wrote large posters to illustrate areas where their leaders could improve. Without exception these critiques occurred all over the country in schools, factories and stores. But the result was unfortunate. It created a division between people with different beliefs and different ways of thinking. Arguments began with words then escalated to beatings and finally, to the use of guns. Many people were killed.

Right up until spring of 1966, our model class had been the center of attraction and the university president was being overwhelmed with invitations from different colleges requesting us to do public demonstrations. The president focused so much of his energy on preparing for the nationwide presentation that he paid less and less attention to other parts of the curriculum at the school. As a result, when the Cultural Revolution began in June 1966, members of the faculty were very angry with him.

The first big-character poster that was painted on paper and hung on the university's outside wall read: *THE LITTLE RED FLOWER IS A REVISIONIST MODEL CLASS!* In half a day, the whole school was targeting the president and our class. The "Little Red Flower" withered. In quick response, the students of our class were mobilized to fight against the president and the other teacher of the class. There were also a few big-character posters criticizing me for teaching the students

Me at age 33 (1966)

"capitalist literature". Both the president and the teacher I had come to help were arrested and detained in the "cow shed[7]". I was lucky that the

---

[7] Spare rooms set up by the Red Guards of different units during the Cultural

students did not turn against me. I thought maybe it was because I did not show myself in public. Instead, I worked very hard in the classroom to guarantee the success of the twenty top students.

School sessions were closed at our university during the Cultural Revolution. Students and non-students were busy writing big-character posters to be hung on the walls of the university. They argued loudly in the classrooms and moved freely everywhere on campus. New organizations were formed one after another; different armbands that carried the names of the newly created organizations appeared; and differing opinions turned friends into foes. The students shared no smiles with their teachers and the teachers stayed in their own offices talking quietly about the current situation.

One day, right after the Revolution began, I was on a bus taking my daughter to kindergarten when I saw members of the Red Guard in the street, chasing women who were wearing high-heeled shoes. They forced the women to take off their shoes and walk barefoot. I also saw some women walking in the street looking very embarrassed; the Red Guards had shaved off the hair on half of their heads. Many girls with long pigtails were forced by the Red Guard to go to an appointed place and have their long hair cut short.

I was so scared because there I was on the bus in my high-heeled shoes. When I got off the bus, I ran with my little daughter to the kindergarten building and requested that she go to class by herself. Then I rushed into the restroom and took off my shoes. I could hardly walk barefoot, but there was no other way out. I thrust my shoes into my bag and fled into the street. In great pain, I got onto the bus and went straight to the university.

When I arrived at our office, I explained to my colleagues what I had just seen. They were all startled. Suddenly, three Red Guard soldiers jumped into our office and pointed their fingers at us women teachers.

Revolution all over China to shut up "the bad people" temporarily.

"You must cut your hair before eleven o'clock", they commanded, "We will come back to check!" The eight women in the room, without a second thought, began to cut off each other's hair. After we had finished, we stared at each other and laughed bitterly. At eleven sharp, the Red Guard came back and looked in on us; they nodded and left. I remained barefoot for the whole day. I finally found a chance to chop off the heels of my shoes and wore them home that evening.

The Suicide of My Favorite Neighbor

With the Cultural Revolution, things changed every day. I heard that many high school students began to physically beat their so-called "problem" teachers. My closest neighbor Gu, was a model high school teacher and she had very good relationships with her students. Often on Sundays, her students would come to her home and enjoy the day with her. I sometimes joined them and shared in the wonderful feelings. I had never seen a teacher so respected and loved by her students.

For over three years, we two families lived in the same apartment where we had separate bedrooms, but shared the same kitchen. We got along very well. Every Saturday evening, Gu brought her son, Xiao Hong, back from his kindergarten and they had dinner with my daughter, Sha Sha and me. The two kids became very good friends. But, with the onset of the Cultural Revolution, she came home much later than she had previously.

One Friday evening when she returned, she came into my room looking very pale and distressed. She told me that the Red Guard had beaten her best friend to death for the mere reason that her father had been a policeman before the liberation. She was so afraid that she requested that I take care of her son should something happen to her. I did not have the least idea what she was planning to do. So, I promised.

The following evening, I picked up my daughter from her kindergarten and on the way home bought food. As usual, I cooked a good dinner and waited for Gu and her son to arrive so we could eat. Sha Sha and I waited and waited. Nobody came to the door, not even Gu's husband. Sha Sha began to cry. She was hungry and had expected her little friend to come and play with her. We had to eat without them. Around nine o'clock, we heard a key turning in the lock, so we rushed to the door. But only the father and his son walked silently into the apartment. The father said to me in a very low voice, "Come to my room and I will tell you." We left his son sitting at the desk, not even talking to Sha Sha, who simply stared at her little friend and said nothing.

The father told me that his wife had killed herself in the Kunming Lake at the Summer Palace that afternoon. After she had seen her best friend beaten to death she was afraid that the same thing would happen to her, because she came from a similar family background. During lunchtime, she had slipped out of the school and had gone straight to the

Summer Palace. He said that she had put a letter into the post box in front of the Summer Palace. Then she walked to the Kunming Lake and jumped in. That afternoon, a visitor to Beijing found her body floating in the lake and reported it to the local police station.

Gu had laid her shoes, her coat, and her school badge on the shore as she clearly wished her body to be identified. Her husband was told the horrible news and went to the Summer Palace with their seven-year-old son, Xiao Hong. I couldn't help crying aloud at this shocking news. I looked at the boy sitting at the desk, drawing. The room was poorly lit and vaguely I could make out that he had drawn a wreath. I held him in my arms, tears dropping from my eyes. At such a young age, he had become motherless.

During those days, nearly every day, I heard similar stories of suicide. The Red Guard was beating people to death. People were killing each other over different political views, etc. The whole country was in chaos. Nobody could control the situation. Even some old revolutionary cadres were tortured to death. Who were your friends and who were your enemies? Nobody could distinguish. Everybody was defending himself or herself. It was Mao, Ze Dong who had started this Cultural Revolution and the people followed him blindly.

A Stranger Visits

The following Monday, I went to school. In the middle of listening to a political report, someone called me out of the auditorium. A middle-aged woman, whom I had never met, came up to speak to me. She introduced herself as a high school teacher from Sichuan province and said that a friend of hers recommended that she come see me in Beijing. In tears, she told me that her students had beaten her black and blue. They had forced her to drink the mucus from the mucus pot and some male students had taken turns in raping her. It made me so angry to hear about the brutal behavior of her students. She began to cry loudly and I got worried. So I asked her to be quiet lest other people overhear our conversation.

Then she informed me that she had run away from her school's "cow shed" and with the help of her friend, she boarded a train to Beijing. She asked me if she could hide in my home. It was really a tough decision. At that time, there were very strict rules; no one was allowed to host anyone without reporting it to the neighborhood committee. Though she had my full sympathy, I could not help her in this way. I could not risk my family. After giving her some money, I had to send her away. For many days after that, I condemned myself for not having helped her. To this day, whenever I think of her, I feel bad about it. It was the only time in my life that I refused to give help to someone in need. I have often wondered where she went and what had happened to her.

There were so many people like this desperate woman. There were so many similar stories of brutality happening everywhere in China. How could this be called a Cultural Revolution? What had happened to our traditional culture?

Chaotic Times

The whole school was in chaos. The whole country was in chaos! One never knew who their friends were and who their enemies were. There was only fighting and more fighting. At any time, a person like me with a bourgeois family background could be chosen as a target. And sure enough, there appeared a big-character poster entitled: *An 'Escaped' Rightist–Chen, Hui Xian.*

The poster stated that in 1957 I had been classified as an "unannounced rightist". I had never been aware of this. But then, it suddenly occurred to me why I had been sent to the countryside to do physical labor in 1957 and why I was transferred from the foreign trade company to teach at a college. I had simply believed that the change of my job had been because the school needed more teachers. I had not had any suspicion about having done something wrong politically. Because of my naivete the many changes that had

Me with Sha Sha at 7 years old (1967)

happened in my life did not affect my way of looking at the leaders. Instead, I remained active and enthusiastic in my work and had kept a good relationship with my comrades and leaders.

One morning, soon after the poster appeared on the wall of the university, I entered the office to find some of my former students from the "Little Red Flower" class sitting there, looking very stern. I sensed I would be the subject of this meeting. The group leader of our office announced that I had to say something about my teaching in the "revisionist model class". A bit nervously, I began to do self-criticism. I spoke honestly about what I had taught and how hard I had been working to make this class successful. I knew that the materials I had selected for teaching were not revolutionary. I only wished that the students could learn more idiomatic English, while not ideologically poisoning their minds. I admitted that I had been wrong. I gave several examples to show my mistakes. For two hours, I spoke almost non-stop. The whole room of thirty or more people listened quietly. I thought they would "fire back at me" afterwards, but to my great surprise, nobody spoke. In that moment of silence, the group leader announced, "Since nobody wants to say anything, this meeting is over!" People stood up and left. I was so relieved and so thankful to the group leader who had definitely protected me.

Free-Travel Throughout China

A short time later, many students and teachers left the school and headed off to different places to "do revolution". By showing their school badge, students and teachers from any school could get onto a train for free and head anywhere throughout China. Together with three other teachers, I went to the train station carrying a small bag. We were aimless and not entirely clear where we should go, so we got on a train bound for Xi'an. The train was so crowded that the passengers had packed themselves in like sardines.

All we could do was stand close to the door. With each stop, more people squeezed in and we were eventually pushed into the toilet room where we could only stand on our toes. Xi'an was a long distance from Beijing and we had to spend the night on the train. Near midnight, a man squeezed into the toilet room and said he had to use it. There were already four of us women wedged in, there was no way we could make room for him to relieve himself. So, we had to close our eyes as he did his business. Over time, more and more people wanted to use the toilet. We could only shut our eyes and try not to breathe too deeply as we could barely tolerate the odor.

About midnight, somebody in the middle of our train car shouted, "What's going on up there?!" The man lifted his head, looked up at a high school student who was curled up on top of the overhead luggage rack. "My God!" the man yelled, "You are peeing right on top of my head." The boy said nothing. He just covered his face with his overcoat amidst the laughter in the whole coach.

Visiting Yan'an during
The Cultural Revolution (1967)

The next morning, we arrived in Xi'an, the capital that served many dynasties throughout Chinese history. We were truly excited to have this free trip. By showing our school badges, we were warmly welcomed and told we could spend nights in the classrooms of any local school. The weather was getting cold and quilts and blankets had been provided for travelers.

We enjoyed sightseeing around the city and visited many places of historical interest. Two days later, we climbed into a truck that was taking people to Yan'an, the revolutionary base. The road was rough and dusty. And soon we were all covered with dust. And, because I sat on my small luggage bag near the back of the truck, the rough ride made me sick to my stomach.

Along the way, we saw many young boys and girls walking alongside the road. They appeared energetic and happy–some even sang revolutionary songs while they hiked. They were learning about the Long March from the old revolutionaries of the Red Army. We found out that some of them had been walking for days from Beijing to Yan'an. I admired those youngsters and felt encouraged to move on no matter what hardships we might encounter.

By the time we arrived in Yan'an, I was totally worn out. There, we were permitted to stay in a cave dwelling. We were put on a big *kang*[8]. It was very large and could hold more than ten people. But, since there was no fire underneath to warm it up it was so cold. I could not fall asleep, even though under the quilt I wore my overcoat, a hat and a thick scarf. I held onto another teacher's feet, but at daybreak, her feet were icy cold and so were mine.

For breakfast, the local people provided us with millet porridge and corn bread. They were very warm-hearted and spoke in a local dialect that sounded very dear to us. The places we were taken to visit looked familiar as we had seen them in movies many, many times. We could even tell which cave belonged to which revolutionary leader. It felt as if we were experiencing the days of the revolution first-hand even though it had occurred dozens of years before. In spite of the hardships we felt satisfied with our trip.

---

[8] A heated, earthen bed

A Return Visit to Guiyang

After Yan'an, we four teachers decided to go together to Guiyang and then go our separate ways. Guiyang was a place where I had spent some time in my childhood and I had a special love for it. Also, my sixth sister, Mao Xian and her family lived there. She and her husband had moved to Guiyang after my mother donated the hospital in Jiaxing to the government. In Guiyang, they had gone to work at the Guizhou Provincial Hospital; it had been years since I had seen them.

There were six in my sister's family, she, her husband and their four daughters. Since all four girls had been born in Guiyang, I had never met them. When I found their home I was so excited, but of course my nieces did not recognize me. It turned out that Mao Xian was serving in the countryside, and would not be allowed home for a visit. So my nieces went to get their father from work. My brother-in-law was so happy to see me. We had not seen each other since I was sixteen. Seventeen years of separation!

In those days it was difficult financially to make the long trip to Guiyang from Beijing; how grateful I was for the free train travel.

I wanted to make this short time with my brother-in-law and my four nieces memorable–and it was! The girls were especially curious about the resemblance between their mom and me. Since I had caught cold in Yan'an, I coughed a lot. Whenever I coughed, the girls would laugh. They said, "Auntie Eight, you look so much like mom and you even cough alike!" Neighbors peeked into the house and one of them said, "Oh, I could easily mistake you for Mao Xian."

In Guiyang along with my four nieces (1967)

The next day, the girls took me to a nearby mountain and to a recently discovered mysterious cave. It was called the "Underground Garden". My nieces told me that one midnight in July of 1966, during the Cultural Revolution chaos, a prisoner escaped from jail and made it to the foot of the mountain. Near daybreak, he decided to look for a place to hide out and was surprised to find a crack between the rocks just big enough for him to enter. As soon as he pushed through the crack, he found a huge, spacious cavern. From the small fissures in the cave, dim light shone on stones of different shapes hanging from the ceiling and growing from the floor. The further in he walked, the more mysterious he found it to be. The stones were long icicle-like shapes and there was even a river running inside the cave. Both startled and excited, he realized this cave must be an undiscovered place. He thought, "If I report this place to the government, I might be set free." Therefore, the next day, he returned to the jail and confessed his escape and also told of his discovery. In turn, the government did, indeed, reduce his sentence and set him free.

At the site, the local government had widened the crack, installed a gate and put lights in the cave. It was not quite ready for visitors yet. However, the Red Guards and young students insisted the cave security workers let them in. My nieces and I had the good fortune to follow them in and we became one of the first groups to visit the fantastic "Underground Garden".

I had never seen such an interesting sight as the beautiful stalactite and stalagmite cave; the stones looked as if they were brand new–milky white and shiny. The shapes that the stones created were amazing. We could make out a peacock with its tail open like a fan, a dragon swinging in the clouds, a crocodile opening its big mouth, two tigers fighting fiercely, fairies dancing gracefully, eight immortals sailing in the sea, four old men playing chess round a table with cups of wine in front of them and many, many other images. Every image looked so realistic that you could have easily believed that great artists from another world had carved them. In all my life, I had never seen a more magical cave. We even got a boat ride inside the cave. It drifted along the river while drops of water dripped on us from the ceiling of the cave.

Three days later, I headed on alone to Guilin, known as the most beautiful city in China. The train left Guiyang in the afternoon and it was as crowded as the one I took from Beijing to Xi'an. But this time I succeeded in finding a space for myself under the seat. The whole time, I was lying on the floor with a piece of newspaper covering my face so that I would avoid looking up into the crotches of those who came down the aisle.

At one point, the train stopped at a small station and there were some people selling food on the platform. People inside the train wanted to buy food, but found it very hard to get out. One man struggled through the crowd to a window and got a bowl of noodles through the window. Afterward, he could not squeeze back to his seat. But he was very smart and figured out a way to use a big handkerchief to hold the bowl and then used his teeth to hold the four corners of the handkerchief. Since the aisle was totally blocked, he reached out his long arms and held onto the luggage rack. Then, stepping on the back of the passengers' seats he walked back toward his seat. Suddenly, a female passenger screamed as she felt his heavy foot on her shoulder. "I am sorry!" said the man, opening his mouth to apologize. Alas! The big bowl of noodles poured onto the woman's head! The roar of laughter from the crowd drowned out the scolding he received from the suffering woman! Nothing could have been more laughable!

But, not everything that happened during the Cultural Revolution was funny. During those days, many young students traveled on top of the crowded trains and were killed when the carriage passed through tunnels. Tons of invaluable books were burnt to ashes; thousands of carders and intellectuals were shut in "cow sheds"; many people committed suicide and countless homes were searched. The whole country had gone mad and still we just followed the government blindly, unaware what would happen to us in the days that followed.

Another "Long March"

During the Cultural Revolution, there was one thing that impressed and touched me deeply. Many students ranging in age from junior high to college organized themselves into groups and launched a long march. Carrying heavy backpacks containing bottles of water and some food, they held up a red flag, as they walked hundreds of kilometers across several provinces, from the south to the north and from the east to the west. The students followed the example of the Red Army in its Long March dozens of years before, during revolutionary times. Encouraged by the great spirit of the Red Army, most of the youngsters walked for more than one month, some even longer. The majority of them chose to walk along the railroad tracks so that they would not get lost; it also meant they might be fed by the local people. I often saw the young marchers in the streets of Beijing looking very happy, energetic and proud.

Once, I was walking in Tiananmen Square when I saw a girl about fifteen-years-old marching towards the Tiananmen Gate. I rushed up to her and asked, "Where do you come from?" She kept marching very fast without even looking at me and answered, "Urumqi!" I was both shocked and touched. How could a girl of this age walk that far?! Urumqi is the capital city of Xinjiang province in the farthest northwest corner of China. It would take more than a week to travel from Beijing to Urumqi by train. Imagine, she had walked all the way to Beijing! As she disappeared out of sight, I looked upon her with admiration and respect as tears rolled down my cheeks.

I recalled, on my trip to Yan'an, we saw many groups of students on long marches of their own. Some of them had their feet bandaged or needed a walking stick, but they were still in high spirits.

One Saturday morning in Beijing, while I was in the kitchen cooking, there was a loud knock at my door. I opened the door and there stood my nephew, Rong Guang, who lived in my hometown, Jiaxing in Zhejiang province. With a big smile, he stood there proudly and opened his long fur overcoat. He said heroically, "I'm here, a Long March cadre!" I was dumfounded. I pulled him into the room and looked at him with affection and admiration. He, too, had marched for months to Beijing. His hair was long and his beard looked like the beard of a middle-aged man. He was actually a senior high student. His image stayed with me a long time as an inspiration to me as I tried to overcome my own difficulties.

Army Soldiers Arrive at School

According to the instructions of the government, People's Liberation Army soldiers were to come to all the universities and colleges to help discipline the teachers and students. There were military-like training drills every morning for all of the teachers and students. Even though there were no classes at the university, we all had to remain in our offices or classrooms for the entire day. We were told to study Chairman Mao's works each day.

The primary task of the army soldiers was to go through the personal files of everybody in the university. One evening, I was called to have an individual talk with one of the soldiers. He told me that they had examined my personal file and read all the information in it. He also told me that I was labeled an "unannounced rightist" during the Anti-Rightist Movement in 1957. But, after discussing my case, they decided that this conclusion should be changed. They had removed from my personal file all the materials that served as proof of the rightist label. The soldier smiled sincerely and said, "In my eyes, you are a very brave woman. You dared to criticize Chairman Mao for having done something wrong to women and you even said, 'If the upper beam is not straight, the lower ones will go aslant.'" He said, "You have a very sharp political eye. You said, 'Nikita Khrushchev is an ambitious careerist' long before the Chinese Communist Party exposed his true face." I felt so relieved after the talk and I respected this army soldier for being so honest and friendly toward me. After the talk with him, I felt much more light-hearted. I had been fairly treated and as a result, I decided that I would work even harder to show my loyalty to the people.

Finally–a Divorce in 1969

During much of the Cultural Revolution my husband Li had been away. By the time he returned, Sha Sha had turned nine years old. My university leaders and colleagues expressed sympathy for me. They had witnessed how miserably my daughter and I had lived. They decided to help me end this terrible marriage for they knew that I was not mentally or physically strong enough to deal with it on my own. Without my knowledge, our leaders called a meeting and most of the women teachers came. They asked if they could encourage and help me divorce Li. When they came to ask my permission my answer was an emphatic, "Yes!"

One day, I was informed that my leaders had talked to the leaders of Li's company about our marital troubles. The leaders of both our units called Li and me together for a meeting. They asked us how we would like to resolve the problematic marriage. We both agreed that we wanted a divorce. Li said, "I would like to have a divorce on the condition that I am not going to give child support, because I am going to marry again." I responded, "I would like to have a divorce on the condition that our child belongs to me alone." We both agreed to the conditions and the next day we became legally divorced. I left our home empty-handed–with only my precious daughter–and moved into the women teachers' dorm. My heart was filled with relief and I felt a great freedom with the shackles of my loveless marriage removed. After twelve long years, it had finally come to an end. And I was very grateful to my leaders and colleagues for helping me through it.

May the 7th School Edict

Soon after my reprieve, the Central Government of the Communist Party called on the governmental cadres, in addition to the faculty and staff of universities, to go to the countryside and receive re-education from the peasants. It became known as May the 7th School after Chairman Mao's declaration on that date.

In winter 1969, like all other universities and colleges, my university closed and the whole school, along with their families, left Beijing to attend May the 7th School. There were many locations for these "schools" and ours was in Xixian, located in Henan Province in the middle part of China. We were given three days to prepare and were permitted to take only a minimal amount of clothing and bedding. The older family members could stay in Beijing without moving, but children over ten years of age had to go to the countryside, along with their parents. Younger ones were allowed to stay in

At May 7th School (1969)

Beijing a while longer, until the adults were settled. Many families had to open their doors, allowing anyone to take their furniture and other things away for free, as no one was interested in purchasing them.

My daughter Sha Sha was only nine years old, so I left her in the care of our former nanny. When she came to the railway station to see me off, Sha Sha's eyes were wet with tears. With a big smile, I said to her, "When your dear ones leave, do not cry!" This quote was from a popular Peking Opera. She immediately gave me a big smile.

The people of our university had moved into a local high school where the classrooms served as bedrooms. About forty people were required to share one big classroom. Our beds were lined up in two rows with only one foot in between them. We put all our belongings under our beds.

It was winter and the weather was extremely cold. In the middle of our room, there was a big iron stove. The restrooms were far away on the other side of the school's playground. Therefore, we had a huge clay pot that held the overnight urine. Every morning, two people took on the duty of carrying the pot downstairs to dump it in the fields. Often the pot was full and the urine would splash along the floor, all the way from our dorm to the fields.

After a month, my daughter came to join me, along with the other children her age. We parents rushed to meet them and the kids were excited to see us. I had to share my twin size bed with Sha Sha. Life was difficult for the kids, but they were still very happy as they continued their studies at the local school.

By July, the weather had gotten very warm and our bedroom was so hot we had to leave the door open at night to cool it. One night, just before we went to bed, a large bat flew in through the open door. One of the female teachers was so scared she let out a scream at the top of her voice. A bold woman hit the bat and killed it. After a while, we all fell asleep.

At May 7th School (1970)

But, in the middle of the night, there was a strange noise in the room that woke us up. "Turn on the light!" someone shouted. As soon as the lights came on, we saw hundreds of bats flying around the room—so many, in fact, that the room was darkened by their presence. The mouse-like birds opened their angry mouths and squeaked as they swirled round the room. Our terrified screams filled the air. Luckily, we were all under our mosquito nets; unluckily, nobody dared to open her net. This meant there was no way that we could drive the bats away. We all assumed that they had come seeking revenge because we had killed their friend in this room.

It was a nightmare! Intellectuals like us had never experienced this kind of horrifying scene. The bats did their "protest" and left about an hour later. After that night, no matter how hot the room got, we would keep the door tightly shut as darkness came.

During the daytime, we basically worked in the rice fields. In the fields, we would see snakes swimming in between the rice plants. After finishing the fieldwork, we would march back to the school like an army. Often we saw some of the male teachers and students holding aloft on the ends of their carrying poles the snakes they had killed. In the golden sunset, the skin of the snakes shone brightly reflecting the sunshine. When the men got home, they would ask the "cooks"–also teachers from our university–to stir fry them and they would enjoy eating the feast.

We had no meat to eat, so those responsible for kitchen duty would go to the nearby river to dig for clams and make delicious dishes for us. However, many people were allergic to this type of clam and they broke out in rashes and blisters all over their bodies. My Sha Sha was one of the ones who got sick. My poor girl could not fall asleep. Every night, because of the itching, I had to use a paper fan to cool her down. I wished I could do more, but since the room was so hot, she sweated all night long. Whenever she turned over, I could see the wet spot her sweat made in the bed.

Heartaches and Political Pressure

One morning, all of the people in May the 7th School were called together to attend a local public trial. We had no clue as to who had been charged or why. When we got to the large playground where the local government usually held big meetings, we saw hundreds of people already waiting there. In front of the square, there was a platform where people stood looking very serious. No one was talking.

A few minutes after we arrived, a young man stepped onto the platform and through the loudspeaker he announced, "Now, the public trial begins! Bring the men onto the platform!" Then, one after another, twelve criminals were dragged onto the stage. They were all men, old and young, their arms and hands bound with rope. Almost as soon as they appeared, shouted slogans from the masses, echoed in the air.

Then, the leader of the local government announced their crimes.

"This person stuck a pin into the portrait of Chairman Mao's head. This showed his hatred for our great leader, Chairman Mao. He is a landlord who did not reform his ideology. He is sentenced to death!"

"This person broke a porcelain figure of Chairman Mao. He is also a landlord. He did it deliberately to show his true feelings. He is also sentenced to death!"

"This person used a page from Chairman Mao's writings as toilet paper. That was a big insult to our great leader, Chairman Mao. How can we put up with that? He is sentenced to death!"

Naming each person, he pronounced, "He is sentenced to death!" "He is sentenced to death!" The government leader went on and on until all twelve men were sentenced to death.

As I stood listening, I was astonished. I could not understand who had given this man the right to kill people just because of mistakes like this. What happened to the principles of the government? Were these local officials crazy? I felt the blood in my body turning icy, but no one dared to say anything on such an occasion. Those poor twelve men, paralyzed with fear, were immediately dragged to the execution ground where they were shot to death.

On our way back to the school, none of us said a word about the trial–which was actually just a gathering to pronounce sentencing. But, who and where were the judges? There were none! An old saying popped into my head, "They treat human life as if it were not worth a straw." I found it hard to believe what had just happened, before my very eyes.

Later that afternoon, we held group political studies. Everyone looked very nervous. It seemed that all of us were checking ourselves to see if we had done anything similar to those "criminals". We kept our eyes only on Chairman Mao's works, as we were not allowed to read anything else. No one talked for the whole afternoon. This had never happened before. I thought everyone must have had the same thoughts and experienced the same feelings as I did. But no one dared to express them. Even in later years, none of us ever mentioned that public trial again. It left a deep wound in my heart.

After that, people around me were often in fear. Everybody was afraid of making a mistake that could be seen as a crime. During the Cultural Revolution, activated by the "revolutionary" atmosphere, some people went crazy. There was lawless behavior everywhere. Some searched other people's homes and took away valuable antiques and burned treasured books. Others, in the name of the Revolution, destroyed buildings and temples of great beauty–all structures of historical interest. What a loss!

Politically–No Improvement

I thought my background had been cleared after the army soldier informed me that the negative material had been removed from my personal file. I felt sure that I would now be treated as an equal by my revolutionary comrades. So, I was light-hearted during my time at May the 7th School. I worked very hard in the fields and I was very active in political studies. In addition, I often went to visit the poor peasants' families to see if I could be of any help in the house.

One day, I visited a woman who had a seven-day-old baby. It so happened that just as I entered her home, her baby had a seizure. He was running a high fever and his face had turned purple. I knew he was suffering from umbilical tetanus. I suggested that we take the baby to the hospital, but the father said that the doctor had already seen the baby and said there was no way to save this child. The only thing I could do was baby-sit him so his mother could rest. Every day after work, I would run to the house to help with the housework and stay with their child until midnight. After four days, the baby died. I tried my best to comfort the mother telling her not to be too sad. I did what I could.

The morning following the baby's death, our whole school attended an out-of-doors meeting. After the leader gave us our instructions, we watched a group of peasants walking towards us. The two people in front were holding a red paper with big characters on it. The rest of the group were beating drums and gongs. They came to a stop in front of our group and read aloud from their letter. This was the normal way to deliver a letter of praise.

People were curious to know what the letter was about. Actually, it turned out to be a thank-you note to me for helping the family while the baby was so sick. Upon hearing the name "Chen, Hui Xian", our leader interrupted the peasants and told them to drop the letter off at the office and leave. The father of the dead baby kept turning his head and smiling to me as he walked away. Our meeting being over, many people came to ask me what I had done. I said, "Something I should do."

People thought our leader would choose another opportunity to read aloud the letter or to post it on the wall. But, nothing was ever said; he was forever quiet. My comrades and I knew very well that the leaders only wanted to give praise to those who came from the families of workers, peasants or soldiers. A person like me, who came from a bourgeois family, should never be praised even though he or she did good deeds. This event made me realize that I would never be treated equally, despite their saying they would treat all people the same as long as they behaved well.

Being born into a family like mine, one had to study hard, be obedient to the leaders and work diligently. Otherwise, it would be very difficult to be admitted to the Youth League, to say nothing of the Communist Party. If it were not for the outstanding work I had done in the anti "Five Evils" movement while in college, I would never have been admitted to the Youth League. After I began work in 1954, I submitted my application to join the Communist Party. There was no response for many years. My application was ignored because of my family background and my complicated social relationships. I gave up the idea of becoming a Communist Party member.

Mother-of-Chickens

I was often sick during my time at May the 7th School. For several months, I felt fatigued and at night I would sweat. Finally, I was diagnosed with pyelonephritis, an inflammation of the kidneys. The doctor suggested I stop working in the rice field, because we stood in icy cold water for hours at a time. Our leader assigned me a new task–to raise chickens. Happily, I accepted the job. An old hut was set aside to serve as the chicken coop. I spent a whole day cleaning the empty hut and got everything ready for the new residents. Two male teachers went with me to the market to buy two hundred chicks. Those chicks were so happy to be moved into the new house and showed it by busily eating food and drinking water while making pleasant peeping noises. I immediately fell in love with those babies with their light-yellow, silky down. When night fell that first night, I reluctantly locked the hut door and went to my dormitory.

In the morning, I got up an hour earlier than usual and rushed to the chicken coop. It was so quiet inside that I thought the babies must still be sleeping. I softly unlocked the door and pushed it open. Oh, my God! The ground was covered with the dead bodies of my chicks! All of them had died. Two hundred chicks were all dead! It was awful. Their brains and hearts were missing; the rest of their bodies were intact. I burst into tears and ran to my comrades for help. They came and looked at the sad scene and discovered many rodent holes in the ground. The leader came and comforted me, "It's not your fault. We should have thought of the rats. They are here and everywhere in the fields."

That same day, he asked some men to cement the entire floor of the hut and pen. Two days later, another group of chicks were brought for my feeding and care. That afternoon, I saw a peasant carrying a basket with three young cats in it. I ran to him and begged him to sell me a cat. After listening to the story about the terrible death of my baby chicks, he gave me a male cat. He looked like a little tiger with his striped light-brown fur. I named him, "Xiao Huang", which means Little Brown Cat, and took him to the chicks' hut. I squatted down and placed him on the ground intending to introduce him to his new friends. At first, both sides seemed a bit startled, but a few minutes later, they all relaxed. The cat did not seem to want to attack my chick babies, so I sat on the ground watching as they became familiar with each other. Later, I fed the cat a meal of fish and kept him in a cage. When it got dark, I placed the open cage in the chicken coop and locked the door on my way out.

The next morning when I opened the door, the cat and the chicks all addressed me in their own language, "Good morning!" My heart was full of joy! In order to train the cat to be the protector of my chicks, I caught small snakes and rats for him to eat. Very soon, Xiao Huang was honored as Chen's Brave Guard. He seemed to know his duty and all day long he stayed around the chicken coop watching the chickens playing in their fenced yard. All my comrades loved him and praised me for training him so well. From then on, I never again worried about my chicks.

In spring, the crops were growing fast. Grain was distributed and I was given a piece of land to grow vegetables for the chicks. The chicks had plenty of vegetarian food, but I wanted to give them a better life. So every night I went to the fields to catch frogs. With a bag over my shoulder and a flashlight in hand, I moved slowly along the paths between the rice fields looking for frogs. As soon as I found a frog, I would flash the light on it. The light would blind the frog, causing it to remain still and making it very easy for me to catch. Sometimes, I would see a water snake and get startled, but I encouraged myself to be brave for my chicks.

Within a couple of hours, I had a bag full of frogs which I carried to the back yard outside the women teachers' dorm. The next morning, many of my roommates complained about the noise from the frogs. When they found out that it was me who hung the bag of frogs outside the windows, they said, "We know that you love your chicks, but have some pity on us, okay?" Thereafter, I put the frogs in the chicken house for the night and killed them the next morning. I chopped the meat up to feed the chicks and mixed the blood with the grain. They grew very fast. The farmers in the neighborhood said that they had never seen chicks grow so big within such a short time.

One day, four male teachers came to my chicken coop and handed me several large eels. One of them said, "Let's make a deal. We four are working in the rice fields and we know how to catch eels. We will supply you with eels. However, you have to cook the middle part of the eels for us. The rest of the eel meat you can feed to your chicks." I agreed. For months, the teachers would arrive during their breaks to enjoy the eels I prepared for them. At their request–to make the eels taste better–I stole some salt from the kitchen. It has remained a secret between us until now. I never told this story to anybody in our university; it was clearly against the rules.

In addition to the frogs, I fed my chicks the heads and tails of the eels as well as the blood. What nutritious food I was feeding my chicks! I also trained them according to a book written by a Soviet expert on how to raise chickens. I used whistle signals to command the chicks to eat, to gather together, to go out to play, and to go back inside the hut to sleep. The expert's advice turned out to be quite successful as the chicks followed the signals very well. Every day, I whistled many times training my chicks like an army. My comrades were amused.

One morning, the school leaders came to observe my chicken farm. The chicks were outside the coop hidden in the bushes, pecking for earthworms. When I saw the leaders, I told them I would call my chicks together to welcome them. They appeared doubtful. I whistled the signal to gather and in less than a minute, all my chicks ran out of the bushes, lined up on both sides of the path and stared at the leaders just like two rows of soldiers saluting their commander-in-chief. The leaders were impressed! They inquired as to how I had trained them, to which I replied that I learned the techniques from a Soviet author.

One day, my comrades came back totally exhausted due to an extremely hard workday in the fields. They knew that they all needed more rest, so they had planned to sleep in late the next morning. But a female leader, whom everyone hated, wanted them to get up and go to the fields at their regular time. She knocked at every door but nobody would answer. She even borrowed my whistle and blew it very loudly again and again. Still, nobody got up. The whole morning passed without anybody working in the fields.

During lunchtime when my comrades appeared, the female leader was very angry and loudly voiced her criticisms, "Why did you not get up to work? I whistled many times, but nobody got up? What's wrong with you? Did you hear my whistle?" Everybody remained quiet. Then, a male teacher answered casually, "Well, we thought it was Chen, Hui Xian giving whistle-signals to her chicks!" The whole group roared with laughter. Actually, she had blown the whistle loud enough to wake up the heaviest sleeper, but the comrades kept silent in protest against this leader's unreasonable demands.

My chicks matured quickly. Every morning around four o'clock, weird sounds would come from the chicken coop. It sounded like ghosts crying. But it was only the young roosters practicing their crowing.

There was another little hut next to the chicken coop where the "problem" teachers lived. One morning, a professor from that hut came to me and said very politely, "You know some of my roommates suffer from insomnia. They get even less sleep close to dawn when your roosters start to crow. Could you please do something to stop this noise?" I felt so bad.

I said, "I am terribly sorry. I did not know the male chicks had already begun to crow." That very morning off I went to the kitchen and told the cooks that I was ready to bring the roosters in so that they could be prepared as a treat for all our comrades. That evening after the chicken dinner, many came to thank me, both for feeding the chickens so well and for the truly enjoyable meal.

A few months later, all my little "girls" had grown into healthy hens that began to lay eggs. I had a beautiful knitted bamboo basket that I carried with me all the time. I used it to carry the leftovers from the kitchen to feed the chickens and upon returning, to hold the dozens of eggs I carried to the kitchen. I became the most welcomed person to the kitchen. Now, my comrades could have either scrambled eggs or boiled eggs every day.

With the purpose of breeding a good quality younger generation of chicks, we bought an imported rooster. He was much bigger and stronger compared to the local roosters. From the beginning, he seemed happy to have so many "wives" under his control. He loved them all and acted like their protector.

One day, two hens got sick; I decided to take them to the vet. But, first I had to catch them. Unexpectedly, the rooster flew at me and angrily pecked me with his big, long beak. Such a sudden attack scared me so I swatted at him with my apron. But he was a very brave guy and showed no sign of retreating. It became such a heated battle it caught the eye of quite a few comrades who laughed and laughed. They thought it was great fun to watch this fight. I did not think it was fun and I would not give in. Then, the vice-president saw us and brought a carrying pole to hit the rooster on the head. The feisty rooster fainted. I grabbed the two sick hens and left for the vet. When I came back, I saw the rooster standing near the corner of the hut with his head lowered. People joked about it saying that he was doing self-criticism for having fought against the Mother-of-Chickens. After that, whenever the rooster saw me, he would walk away. I, however, remained afraid of him.

During those days, I carried a long stick with me wherever I went. I was reminded that in one of the Chinese classics, *Dream of the Red Chamber*, the heroine Lin, Dai Yu who was weak and thin, often carried her basket along with a stick to collect fallen flowers into which she shed her tears. My comrades nicknamed me Lin, Dai Yu. But, they humorously put the Chinese word "socialist" before the name because I was overweight, not weak and slim.

Days went by quickly and it came time to hatch the eggs. In order to keep the hens producing the same amount of eggs for our kitchen, I did not let the hens hatch the eggs. Instead, I took thirty-four chicken eggs and had a mother goose sit on them. The goose seemed very happy and sat there quietly. But, her weight was too heavy and some of the eggs were crushed before it was time for them to hatch. Still, twenty-one days later, beautiful little chicks pecked their way out. Altogether, I counted twenty-five chicks; it was a great success! The mother goose loved her hen babies so much she took especially good care of them. She led the chicks to the fields to find food and walked them along a nearby pond to enjoy the beauty of nature.

One afternoon, while I was chopping vegetables for the chickens, somebody shouted, "Chen, Hui Xian, your chicks are following their mother goose into the pond!" I rushed to the pond and saw some of the chicks faltering in the water. I was so afraid that they would drown that I jumped into the pond, forgetting that I was not a swimmer, either. But, I was able to pick them out of the water and we all made it safely back onto dry land.

After that incident, I dared not trust the mother goose any more. It seemed that she would try to teach the chicks to do everything that she could do. The risk was too great! The next day, I had to shut the mother goose in the hut while I built a little fenced-in playground for the babies. When I freed the mother goose, she walked around and around the fenced area making crying sounds as if her heart were breaking. Watching her, I cried, too. But, what else could I do? From morning till night she stopped eating and continued to cry. Poor mother! Then a comrade suggested that I put another thirty eggs under her to hatch. I did and it worked! The sad mother goose did not come to cry outside the playground fence any more.

There was another smaller group of chicks that were hatched by a hen. The hen was quite large and took very good care of her babies. I did not have to worry about her taking her babies for a swim. One afternoon, while I was studying Chairman Mao's works with my group, there came a big thunderstorm. It was raining cats-and-dogs–so much so that I could not go to my chicken farm. I waited until the storm passed and the rain stopped.

As I ran to the chickens, a "problem" professor saw me through his window and came out of his assigned hut. Full of emotion, he whispered to me, "Chen, I want to tell you something. When the storm came, your hen and her chicks had no place to hide themselves. The hen opened her strong wings and let her babies hide underneath. She stood in the storm without moving, her eyes were wide open and her body was wet through and through. I looked at her thinking, 'How touching her motherly love is.' I was almost in tears when I saw this. But, do not tell anybody about it; they may criticize me for thinking that motherly love is great." The professor's words touched my heart. The image of that hen standing in the storm protecting her babies has always remained fresh in my mind, even though I did not see it with my own eyes.

During those days that I was working on my chicken farm, I was still suffering from kidney problems and arthritis. My daughter, Sha Sha was with me and she was frequently sick because of her many allergies. When my mother learned this, she wrote to me saying that I could bring my daughter to stay with her in our hometown, Jiaxing. I was given two weeks' leave and had to put my chickens under someone else's care.

An Accident on the Way to Jiaxing

We, Sha Sha and I, took the train to Wuhan and then a boat to Shanghai in order to go on by train to Jiaxing. It was dark when we arrived in Wuhan and the Shanghai boat was scheduled to leave port at eleven o'clock that night. The waiting room was big, but the air in it was humid and suffocating. Hundreds of people were there, some sitting on the benches and some sitting or lying on the cement floor. When the time came for boarding, people squeezed tightly together trying to get onto the boat first. Sha Sha and I finally got to our cabin and found our beds, but our clothes were stuck to our skin with sweat.

During the Cultural Revolution, passengers waited to be organized once they were on a train or boat. There were twelve passengers in our cabin and a temporary group leader. They chose me to be the leader. Most of the people in my cabin were women with children, the exception being one young couple. After the boat began to sail, there was only silence in our cabin as everyone fell asleep. Suddenly, at around 3 o'clock in the morning, a loud explosion interrupted my dreams and violently rocked the boat.

We were all fully awakened by the sound of the loudspeaker. "Passengers! A bomb has exploded in the operations room. Stay where you are and wear your safety jacket. We are going to stop at the closest dock. Please be orderly and wait for your turn to get off the boat." I immediately told the people in my cabin to remain calm and get their important belongings ready–just in case we had to make a fast exit. I distributed the safety jackets, but found that there were only ten. When I finished giving away the jackets, Sha Sha looked at me and asked, "Mom, how about you and me?" I patted her on the head and said, "In times of difficulties, we think of others first." Within a few minutes, the young couple left the cabin. I tried to stop them, but the man said, "We are not leaving. We only want to stand outside the cabin."

Very soon, we heard different kinds of sirens sounding from all directions, as the loudspeaker announced to passengers that many boats– large and small–were coming along the river to rescue us. Our boat would soon reach a port, but it was slowly sinking. Passengers from the lower decks had come to the upper decks; there were no screams or shouting, only silence. The calmness of the passengers impressed me greatly.

The only disappointing thing I had witnessed was the disappearance of the young couple from our cabin. They must have found an easier way to escape, but I still felt concerned for them. In about an hour, we reached a dock. The loudspeaker told us to wait until the wounded and dead workmen from the operations room were carried off the boat.

In the dim morning light, I saw nine people being carried out on stretchers. We would learn later that three of them had died on the spot and six were wounded. Among them were passengers who rushed into the operations room to rescue the workmen. I thought of them with deep respect, for they were all heroes. Then, it was our turn, as cabin by cabin, we left the boat and went ashore.

It had been arranged for us to stay in the big waiting hall of the dock. People were tired but remained disciplined. When all the passengers got into the hall, the captain apologized for what had happened and told us that very soon another boat would take us on to Shanghai. It was almost dawn and in the hall, which was brightly lit with electric lights, we could see that there were several hundred people waiting. Some shared their food with the children and older folks, while others took out their musical instruments and played to amuse the frightened group. People began to smile at each other and to chat. It was a very touching sight. A couple of hours later, we all boarded another boat and sailed without incident to our Shanghai destination. It was reported to us later that the first boat sank slowly to the bottom of the Yangtze River, but the criminal who had set the bomb was not found. During the Cultural Revolution, such things often happened; the whole country was in constant chaos.

More Re-Education from the Peasants

After I returned from Jiaxing to the May 7th School, I went to work on my chicken farm again. I had missed my chickens a lot, but they had been well cared for while I was away. The major purpose of our going to the countryside was to learn from the peasants. In addition to the farm work, we often went to visit the peasants' families and listened to them telling their sad stories of the past. The area where we were located was in the middle part of Henan Province. The land was not very fertile and the weather was not agreeable to growing crops. The people, there, had never had a stable life. Before liberation, the peasants often lived on wild vegetables and tree bark when the harvest was poor.

One year there had been a huge flood. Some of the villagers tried to escape but no transportation was available. There was a railway running through that area, but none of the trains would stop and allow the peasants to board. The poor suffering people just stood alongside the railroad tracks and watched the train pass by. Standing in the water for days and nights, they waved to the passing trains but the trains continued on, ignoring them. Hundreds of people drowned or starved to death in the weeks that followed.

A year later, there was a severe famine and many people died of hunger. They had already eaten everything possible to fill their stomachs; grass, barks, leaves and even clay. I remember a story told to us by an old peasant. He had had a family of five–his wife, a son and two daughters. One day, the youngest daughter died of starvation. His wife was preparing to bury her but he stopped her. Through his tears he kept his eyes on the dead girl of seven. "Xiao Hua," he whispered, "the whole family is going to die like you. Could you offer your body to save our lives?" The rest of the family cried bitterly and said in one voice, "No! No!" They all sat by the dead girl staring at her, tears rolling endlessly down their faces. No one moved to touch her.

They sat there for the whole night and then another whole day, until the mother fainted, as did the elder daughter. It was clear that the whole family was going to starve one by one. With a loud cry, the father stood up, took a knife and cut into his daughter's dead body. When the "food" was ready, the father begged the family to eat. Looking at the plate full of her daughter's flesh, the mother fainted again. There was no other way out and they began to eat the flesh of their dear family member. The

137

father finally said, looking at the empty plate, "My daughter, I fed you for seven years. You fed us one meal, but saved the whole family! You will live on within us!" When the old peasant was telling his story, all of us listeners cried with him. What a miserable life they were living before the liberation.

At May the 7th School, after listening to stories like that, we often ate *Yi Ku Fan*[9]. Most often, our meals were prepared with wild vegetables mixed with course corn powder. It tasted awful. We were asked to eat this so that we could remember the bitter life the peasants had lived in the past in comparison with the good life they lived today.

During the years of the Cultural Revolution, I seldom heard from home. But, one day, news came from Hangzhou that my grandfather, who had lived for an entire century, had passed. Because of the Cultural Revolution, I could not attend his funeral, but this is what I was told. One morning during that hundredth year, he was reading his newspaper in his sunny, cozy room. Suddenly he called out to my auntie's son and asked him to go get his old friend who lived near the West Lake. About two hours later, his old friend walked with the aid of a stick ever so slowly into my grandpa's room, calling out to him in a quivering voice, "An Fen, I am here." There was no response! "An Fen, how are you?" The ninety-nine year old friend moved closer to my grandpa who was sitting in his armchair holding the newspaper. My grandfather's soul had already left his body. His heart had ceased beating, yet his death was such a perfect one. No pain, no suffering.

Years later when I was in my late thirties, I revisited grandpa's old home. The room was still there and the bamboo bushes had grown wild. The date tree by the well had grown taller and older–still a source of shade for the backyard. It was so quiet and peaceful. I sat down on a small stool as if waiting for my grandpa to again tell me the story of the crying calf.

---

[9] A meal that reminds you of what the poor peasants had to eat in the old society

I Depart from May the 7th School

In the summer of 1971, my leaders told me that along with nine other teachers, we were to leave the countryside. I was assigned to teach English at the Liaoning Institute of Finance and Economics in Dalian. All ten of us were to teach different subjects: international business, foreign languages and politics. Most of our comrades in May the 7th School admired us and congratulated us. But, one of my friends confided to me, "It may not be a good thing to be chosen to go to the Institute." He was right. The transfer meant we would never return to our original university. But, what else could we do? We had to go wherever the leaders wanted us to go; we were taught to be obedient. Even if someone tried to resist, he or she would be persuaded to go anyway. Besides, to leave the countryside for the city was what everyone had wished.

So, I was happy to be chosen to leave. But, it was hard to tear myself away from my lovely chickens. On the day of my departure, I went to the chicken coop and opened the door. As usual, the chickens flew out into the fields happily. I fed them with the best food I had prepared. Then I squatted down weeping. It seemed that the young chickens knew what was going to happen, for they gathered close to me. Some of them jumped up onto my shoulders and gently pecked my head and ears. I held one of them in my hand and smoothed her feathers. I had no way to know if they could sense my feelings. I was their mom and I was going to leave them forever. On that afternoon, we ten teachers left our comrades, the peasants and the farm. But, I left part of my heart in the chicken coop that day.

After a long train ride we arrived in Dalian, a coastal city in Liaoning Province. Our new institute was very close to the seashore. I moved into a 12 square meter room. It had a small kitchen and a restroom which I shared with an apartment mate. Once I unpacked my simple luggage, I ran to the seashore. Ever since I was a child, I had a fascination for the sea and had dreamed of living near it. My dream had come true.

I was filled with excitement as I looked out over the boundless blue ocean. Along the shore it was very quiet. There was only one man walking along the water's edge. He must have felt my excitement because he asked me, "Is this your first time here? Where do you come from?" I answered honestly. Just then, I saw something fluttering across the surface of the water. I asked the man, "Is that a flying fish?" He laughed and said, "No, they are only sea shrimp. You have a big imagination."

I was really enchanted by the sea. Early the next morning, I went to the seashore, again, to watch the sunrise. I lay back on the sand and read a novel. Ever since I was a little girl, I loved being in nature. I loved mountains, rivers and forests, but I never had a chance to live by the sea. I was so happy I sang as I watched the seagulls flying overhead.

Nevertheless, I couldn't live on beautiful scenery alone. I had to eat, but there was scarcely anything in the grocery stores. Whenever edible supplies were unloaded at the store, people would immediately line up in front of the store and buy up everything. I had never seen anything like these stores before. Usually, grocery stores would not sell anything unless people showed their residential food-purchase book. Each month, a person was allowed to buy 3 ounces of vegetable oil, 5 ounces of pork, 1 *jin*[10] of flour, 2 *jin*[11] of white rice, and a limited quantity of vegetables. Only for special occasions, like the New Year or Spring Festival, people could purchase eggs or fish. I soon realized that life in Dalian was much like it had been ten years earlier when the whole country was starving. And yet, we were supposed to live there for the rest of our lives. I soon felt very depressed.

As school began, I was appointed to be the English teacher of a class formed of young people who had come from different places such as factories, armies and the countryside. They had been in high school when the Cultural Revolution began and were sent to receive re-education from workers, soldiers and the peasants for several years. I found these students to be very disciplined and they valued the opportunity to study at the institute. They had all suffered so much before entering the institute and they knew very well that they had been selected from among thousands of young people in similar situations. So, they all studied very hard.

In my class, there was one boy who had never been out of his hometown, so he found it very difficult to imitate the pronunciations of the English language. In order to help him, I gave him some special oral exercises to do. Every morning before I entered the classroom, he would

---

[10] See page 19
[11] See page 19

be waiting for me at the door to check his homework. One day I found that his lips were full of blisters and cracks. I asked him what had happened. He just lowered his head and without saying anything looked at the exercise book. I was touched to tears. I would learn that he got up at 4 o'clock every morning and did his pronunciation exercises for hours. Owing to his persistent hard work, half a semester later, he became one of the best students in the class and his pronunciation was excellent. All my students were hard working. I loved them and I tried my best to teach them well during class and coached them in the evenings as well. They advanced in their studies and the relationship that developed between the students and me was very close.

After I had settled in Dalian, I went back to my hometown, Jiaxing, to get my daughter. Sha Sha had grown into a very pretty girl and was really happy to be with me again. She attended a local elementary school nearby my institute. Whenever I went back to the classroom to coach the students in the evenings, she would come with me, because I could not leave her alone at home.

Every Sunday, we would go to the seashore and gather seafood. We collected seaweed, sea cucumbers, clams, oysters, etc. It was great fun to spend our Sundays in this way. We could enjoy the beautiful scenery, breathe fresh air and be with nature. Often, we brought something back for dinner. We especially liked oysters, but they were difficult to collect. They attached themselves to the rock and we had to crack their shells to remove them. Only when the tide was low, could we reach the bigger ones.

Early one Sunday morning before sunrise, the two of us climbed onto a huge rock that had emerged only because the tide was very low. We were excited to see that it was dotted with oysters. Being careful not to slip on the seaweed, we squatted down and began to crack open the oysters with our homemade tools. We then put them into the basket we carried. Bent over, we moved slowly around the rock. When the sun rose, the rock brightened in the morning light. Again, I was so happy I began to sing a folk song.

Time quickly passed. About an hour later, Sha Sha suddenly lifted her head and shouted in terror, "Mom, we are surrounded by the sea!" I looked up and was shocked to see that we seemed to be in the middle of the ocean surrounded by water. I could not think how we would get back to shore, which was at least one hundred meters away.

What to do? I was really scared; I did not know how to swim! Just then, we saw a teenage boy walking along the shore and we shouted to him for help. In no time, he came out to us–half swimming and half walking through the water. I put Sha Sha on my back and followed closely behind his every step. Sometimes the water was so deep I could hardly touch the bottom and he had to pull me by the hand. When we got to the shore, we were completely soaked; the basket and tools and oysters were lost, but this kind boy had saved our lives.

A Second Marriage—a Second Baby

Life was hard in Dalian, especially in winter. We had to burn coal to heat our room. We also had to store large quantities of cabbage and turnips for the entire winter, because there were almost no vegetables at the market. To carry coal and cabbage required a man's strength, so I had to depend on other people for assistance. Many of my friends advised me to find a husband, but I hesitated because of the misery of my first marriage.

In 1972, I met a man named Li, Zhi who was a Chinese teacher at a high school in the same neighborhood. After dating him for several months, we decided to get married. We were both middle-aged and there was no romance. In fact, neither of us had much love for the other. I needed a man to complete the household and he needed a wife with whom to have a family. Life was dull, but practical. What we mostly talked about was how to make ends meet every month and how we could get enough food to eat. We did not have much else to talk about and our personalities were very different. I was a people-person and he liked to be alone.

Then in 1973, I became pregnant and was quite ill. I suffered from severe insomnia and neurasthenia and was plagued by terrible headaches every day. I slept only a couple of hours each night–even with sleeping pills. But, I still had to teach during the daytime. In addition, the heavy housework wore me out.

Since the food supply was so poor in Dalian, I decided to return to my hometown two months before the baby was due. In Jiaxing with my family, I knew I would have better food. It would also mean that I would deliver my baby at the same hospital my parents had founded and later donated to the local government.

Unfortunately, I would learn that the medical service was not as good as before. They had "bare-foot doctors" working there. They were called "bare-foot doctors" because they did not receive strict training in medical schools; they primarily served people's basic needs in the countryside. According to Mao's policy at that time, the public hospitals had to accept them as assistants to the regular doctors. In this way, their medical knowledge and techniques would be enriched.

On the evening of November 20, I was sent to the hospital to deliver my baby. After she was born early the next morning, the obstetrician left the delivery room, leaving only a bare-foot doctor to attend to me. She examined me and then violently pulled out the placenta. Immediately, a large quantity of blood poured out of me. I knew something bad had happened. As the blood flooded out of me, I could feel its warmth. When I looked at my fingers, they seemed to be shrinking fast right before my eyes. I thought to myself, "I'm dying!"

Within a few minutes, I was almost in a coma. Vaguely, I heard the footsteps of people running into the delivery room. The bare-foot doctor brought the obstetrician back. The doctor quickly put on her rubber gloves and pushed her hand into my vagina, which caused a very sharp pain. I screamed at the top of my voice. The doctor said, "I am saving your life! You just have to bear the pain." She began peeling something from my womb as I lay bleeding. After a while, she stopped, and with a deep sigh showed me a half-inch long piece of something bloody. I was too exhausted to look or to hear any more. The doctor said to me, "This small thing would have killed you!" Then, they took some tests and gave me shots to stop the blood-flow. As a nurse was wheeling me out of the delivery room, I saw my 79-year-old mother awaiting me in the corridor. She put her soft hand on my forehead and said with emotion, "You have suffered a lot!" I broke down; I could not hold back my tears.

While I stayed with mom, she hired a nanny for the baby. The weather was very cold and there was no heating system. My health was not good and I was unable to breastfeed my baby. We had to feed her powered milk and rice powder, because fresh cow's milk was not available. Times were difficult during the Cultural Revolution, but my mother tried in every way to get nutritious food for me. The nanny was a very good woman and took good care of my baby and me.

Ping Ping at one year old (1974)

Li, Zhi followed tradition and named the baby Ping Ping. The character for Ping can be translated as "peaceful", "balance" or "safe". It was a good name. When she was only four months old, Ping Ping started calling all men "Da Da", which means "uncle". People could hardly believe it and often tested her, but she never failed to prove her ability.

The Death of My Dear Mother

One sunny morning when we were sitting in the courtyard, my mother abruptly turned the conversation to the topic of her death. She told me that she had prepared everything. I hated to hear her talking about death and said, "Mom, you will live for many more years. Stop talking about death."

Upon her retirement, mother liked to travel to visit her children's homes. During those years, mom lived primarily with my second eldest brother De Xian and his family, in Jiaxing. My sister-in-law was a very nice lady; she was the most loved person in our family. So, mother was happy with them and enjoyed her life there.

My other brothers and sisters often came to visit mom, even though all but my youngest brother lived far away. Mom lived a very simple life and she cared about all her children. Some of us were better off and could give mom money every month; we knew she always shared her money with those who had financial difficulties. We all felt love from her, even though most of us were not able to be with her often.

About twenty days after I gave birth to Ping Ping, my mother came into my room. It was in the afternoon and I invited her to eat some chicken broth. She smiled and told me that I was a very filial daughter. She said, "You always give me a share of whatever you eat, as if I am also having confinement of childbirth." As I sat up in bed, she came to me and picked up the baby. She felt Ping Ping's hands and said. "This baby girl has beautiful long fingers. She should learn to play the piano." We both smiled.

Looking into my mother's face, I was shocked to see something hidden deep in her eyes. It was not my mother's usual kind face, for it seemed as if there was the shadow of a different, terrifying spirit under its surface. But I did not say anything. As she walked slowly toward the door, my mother said, "I am going to cook dinner for your brother's family." Then she left us. About ten minutes later, my niece Zhen Guang rushed to my room calling out, "Auntie 8, Grandma fell, I think she had a stroke!"

I quickly jumped out of bed and ran to the kitchen where I found my mother lying on the floor. Just at that moment, my youngest brother Kai Xian, arrived home, noisily ringing the bell of his new bike. He could not have known what had happened when he shouted, "Mom, look, I have bought a new bike. Thank you for your wonderful gift to me!" As soon as he saw the scene, he quickly put his bike against the wall. We placed mom on a bed. As we were leaving the house, mother stretched out her hand and motioned for us to lock the door; she had already lost her ability to speak. We answered, "We will, mom!" Then, with all of us following along, my brother and our neighbors carried her to the nearest hospital.

She was diagnosed with a severe stroke. All my brothers and sisters were informed of the terrible news and one by one, they came from their homes around the country to see her. Mother nodded and moved her lips a bit when she was told of the arrival of each of her children. Nearly all my brothers and sisters came to visit and we took turns keeping her company day and night. She was only able to drink chicken broth; she never fully recovered. And later as she slipped into a coma, she never regained consciousness. The hospital tried every means to save her life but it was in vain. Ten days later, she passed away.

One could only imagine how heartbroken we were over her death. She was a great mother and was deeply loved by us children. She died on December 21, 1973 at the age of seventy-nine. Due to the political situation during the Cultural Revolution, it was impossible to have a big funeral. Only our family, some close friends and neighbors accompanied her remains to the cemetery.

After burying her ashes in the same tomb as our father, we all came home feeling very sad. My fifth oldest brother, Gong Xian suggested that we hold a farewell gathering after dinner. He said, "It is the law of nature that the old generation will die. As the younger generation, we should do things according to what our parents taught us. Let's not separate in tears. We should follow their good example in serving people with our heart and soul."

That evening, we gathered in the sitting room and talked about the good deeds that our parents had done during their lifetime. Reminiscing about the jokes our father had told us, we laughed a lot. The next morning, those who came from afar left for their homes. When everyone had gone, the house was very quiet. It was not until then I realized what my mother's death meant to me. I stayed awake through the night without a wink of sleep. Whenever I closed my eyes, I would see the image of my mother sitting beside my bed. I totally broke down and could not stop crying. I became very ill myself.

At the urging of my youngest brother's wife He Ying, I left my hometown for Shanghai where their family lived. I wrapped my month-old baby in a thick quilt, and putting one of my mother's long silk waist bands over my shoulder and around my waist, I fastened her to my chest so that my hands were free to carry other things. Sha Sha, only 13, had to handle a big bag full of our belongings by herself. On my way to Shanghai, I simply could not control my tears.

Upon arriving at our destination, I lay Ping Ping down on the bed. After I untied the silk waist belt, I placed it on an armchair asking Sha Sha to put it away. As she went to pick it up, the waist belt disintegrated. With great surprise she exclaimed, "Mom, the silk belt has melted." I looked at it carefully and was shocked at this strange phenomenon. It had been so strong and I had used it the whole way to hold my baby to my chest. So, why had it shredded? I sighed and without much thought I said, "Mom has guarded Ping Ping on our way here!"

During our stay, my youngest brother, Kai Xian, often came home to Shanghai from his job in Jiaxing. His wife, He Ying and his son, Yue Guang cared for us and treated us very well. I still had trouble sleeping and was very depressed. But, finally one afternoon I somehow fell asleep. Yue Guang saw me and got very excited as he ran to tell his parents, "Auntie 8 fell asleep!" Later, when his parents told me this, I was very touched by the boy's concern for me. He was such a kind-hearted soul. I liked him very much.

In Shanghai, I went to see both Western and Chinese medical doctors for my illness and they all told me that I was suffering from neurasthenia. They said the syndrome was severe. Every evening I took sleeping pills and would sometimes faint after taking them. My mind just did not work! I forgot how to cook simple meals and I could not figure out how to change Ping

My brother Kai Xian, his wife He Ying and son Yue Guang (1972)

Ping's diapers. I cried whenever I realized that I had lost the ability to do even the simplest housework.

Dizzy all day long, I could not think properly. I was unable to even recite the 26 letters of English alphabet. It felt as if I were in a bad dream, as if I were controlled by somebody else. I was desperate! Finally, I was taken to a very popular old Chinese doctor who advised me not to feel too sad over my mother's death. He said, "My medicine can only partly help you. You have to depend on yourself in order to make a full recovery." After taking his herbs for ten days, my mind half-cleared, but I still felt as if I were living in a dream.

Then one day, my husband came to Shanghai to take us back to Dalian. But first, it was important that I return to my hometown, Jiaxing, to visit my mother's tomb to pay my respects. The day we arrived, I was still in a half-dream, half-awake state, but as soon as I stepped into my mother's bedroom, I suddenly and totally woke up. It was such an amazing experience that I will never forget it. My mom was still taking care of me.

We Return to Dalian

At the end of February, 1974, our trip from Shanghai to Dalian by sea was a 48-hour journey. The weather was cold, the sea rough, and my health was still poor. Upon arriving home, I found my kitchen counter piled high with dirty dishes. With Ping Ping strapped on my back, I did the dishes and cleaned up the apartment.

On March 1, our school began. I had to teach every day, even though I became breathless whenever I talked. The food supply at the market was very scarce. In fact, nothing had improved much since I had left six months earlier. We still had a ration of 3 ounces of vegetable oil and 5 ounces of pork per person each month. For our survival, the government provided us with limited amounts of rice, flour and corn powder. But milk for the baby was insufficient, so we also had to feed her ground rice powder mixed in warm water.

Life in Dalian was extremely difficult and help was nowhere to be found. The only way to improve our life was for me to grow vegetables and raise chickens. When spring came, I planted more than ten different kinds of vegetables on a small piece of land outside our home. I built a large chicken coop under the bedroom window, using cobblestones. There, I raised more than ten chickens and a female goose I called Ms. Goose. With my prior experience in raising chickens, the chicks grew fast. But actually, most of the credit belonged to Sha Sha. She ventured into the nearby fields to collect the farmers' discarded vegetable leaves, or she would go to the seashore and pick seaweed to feed the chickens. By summertime, our family had plenty of eggs to eat.

We hired a nanny from my hometown to take care of Ping Ping. That meant five people lived in our 12 square meter room. The large bed and double bed nearly filled the room, and there was no space for a desk. So, I had to prepare my lessons or correct students' papers while sitting on the double bed. I hid myself behind a sheet so that Ping Ping could not focus on me. It seemed that Ping Ping was an outdoor baby; whenever she was awake she would want to be taken outside. She especially loved being near the sea and always wanted to go into the water.

Once, while at the seashore, I held her in my arms as we stood in the shallow water. She kept urging me to go further into the water. She pointed to the middle of the ocean with her little fingers and screamed, "Wai wai!" She was saying, "Go out there!" I could not swim and I was also pretty short. Could I dare to go out further? I cautiously moved forward, until the water was almost at the level of my waist. Ping Ping was not satisfied and kept saying, "Wai wai!" Suddenly a big wave crashed high against my face and I realized I had ventured too far, so I turned around and walked back to shore with Ping Ping crying and screaming. Our adventures to the seashore were the only fun we had during that time. There were no movies or other recreational activities. Life was very dull in Dalian.

The families of the ten teachers that had gone directly to Dalian from May the 7th School remained close. Whatever problems arose in health or finances, we would offer each other help. And we were all truly in need. Close to the end of every month, inevitably some families would be short of money or food. The rest of us were quick to share whatever we could spare. We often said that our shared suffering had made us friends indeed.

None of us liked the leadership provided by the heads of the institute. There was no democracy; whatever the leaders told us to do we had to obey. In Beijing, at least we had been able to express our own opinions when we disagreed with the leaders. None of us were happy in Dalian. Often, we would put our heads together and discuss the idea of asking our original university to take us back. We would learn later that not long after we had left May the 7th School, the rest of faculty and staff of our original university had been taken back to Beijing at the request of the central government.

There was no freedom to choose one's job or place of work in those days. In my thirty-five years of work experience in China, I had never had a chance to choose my own career. We were taught to be obedient and be a "tamed tool" of the Party. When you were transferred to another job, you should not ask for the reasons. The personnel department would simply tell you that you were needed there and you should just go for the sake of the revolution. If you refused to accept it, you would be seen as denying the needs of the revolution. It was very difficult for us teachers from the May 7th School to go back to Beijing. It took ten years and a lot of money from the original university in Beijing to "buy" us back. Hundreds of couples worked and lived in different places for tens of years, and even from young age to old age. They could only be reunited for a short period of time once or twice a year. The personnel system of China at that time was merciless.

Earthquake, Premier Zhou Dies, Chairman Mao Dies, the Fall of the Gang of Four[12]

Many terrible events occurred throughout China during 1975 and 1976. On February 4, 1975, an earthquake happened in Haicheng, Liaoning province. The earthquake made us "crazy" as the whole city of Dalian shook when it happened. We were not allowed to live in our homes because they were deemed unsafe. In the freezing weather of northern China, we had to stay outside in a temporary earthquake shelter day and night. Sha Sha helped me cook outdoors in the open, while Ping Ping, wrapped up in a thick quilt, had to be carried all the time to comfort her. Because of the cold, she could not sleep and her constant cry was heartbreaking. From our indoor kitchen to the shelter, back and forth, I carried water, with two-year-old Ping Ping tied on my back. Her father had left for his hometown before the earthquake occurred and could not make it back to Dalian. This horrible situation lasted about ten days.

By the end of 1975, it became known that our beloved Premier Zhou, En Lai was ill with cancer. Under the suppression of the Gang of Four, he had suffered tremendously. Having done so much for the revolution, he then tried his best to prevent the Gang of Four from bringing further harm to the country.

Since I had worked as his translator on several occasions in the 50's, I had a special respect and love for him. On January 9, 1976, as I was making up the bed after I got up, the loudspeaker announced Premier Zhou's death. I burst into tears. Ping Ping asked in surprise, "Mom, why do you cry?" But there was no way to explain my sadness to such a small child.

At 8 o'clock that morning, I entered the classroom and noticed that the students were very quiet. I stood on the platform wanting to speak,

---

[12] The name given to a political faction composed of four Chinese Communist Party officials. They came to prominence during the Cultural Revolution (1966-76) and were subsequently charged a series of treasonous crimes. The members consisted of Mao, Zedong's last wife, Jiang, Qing, the leading figure of the group, and her close associates, Zhang, Chunqiao, Yao, Wenyuan, and Wang, Hongwen. Their downfall in a coup d'etat was on October 6, 1976, a mere month after Mao's death.

but I could not. In an effort to try to control my feelings, I turned to the blackboard and wrote in big letters: "Premier Zhou will live forever in the hearts of the people!" Upon reading my words, the whole class burst into tears. They sobbed for a long time.

Not long after that I began to feel political pressure from our institute leaders. They frequently held meetings insisting we discuss our true feelings for Premier Zhou, En Lai. I felt they were overly focused on me, as if it were a sin to love Premier Zhou. I spoke my truth, yet they often hinted that there was something wrong with my position. Even the head of our department talked to me, privately, trying to convince me that Premier Zhou had not been a good leader. But, I stubbornly refused to accept what he said. The political atmosphere was so restrictive that I always felt I might be enfolded into a "reactionary" group. Accordingly, the attitude towards me of the leaders and "progressive" comrades became totally negative.

Then, as if to top all of China's miseries, in July, 1976, the Tangshan earthquake struck. The whole city of Tangshan was crushed, burying millions of people alive. Two months later, on September 9, Chairman Mao died, which saddened the entire country. The Chinese people were in great despair!

Political pressure became more intense. One day, in early October, I was informed that I needed to attend a meeting the following day. I had a strong feeling that something bad was about to happen to me. However, before I fell victim, a friend from another university came that night to secretly tell me about the fall of the Gang of Four. He said, "Beijing people are hailing this victory over the fall." The news sounded as though it would be my salvation.

I could not sleep the whole night in hopes that the news would be announced first thing in the morning. And it was! The whole institute turned out into the streets shouting slogans and cheering for the people's victory. During the celebration, I was extremely excited and told everyone around me, "Today is my second liberation day!" And just as quickly as things had turned against me, everything changed as the worker-leaders left our institute. No longer would anyone be condemned for saying they loved Premier Zhou. At last, the political pressure had been lifted from me.

Truly, Premier Zhou, En Lai was a great leader who had done so much to build a new China. During the Cultural Revolution, were it not for Premier Zhou, many more good revolutionary leaders and prominent scholars would have been killed and more valuable historical architecture would have been destroyed. His whole life was dedicated to the people. He would not even permit a tomb to be built for him. Instead, his ashes were scattered in the ocean. In the Chinese people's heart, he stood much higher than Mao, Ze Dong. It was due to his humanity, his merits and his love for the people.

A Fighting Spirit

Soon after the fall of the Gang of Four, instructions came to reform our system of education. We were encouraged to teach students skills and techniques that would be relevant for their future. Two years prior, we had been ordered to eliminate the examination requirement, as both students and teachers were frequently sent to work in the factories, or to do physical labor in the countryside. This education was termed the "Open Door School".

Under that system, students learned almost nothing related to schoolwork. Now, they were studying hard, especially their English. The new goal was to be able to communicate with foreign businessmen after graduation. I tried in every way to help them catch up on what had been lost to the past. With the students closely following me, the atmosphere drastically changed. Not only did I hold classes, but I also organized many after-school activities, such as teaching them songs and short plays which they all performed in English. The result of my efforts was very positive.

Quite naturally, I proved to be very bold in expressing my opinions whenever I found injustices in our institute. But two leaders were not happy with me. These two were very self-centered and whoever disagreed with them would be given "small shoes to wear".

Around this time, a male teacher and I were invited to teach English together on the Liaoning Province Radio Station. Our English instruction program went on at 7 a.m. following a morning exercise program. It went beyond Dalian; it was broadcast over neighborhood loud speakers and into high schools all over the province. Many of our colleagues and students regularly listened to us and naturally knew our voices. But most people had no idea what we looked like, or who we were. The listeners seemed happy with our teaching and I was glad to be respected and loved. On occasion I would be out in Dalian or in another city and I would overhear conversations where people were discussing the English teachers on the radio. It seems that we had become famous for our listeners had made up stories about us. While riding in a tram, I overheard two women who sat next to me telling a grand story! They said that when I was a teenager I returned from the USA where I had studied English. They described me, sight unseen, as a pretty lady and they had me romantically coupled with my co-broadcaster.

The station paid our institute 1.50 *yuan*[13] per hour, or 6 *yuan* for our four hours a week. We two broadcasters received half of the income because our department leader took the other half for office expenses. Not satisfied, our leader kept pushing me to ask the radio station for more money. One day, he told me to demand higher pay from the station. I refused! He got upset and punished me by adding another class to my teaching schedule. I knew what he was doing and I would not obey his unreasonable requests.

Our English instruction broadcast went on for two years. Overloaded with work, I again became sick. I passed blood all the time due to kidney problems. My friends told me not to work so hard but I would not stop. Both teachers and students hated these two leaders. But, with them in the lead positions, there was nothing that we could do.

Then, out-of-the-blue, came two new leaders to our institute. I decided that I would tell the new president and the new secretary about all the hurtful things that our current leaders had done to our department. Having no opportunity to meet either of them, I chose one evening to go to the president's home. As it turned out, the new secretary was also there to dine with the new president.

After I introduced myself, the president said, "Oh, you are the English teacher I have heard so much about. You are the trouble-maker in your department." "How do you know I am a trouble-maker?" I shot back, "You have just arrived at our institute and without any investigation you have already come to that conclusion. You have only listened to the reports from our hated department heads. You should go to the students and teachers and listen to them. What you are doing is against Chairman Mao's teachings!"

Seeing that I dared to talk back to him like that, the president flew into a rage and yelled at me, "Get out!" The secretary stood up and tried to calm both of us down. But, I would not let the president treat me like that. In retaliation, I overturned their dinner table and left in tears.

Even though I remained upset, I was not afraid of anything they could do to me. Yet I felt desperate that there was no place for the truth to be told. I hated the institute. I wanted, with all my being, to return to our Beijing university where we had such good leaders.

---

[13] Equal to 1.71 U.S. dollars in 1981

One evening about a week later, there was a knock at my door. It was a young man who introduced himself as the son of the president. I let him in and he handed me a note from his father. It said, "Please accept my son as your student." I was shocked by this and asked the young man why he wanted to study with me. He said, "My father said, 'I have never seen a woman intellectual as bold as Chen. She is an outspoken and honest person, and she teaches well. Go, study with her'. My father also said he likes your personality and wants to become friends with you." I was touched by his words and I promised to accept him as my private English student. I would later learn that the president had been an army official before coming to be president of our institute. In his way, he was simple and straightforward. I later apologized to him, telling him that I was wrong to have been so rude to him that night. He smiled and said, "It's okay".

Shortly thereafter, a special class was organized, made up of the sons and daughters of the important cadres and teachers at our institute. The request was made for me to teach this class. This meant I had to leave my original class in the Foreign Trade department. One afternoon when I was at a high school teaching a class in preparation for their entrance examination, the dean of my institute rushed in and said, "Come back to our institute with me right now, it's an urgent matter!" She would not tell me what had happened. After getting into her car, she just drove directly to the president's office without talking. As the car passed the playground, I saw a big crowd of students shouting slogans, but I could not understand what they were saying. When we entered the president's office, I saw that the room was filled with major leaders, all of whom were smiling at me.

I was puzzled, then relieved when the president said, "Will you please go back to teach your original class? Students from your Foreign Trade department are having a demonstration against the institute leadership because you have been taken away from their classroom in order to teach the children of our institute's major cadres. They say it is discrimination."

I responded with, "It is only right that the students are upset. It was not me who wanted this new class. Certainly I will go back, but I also have a request. The institute's top leaders must investigate the bad things done by the Party secretary of my department. Otherwise, I will not teach under his leadership." The major leaders agreed. An hour later, the president admitted it had been a mistake to organize the special class for me to teach. The class was officially disbanded and the demonstration came to an end. The next day, I was happy to go back and teach my dedicated students. After that the leaders of our department did not dare to challenge us as they had done before.

At Last, Our Housing Problem Is Resolved

When our institute built some new residential buildings, they were to be distributed among the faculty and staff. Although my family had a small kitchen, the four of us basically "lived" in the 12 square meter bedroom, where we slept, ate, played, and prepared our lessons. It was very crowded. Ping Ping's father taught at a high school that was unable to provide any living space for its teachers. Therefore, I applied for a larger space through my institute. But, the institute leaders refused me. Their excuse was that the husband of the couple should be responsible for housing, not the wife.

I was very upset and thought that this policy was unfair to women. Female teachers, like me, worked as hard as the male teachers, so I didn't understand why we were treated differently. No matter how hard I tried to reason with the leaders in charge of housing, they would not provide me with additional space. At the time, I knew many people were bribing the cadres who were in charge of allocating the new apartments, giving them all kinds of gifts such as meat, oil, clothing, etc. Since I would never consider handing over a bribe, it seemed that my request would never be approved.

Once the distribution ended and I obviously had been overlooked. I decided to rebel and take action. I told my students the truth about the housing allotment policy. The students thought of various solutions. The monitor of my class put forth a great idea. The students would remodel my kitchen into a bedroom, and then build an extension to serve as the new kitchen. With our bedroom on the ground floor, it was easy to do. Of course, I quickly agreed with his recommendation. All of my students knew how to build houses and readily volunteered to help. My plan was that I would buy the materials and they would do the building. However, the students refused to take my money. They said, "It is unfair for you to have to use your own money. The institute has lots of building materials left out on the playground. We will just go and get some."

Within two days, a new kitchen was built and the old kitchen remodeled into a small bedroom. Once the institute leaders found out, they were furious. They publicly criticized me, stating that I would be punished. A few days later, I went to the offices of the leaders in an effort to reason with them. Afterward, our institute's Party Secretary Li came to my remodeled apartment to have a look. When he saw my small room, he said, "I had no way to know that you had such a small space to live in. I came to know too late." His attitude touched me. So, he gave his permission for the students' renovation and did not punish me. I of course continued to work as hard as ever.

A year later, another new residential building went up and this time I was allotted a two-bedroom apartment. It was on the seventh floor and there was no elevator, so we had to climb many stairs every day. But, it was so much better than my whole family being crowded into one small room. I felt that I had succeeded again through my fighting spirit.

Justice Is Granted in My "Reactionary" Uncle's Case

In the spring of 1979, my youngest aunty and her husband, Wang came to Dalian for a visit and stayed in my home. She was a musician and her husband had studied abroad in England. He taught International Finance at the Northeast Finance and Economics University in 1953, where he was labeled a "reactionary". Sent to prison for years in northeast China, he suffered from the extreme cold. Owing to the hard labor he had to do outdoors, the ends of his fingers froze. After getting frostbite, he eventually had to have half of each finger cut off, which made it very difficult for him to use his hands.

After his release from prison, uncle was assigned to teach English at a high school in the south. But, life was so hard for him during the Cultural Revolution that twice he tried to commit suicide. So, it was my aunty who had to work as a music teacher to feed their two children. When they came to Dalian, both had retired. Since he was not healthy or happy, my aunty tried to cheer him by taking him traveling to different places.

I had never really had the chance to ask my uncle about this sad history. All I knew was that I had a "reactionary" uncle. By the time they came to Dalian, the political situation had completely changed. In fact, the government was trying to correct the injustices they had carried out, especially those occurring during the political movements of the past 30 years. One evening, I asked my uncle, "Can you tell me the real reason as to why and how you were deemed a "reactionary"? He said, "I made three mistakes:

"First, right after the founding of the People's Republic of China, a high-ranking general crossed over from the Kuomintang in Taiwan into China via the United States. While I was reading about it in the newspaper, I said, 'Oh, I know this man. He is also a very famous geographer; it was he who drew the first map of China.' Second, when the Korean War started in 1950, many young people joined the Chinese Volunteers and left the university. I remarked, 'If all the students go into the army, who will be left to study at the university?' And lastly, in 1953, I was the vice-director of our department at the Northeast Finance and Economics University. In our unit, we had quite a few professors from the south who were not used to the hard life of the north. They all wanted to return home. So, they came to me for permission to leave the university. I told them, 'I am sorry to tell you, but I do not have any say in this matter, for I am not a Communist Party member.' In 1953, I was arrested for having said those 'reactionary' words. And I was sent to be reformed for more than ten years in a northeastern prison where I lost my fingers to the freezing cold."

After listening to him, I figured that if what he told me was true, he should have an opportunity to have his unjust case corrected. Starting the very next day, I began investigating. Actually, part of the institute where I worked had been transferred from the original Northeast Finance and Economics University. Some of our older professors used to be my uncle's colleagues. I visited them, one-by-one, asking them if my uncle's words were true and if they also thought it was an unjust case. I got the same answer from each of them; they wanted to support me in getting his case reviewed.

Once I learned that Party Secretary Li had been head of the security department at my uncle's university, I paid him a special visit. In turn, he also supported me in getting my uncle's case reviewed. After I summed up his case and had written all the information out, I went to the Northeast Finance and Economics University in Shenyang to meet with President Sun. He was the person in charge of correcting the injustices at his university. Sun was a wonderful man and was very pleased that I had come for this purpose. He knew my uncle well and told me that he truly thought my uncle was wrongly punished for the things that he had said. President Sun also helped, by gathering even more information. Then, he encouraged me to submit the case to the Ministry of Finance in Beijing for a settlement.

Off to Beijing I went. Upon my arrival, I went to visit a former student of mine, Fei Fei, whose mother worked at the Ministry of Finance. I had hopes that she might give me guidance on how to submit my uncle's case. It so happened that just when I arrived at my student's home, her son was having a severe seizure. Without a second thought, I helped Fei Fei carry the baby to the emergency room at the nearest hospital. We stayed overnight to take care of the baby and when he was better, we took him home. Once everything settled down, Fei Fei's mother, a very nice old lady, asked me why I had come to Beijing. After I told her the whole story, she said, "I can help you. I know the person in

162

charge of correcting the unjust cases in our Ministry." Upon hearing this, I was truly excited and happily handed over the thick pile of papers that I had written and had collected. Fei Fei's mom said, "Don't worry, we will resolve this problem. You just tell your uncle to rest assured as he waits for the answer."

A few months later, my uncle's unjust case was settled in our favor and the corrections were made. An apartment was assigned to him and his family and he was awarded a monetary settlement to compensate for his losses. My uncle's life changed completely. He was so enthusiastic that he wanted to go back to work in the original university. But, he had already reached retirement age and his mind was not always sharp. We friends and family advised him to give up the teaching idea–which he did. Later, he spent his old age in Hangzhou where he mostly read books, and seldom talked. He became a true bookworm.

Years later, after the death of both my uncle and aunty, I was with their son. In the presence of many relatives, he said to me, "Cousin, I am so thankful to you. During my childhood and youth, I was never fairly treated politically. I lost many opportunities for a better career because of my father's case. Only after his injustices were corrected did I have the suppression lifted from me." He told us that he had since become a very successful entrepreneur. I learned an important lesson from helping resolve my uncle's case: *So long as you have the courage to strive for something, you can succeed.*

Though my uncle was granted justice, it set me thinking: "Why did the Party so often make mistakes and then correct them years later?" It was easy to label somebody a "reactionary", a "rightist", a "revisionist" or some such and put them in jail or send them to the countryside to do hard labor. But, what did this mean? It not only brought personal disaster to the person being labeled, it also marked his family and especially his children. They were all seen as guilt by association. Years later, when the Party discovered and admitted their mistakes, the damage had already been done. They could offer an apology or compensation, but those affected had already aged and in many cases lost their career, property, or in some cases, a lifetime! What a tremendous loss to the country and to these individuals!

An Ever-Increasing Workload

In the beginning of 1979, my daughter, Sha Sha was about to graduate from senior high and needed to prepare for her entrance examination to college. She did very well in literature, but poorly in mathematics. Sha Sha really wanted to study medicine, but without good marks in mathematics, it would be impossible for her to be admitted to a medical college. If she majored in literature, most likely she would be assigned to teach at a high school after graduation, however, Sha Sha was clearly not interested in becoming a teacher. Her only way out was to enter a foreign language institute. Unfortunately, she had not studied a foreign language while in high school. So, I decided that I would tutor her in English with the goal of having her pass the exam in half a year.

After compiling an accelerated learning booklet, I worked with her every evening. Sha Sha studied hard and learned enough words, phrases, and grammar to do well on all the practice examination tests that I

Sha Sha, my niece Xiao Hong and Ping Ping (1977)

prepared for her. Since I had been teaching basic English for years, I knew the areas she had to master in order to pass her entrance examination. Sha Sha took several practice exams. I found her weak points and gave her extra make-up exercises to do. Six months later, she passed the national entrance examination. Then, she was told to prepare for the oral exam that would be given at the Second Foreign Language Institute in Beijing.

At the same time, I caught a severe cold and lost my voice, so I had to go to Beijing in order to receive special medical treatment. As it turned out, it was fortunate that I could be there to help Sha Sha prepare for her oral exam. I had had made copies of one hundred short stories and articles to aid her comprehension. She would practice by reading them and then answering relevant questions. Our ten-day training went very well. The stories and articles covered various topics, such as history, geography, the sciences, etc. I had never noticed Sha Sha's amazingly good memory until then. She only had enough time to read each story only once. But, she not only correctly answered all the questions I asked, she could re-tell the story as well. Our confidence was high that she would pass the oral exam.

On the morning of the exam day, we rode together in a minibus to the institute. On the way, I prepared her by asking what she had been doing that morning and what she saw from the minibus windows. Her answers came promptly in very good English. But I did not stop questioning her until the very minute that her turn came for the oral exam. After she finished the exam, she came out with a big smile on her face. She said excitedly, "Mom, you know what? The questions the teachers asked me were exactly the same questions you asked me on our way here this morning. I answered fluently and all the teachers were satisfied with my quick responses. I believe I have received a good mark."

Several days later when some of her schoolmates received their admission letters, Sha Sha still had not heard from the Second Foreign Language Institute. We began to wonder if something had gone wrong. Then two days later, Sha Sha received word that she had been admitted to the foreign language institute. We puzzled as to why it was such late notice. It turned out that there was an interesting story regarding the delay.

At the admissions office in Beijing, there were teachers working on admitting students for their different colleges. The Second Foreign Language Institute had a list of students whom they had decided to admit, according to the results of the students' written English test and their oral exams. Sha Sha's name appeared on the list as one of those that had passed successfully. But, after all the other students' files were admitted, they realized that Sha Sha's file had not been reviewed. While they were trying to determine what had happened, one of the teachers took a break and walked over to another group of teachers. These were teachers from Beijing Normal College. She told them about the missing file. The teachers of Beijing Normal College said, "Oh, we have her file right here. Her marks in Chinese and geography are very high and we would like to admit her to our college." Then the Foreign Language teacher said, "Oh, let's look at her application. If she applied for your college as her first choice, you can have her. But, if her first choice is our institute, you must allow us to have her." Finally, the Foreign Language Institute won out. It turned out that the reason for Sha Sha's late admission letter was that two colleges had wanted to admit her!

News spread rapidly that Sha Sha had studied English for only six months and was admitted to a foreign language college. As a result, many parents and teachers came to me and begged me to teach their children English too. Teachers from high schools even invited me to instruct their graduating classes. I could hardly say no to any of them, so my workload increased. Apart from the regular students I was teaching at my institute, I taught one class at a high school and a private group of students in the evenings at my home.

Nearly all the students that I taught got high scores in the English portion of their entrance examinations. That led to even more people requesting my help. So, I ended up teaching in a large hall instead of a classroom. The ten English practice-exams and the hundred short stories and articles for the oral exam that I had prepared for my daughter were circulated among many of the senior high students all over Dalian.

Being Popular Is Not Always Good

In China, to be admitted to a college was of great importance to senior high graduates. In general, most high schools were weak in the teaching of English, so experienced English teachers were badly needed to coach the students for the entrance examination. More and more people came to me, pleading with me to help them. Even my own brothers and sisters sent their children to Dalian for me to tutor.

There were two brothers in my evening class that were from a poor family with the last name of Hu. During his summer vacation, the older one sold popsicles nearby our residential building. Every day, when I passed by him, he would address me as "Aunty Chen," even though I did not know him. One day I stopped and asked him if he had finished his high school studies. He said, "Yes, I have just graduated from high school. It's my strongest wish to enter a college, but my English is so poor that I don't think I can pass the examination. I have heard that you are very good at coaching students in English, but I was afraid you wouldn't take me as your student. I have been selling popsicles here every day so that I might get a chance to talk to you." His words surprised me. His look softened my heart so I said, "Oh, no problem, you can come to my home tomorrow and I will teach you."

The next evening he came along with his younger brother who had also finished high school. The brothers stood before me, asking me to take them both on as my students. Of course, I said yes. The younger one was very handsome and smart. I was told later that he was notorious for his bad behavior, both at school and in the neighborhood. People even called him a little

Teaching English to my nieces in Dalian (1981)

gangster. While he was studying with me, I never witnessed any trace of 'bad boy' in him. But one day, he showed up black-and-blue; his gang had beaten him and they threatened him, saying, "You are now studying English and want to change. No way! You have to come back and be with us." He asked me if he could come to study in my home from early morning until late at night so that he could avoid meeting the gang on his way home. I told him, "You have been a very good boy since I have known you. You are smart and study hard." From then on, I let the two boys come early and stay until very late at night.

My first private English class consisted of nine students. They all studied hard and improved quickly. A year later, all received good marks in their English exams and most of them were admitted to college. The elder of the Hu brothers was admitted to the Foreign Trade Department of the institute where I worked. The Bank of China in Dalian hired the younger one due to his good English skills; it was a decision that changed his life forever.

Me with my students (1974)

During that time, the University of International Business and Economics in Beijing was working hard to get all us old teachers back to work there. It turned out the institute in Dalian would not let us go. A plan was devised: In order to get me back to Beijing, our Beijing university transferred my husband from the Dalian high school to teach Chinese literature in Beijing. Li, Zhi took our daughter Ping Ping with him, thinking in this way, my leaders would allow me to go, too. But, to our great disappointment, they still said no. I was alone in Dalian, teaching one class after another. But, I was so busy that I hardly found time to cook for myself. Lacking sleep and sufficient nutrition, coupled with all my worries, nearly drove me crazy. Sometimes, I would feel nauseous as I talked or listened to other people, my head kept swimming all the time and I had no appetite.

One day, while I was teaching, the blackboard seemed to be spinning in front of me. I could hardly stand up and almost fainted. Taken to the hospital, I was diagnosed with severe neurosis, so I had to stop teaching. With the help of a student's father, Director Wang, I was sent to an army sanatorium. Director Wang was a good man and took special care of me. Despite the bed rest, my health did not improve. Depression was among the most severe of my symptoms. The sanatorium was located on the top of a mountain surrounded by thick woods with a beautiful view of the broad sea in the near distance. I often sat crying as I looked out of the window in no mood to enjoy the beauty. I had always loved the sea, but now I felt so sad when I looked at it. Without any peace of mind, my temper would flare easily and I had no energy at all. Having no interest in anything, I did not know how to pass the days. Sometimes, my head seemed as if it would burst with pain. Night always seemed too long and I was often startled awake by horrifying nightmares. I began to feel that my days were numbered and longed for death.

A Fatal Diagnosis

Finally I was granted sick leave, and I returned to Beijing where I rejoined my husband and child. Not healthy enough to work, I was paid half of my salary. Life became even more difficult, especially financially. In order to make enough money to survive, I taught a group of private students, which included children of Beijing's high-ranking officials. Even though I only taught about six hours a week, I was exhausted.

Then, one day while taking a shower, I found a lump in my right breast, which really hurt when I pressed. The next day, I went to Beijing's Union Medical College Hospital. After the doctor examined me, he said, "Don't get nervous, but you have breast cancer and you will need to have surgery. However, beds have not been available here for some time. You will probably have to wait for a couple of months before you can be hospitalized." I did not get nervous about the diagnosis, but I knew it was necessary to quickly find a way to get admitted to the hospital. I asked my oldest brother, Cheng Xian, a surgeon, to talk to his former classmate who was a doctor at the Beijing Union Hospital in an attempt to get me in at the earliest possible date.

I soon became too ill to continue my private classes with my students. One of them, Wan, Lao Er, learned of my illness and that I needed assistance in getting admitted to the hospital. He talked to his father who was the mayor of Beijing and very soon, I was hospitalized through the "back door". The plan was for me to wait at the nurses' station. When another woman was released from the hospital I was to be immediately taken to her bed. This way, the doctor would see me on his rounds and I could get scheduled for the required surgery. I truly believe if I had been kept waiting for two more months, I likely would have died.

The news of my breast cancer quickly spread among my family, former students, and friends. Letters came in one after another from each of them expressing their great concern for me. As expected, before performing the surgery, I received chemotherapy to block the cancer cells from spreading too fast.

When the time came for the surgery, I was only given a spinal anesthetic, so I remained conscious during the whole operation. I could actually feel the scalpel cutting my flesh but I felt very little pain. The doctor performed a radical mastectomy and also removed nineteen lymph nodes, which he sent off for immediate lab testing. The test results were all positive; the cancer cells had already spread throughout most of my body.

Near the end of the seven-hour operation, the doctor told me, "Now, I am going to peel off a piece of skin from your lower abdomen. This area is not anaesthetized. It will be very painful, but only for a moment. I want to have this good piece of skin to patch onto your breast area. It will do you good. Put up with the pain, okay?" I nodded. Then I felt the sharpest pain that I had ever experienced in my life. In a loud voice I cried out, "You are killing me!" Then as quickly as he could, the doctor put a cooling patch of Chinese herbs on the wound and the pain was soothed away. I was totally exhausted when the doctor finally said, "You are done!" As I was being wheeled out of the operating room, I smiled to all the doctors and nurses and said, "Thank you all!"

A few hours later when the anesthetic wore off, the pain came back and I hurt terribly all over. I could hardly breathe. Fortunately, my daughter Sha Sha was there to help me recover after the surgery. It turned out that lying down was the worst position for the pain. I just

With President Sun, Wei Yan of UIBE (2008)

thought that if I could sit up, maybe I could get some sleep. As Sha Sha helped me sit up, the pain subsided, but I didn't have the strength to remain upright. So, my loving daughter offered her help by sitting behind me on the bed with her back up against mine.

It felt much better that way and I was able to sleep for a short period of time. The next day, I felt better and Sha Sha returned to her studies at college. During my month-long stay in the hospital, Sha Sha came to care for me every day, right after she finished her morning classes. The distance from her college to the hospital was long and she had to take two buses to get there. I was very thankful for her presence during my recovery.

Ping Ping was nine years old and too young to come to see me alone. So, her father would bring her along during his visit, which was only about once a week. Many of my friends came to visit, carrying all kinds of gifts including fruits, cakes, canned food, etc. The Hu brothers, who were my Dalian private students, mailed me a package of dried sea cucumbers, which they dived deep into the cold ocean to harvest. After they had dried them, the boys would mail them to me. I was touched to tears when I received their special gift. My niece, Xiao Hong mailed me five *yuan*[14] that she had saved up. At that time, she only had ten *yuan* per month to spend on food. My brothers and sisters also gave me money, which I desperately needed. The love that I received from my friends and family encouraged me to recover quickly. One student wrote to me, saying, "Teacher Chen, please live on, we need you." This letter especially moved me.

After a month's hospitalization, I returned home where my neighbors and colleagues brought me old clothes to wear and small dishes of food to eat. It was a Beijing custom that the one who is sick should wear other peoples' clothes and eat food which had been prepared by other families. In this way, it was believed the patient would recover faster. To this very day, I remain thankful for all the kindness they showed me during this difficult time.

President Sun, Wei Yan of my original university, the University of International Business and Economics, said to me, warmly, "Do not think of anything else now. Only focus on recovering your health." Also the head of the personnel department, Miao, Jun Qing told me with a sincere heart, "We are definitely going to have you back at this university, when your strength returns. If you came back today and died tomorrow, we would hold a memorial gathering for you the day after tomorrow!" I broke down when I heard his words. How kind the leaders of my university were.

A month later, my official transfer was made from Dalian back to my original teaching post at the university. Later, I would learn that in approving my release, the Dalian institute's leaders said, "Since Chen has cancer, we should satisfy her wish and let her go back to Beijing." What a hypocritical statement, I thought. It took a

With Miao, Jun Qing – head of the HR Department at UIBE (2008)

health crisis for them to finally grant my request for a transfer.

---

[14] See page 156

The Turning Point

As a follow-up to the mastectomy, my doctor tried to give me additional chemotherapy. However, my white cell count indicated my body could not tolerate the treatment. Instead, he scheduled me for radiation therapy. Since I could barely walk I was uncertain that I could make it to these treatments. Since my home was so far away how was I to get to the hospital? Upon learning of my situation, one of my former schoolmates, Gu, Ze Qing, who lived very close to the hospital, offered me a room in her home while I received the radiation treatments. After she left for work in the morning, I would make my way to the hospital's radiation room one step at a time, using the wall that ran along the street for support. After the treatment and drained of energy, I would struggle in the same way to make my way back to her home.

Ze Qing was such a kind-hearted friend, but she was at a loss as to why I could not take in any food. I was in a bad way and I had no appetite for anything. It didn't matter what food I tried; I would vomit immediately. As I lay in bed those days, I kept thinking that I might not have much time left to live. Having had three days of radiation treatments, my blood tests showed that my white cell count had dropped to the minimum. The radiation treatments were stopped.

Following a few days' rest, I felt a bit better and finally regained my appetite. Then, when my counts went up, I resumed the radiation therapy. My life became torturous. With the exception of Sha Sha, nobody came to see me at Ze Qing's home. Without a telephone at her home, I was unable to tell my friends that I was staying at Ze Qing's apartment. I became very depressed, but I had a strong will. It was important for me to live for my children and to return to my work. Ping Ping was only nine years old; I could not leave her at such a young age and Sha Sha would be miserable if I died. I also wanted to live, so that I could serve at the university in Beijing and show my appreciation to all my leaders. At the age of forty-nine, I was too young to die.

One day at the hospital while awaiting my treatment, a man wearing an old People's Liberation Army (PLA) uniform came into the radiation room and sat down next to me. This man was tall and healthy-looking and he seemed very friendly. He started up a conversation by asking me, "What's wrong with you, why are you here?" I spoke to him honestly about my disease, in a way I had not been able to do with others. As I continued talking about my daughters and my family, tears streamed from my eyes. The whole time he was listening to my sad story, his smile grew wider and wider. I started thinking, "This man has no heart!"

When I finished my story, he said, "Don't worry. Listen to *my* story. I'm a retired PLA official from a small town in Liaoning Province. My doctor told me that both of my lungs were full of cancer tumors, big and small. Several months ago, I came to Beijing seeking a cure. But, all the doctors I saw here refused to treat me because they said I already had late-stage lung cancer and there was no cure. They all advised me to go back home, to eat well and rest well. I knew they meant: 'Go back and wait for death.' But, I was only in my early forties so why must I die so young?

"My wife and I decided to stay in Beijing; we knew that going back home meant there would be no further treatments. Every morning we went to the parks where we observed people doing all kinds of exercises. Finally one day, we were sitting on a bench near one of these groups. I asked them, "What kind of exercise are you doing?" They told me they were practicing Chinese Soaring Crane Qigong. They went on to explain that many people had really benefited from this practice, including people with cancer. Not knowing anything about qigong, I decided to sign up and study with this group. I had nothing to lose.

"After learning the form, and seeing the visible changes in me, and in others, I was convinced of its effectiveness. I practiced daily with great confidence and was feeling better day-by-day. In about a month's time, I felt so much stronger that I went to revisit my doctors to tell them. But, the doctors thought it was impossible for me to have had any real change for the better. Sometime later, I came back to this hospital. A doctor agreed to give me a CT test and he found that my lung cancer was gone–except for one big tumor in my left lung. With that improvement, I am here today for a radiation treatment."

I was amazed by his story and quickly saw hope for my own life. He advised me to learn qigong in the park with his group. The next day, when I saw him in the radiation room, he gave me a monthly entrance pass to the Laboring People's Palace and told me that he had registered me with his qigong group. He would not allow me to pay him for it, but said he would be there to introduce me to the qigong teacher.

The following day, I was anxious as I walked to the park to meet the qigong teacher and to begin practicing qigong. It was strange, but I did not see the PLA officer in the park that day. In fact, he was not at the hospital either when I received the last of my daily radiation treatments. Since I never saw him again, I decided he must have been my guardian angel. While I never had a chance to thank him, I am certain he helped save my life. I continue to be thankful for him and think of him often. Since taking up the practice of qigong, my life has turned a new page! A dramatic page! A wonderful page!

PART II
I Begin Qigong

I took the monthly pass the PLA gentleman had purchased for me and went to the Beijing Laboring People's Palace Park adjacent to Tiananmen. (At one time, it had been part of the famous Forbidden City grounds.)

Once I had entered through the park gate that morning, it took me a while to locate the cancer group that was practicing Chinese Soaring Crane Qigong. I kept looking for my generous benefactor, but the search was in vain. As I stood there wondering why he was not among the group, the qigong instructor came up to me and asked if I was a new student. I told him I was and my purpose in coming. He welcomed me warmly and asked me to follow along with the group. They were already practicing Routine Two of the Five Routines. It was hard to copy the movements, because I could hardly lift my right arm due to the tremendous pain in my right shoulder and the numbness from surgery. In fact, all the fingers on my right hand were numb. So, I decided I would imitate the teacher as best I could. Fortunately, the teacher did not expect me to do the movements accurately. On the contrary, he encouraged me just to follow the group. He said, "Being in the group, you are already receiving a lot of qi."

Later, I would learn that 'Qi' is a Chinese character, meaning a bio-energy that exists in the body as well as in everything in the universe. In essence, the whole universe is formed of qi. Qigong is a method that opens the acupoints[15] and meridians[16] in the body for an exchange of qi with the universe. As a result, the qi helps suppress disease and strengthen the body.

Although it was initially hard to follow the group, I caught up with them quickly after being coached individually by our teacher. After several days' practice, I began to experience changes. Following the chemo and radiation therapies, I had lost my appetite; I could hardly eat anything. My body was puffy and I had no energy at all. However, every morning before 4 o'clock, I would get up and put on my thick padded

---

[15] The same as acupuncture point
[16] A network through which qi travels

coat and pants. It would be pitch dark and icy cold with nobody else on the road. I would walk slowly toward the bus against the howling north wind. Sometimes I would make my way through heavy snow. The bus stop was quite a long distance from my home, so I would walk with my hands over the sore wound on my abdomen from where skin had been taken to patch the hole where my right breast had been. As I trudged along, both wounds hurt badly.

After boarding the first bus, I would have to transfer twice to get to the practice site. It was a journey of approximately two hours one-way. I was always the first student to get there, well before our practice, which began at 6 a.m. But, no matter how early I arrived, there was always a figure standing under the dim light in the park. He was either stepping in place, or swinging his arms to warm up. It was our teacher Chen, De Yi waiting patiently for his students. He had once been wheelchair-bound for several years following a severe stroke. After he learned Soaring Crane Qigong under the tutelage of Master Zhao, Jin Xiang, the creator of the form, Teacher Chen walked away from his wheelchair and was later trained to be an instructor of the form. His devotion to qigong was beyond description and his love for his students touched everyone's heart. Even though on some mornings I initially didn't want to go out, I was encouraged by the thought of my teacher waiting in the park. So, I got up on time and was never late for practice.

I discovered that my husband's sister Li, Zhi Lan and her husband Hao, Zhong Zheng lived very close to the park and our practice site. When they learned of my daily visits, they offered me a bed in their home, so that I could save time and energy on my daily trip. Staying with them made my life so much easier. Not only did they provide me a place to live, but they also offered to cook for me. They had three children, a son and twelve-year-old twins; a boy and a girl. The male twin was Hao, Gang; at home he was called Xiao Ming (Little Brightness). He was a very loving boy, and since it was during the winter school break, he volunteered to accompany me to the park each morning. Just imagine, a boy of twelve offering to get up at 5 o'clock on cold winter mornings and take his aunty to the park. Each morning, as soon as the bus pulled in, he would quickly squeeze onto the bus and find me a seat. Then at the park he would stand out in the open, in the cold air, waiting as we practiced qigong for a whole hour! It was very cold but he never complained. He could have slept later than usual in his warm bed during his vacation, but he chose to take care of me instead. His love meant so much to me. To this day, I remain grateful for his help.

His parents and his brother and sister were all very kind to me, too. During the daytime, the kids kept very quiet so that I could rest and even nap. Life was not easy for the family because of the couple's low income; both of them were elementary school teachers. But, while I was staying with them, I was given the best food they could afford. They also comforted and encouraged me to fight against the cancer. All the members of the family were like my saviors; they helped me to recover very quickly. In a short time, I could eat and sleep much better. After a month's qigong practice, the insomnia that had bothered me for more than ten years completely disappeared and I found myself happier than I had been in a long time.

Soon, I was trained in the second level of Soaring Crane Qigong, following a series of preparations, which included the spontaneous movements of the Standing Meditation. For the first three days that I did it, I strictly followed the teacher's instructions, but there were no spontaneous movements. Around 4 o'clock of the fourth day, I went to the park to practice qigong on my own. As soon as I finished doing the preparation, a strong force from nowhere knocked me onto the ground. I struggled to stand up and again I was pulled down onto the ground by some unknown force. I got up, and again I was pushed down to the ground. The same sequence repeated seven times in a row. The strange thing was that I was not hurt at all. It felt as if I had been thrown down onto something soft, as if there was a thick layer of blankets between the hard ground and me. I decided to surrender to it. I rolled and rolled on the ground for a long time until it was almost dark. What an experience! I felt very light and happy, even though I looked like a dirty monkey.

My excitement and interest in qigong kept me going. Religiously, I practiced every morning with the group. In the evening, I would do qigong alone at the park closer to my temporary home. Day-by-day I found recognizable changes in both my health and my emotions. One morning after our group practice, I asked Xiao Ming to accompany me to the children's shop. Typically, it was very crowded; people pressed against each other as they shopped. In reaching for an item, I accidentally touched the button on a woman's overcoat. She let out a scream, yelling at me loudly, "Why did you stick a knife into my chest?" I was shocked by her accusation. I stood there dumbfounded with everyone's eyes fixed on me. Looking at my hands, I murmured, "No, I did not." After pausing a few seconds, I spoke in a very low voice to myself, "Maybe it's electricity?!" Upon hearing what I said, the woman ran out of the shop and the people standing nearby scattered as if I were a murderer.

When I returned to the park with Xiao Ming and told my teacher what had happened, he smiled and said, "Oh, it is qi. You have been practicing for quite a while and have accumulated a lot of qi. It flowed out from your fingers when you touched the button on her coat. She felt as if you had stabbed her in the chest. But this was a good lesson for you. Be careful. Save the qi you have obtained from the universe for healing your own diseases. Sending qi to others before you are well and before you have learned the healing techniques depletes your qi and will be harmful to your health." Until then, I had no clue that people could have the ability to heal others by emitting qi. From then on, I became even more fascinated about the power of qigong.

When spring arrived, I moved back to my own home, but I still practiced qigong twice a day, at 6 am and 6 pm. On Sunday mornings, I would go back to the Laboring People's Palace Park for our group practice. After qigong, our teacher would encourage the students to share their qigong experiences. People were very enthusiastic, whether telling their own stories, or just listening to others. All of the inspiring stories I heard from my fellow practitioners encouraged me to practice even more diligently. And my efforts paid off more than I ever imagined possible. After only three months, I had totally recovered from cancer and was told by my doctor that I was cancer free!

Finally—Back to the University!

In the spring of 1983, I was strong enough to return to work in the English department of the University of International Business And Economics. I had begun teaching at this school in 1960, and I had many wonderful memories and a deep love for it. Now, after twelve years' absence to work in Dalian and half a year of sick leave, I was finally able to return to teach at my original university. What a joy!

Returning strong and energetic, I was admired by all my old and new colleagues. Everybody knew that my quick recovery had come from my diligent practice of qigong. It was true that reaping the benefits of qigong took time and the discipline of regular practice. But, I also needed to learn the theories and philosophy behind it.

During that period, apart from preparing my English lessons, I spent all my time on my daily practice and reading books on qigong theory along with relevant philosophies. All my old diseases such as neurosis, arthritis, kidney problems, stomachaches, headaches and insomnia had disappeared without my awareness. However, everyone else noticed the changes in me.

Our university clinic organized an overall medical checkup for all the staff and faculty. Most of the important examinations were done in a large Beijing hospital. Then the test results were sent to the university's clinic. Once the results of my tests arrived, the clinic director called me into his office. He said with a big smile, "Professor Chen, the results of your medical examinations are unbelievably good. But we have our doubts, and wonder if the hospital could have made some mistakes. Would you please consider having a second-opinion checkup at the same hospital?"

I was not surprised. In the past, I had been a frequent visitor to the doctors at the university clinic. All of them knew me well, as I was a famously "sick person". However, in my heart I was very proud to hear the good news about my improved health. I knew that I owed all the improvement to qigong. Of course, I went to the hospital and repeated all the examinations. A few days later, the same positive test results were reported to the clinic. The good news spread fast and wide throughout the university.

Qigong Is Introduced at Our University

In summer of that same year, the university's trade union asked me if I would teach qigong to my colleagues. I was overjoyed that they had decided to offer the teachers and staff this opportunity. Ever since I had

Qigong dance with Ping Ping

learned qigong, to my eye, almost everybody around me appeared sickly. I so wished that everyone could learn qigong.

However, since I had not been trained as an instructor, I asked my teacher, Chen, De Yi for his assistance. He was very humble and recommended I ask another teacher Sun, Ji Xian. When Master Zhao learned that qigong was going to be taught at the university, and knowing how important it was, he decided to come along with Teacher Sun. More than 300 people participated in the qigong program. Most of them were from our university's faculty and staff, but about fifty others were regular students.

It was a big event. Both the master and teacher came to instruct at our university once a week. I led the group practice on the playground every morning. Since it was such a big group, I had to stand on a platform and use a microphone in order to lead the group. Things went very well. Even the president of our university, Mr. Sun, Wei Yan, took an active part in the practice. Very soon people began reporting on

Qigong practice on campus (1984)

the benefits they felt from practicing qigong. In order to enrich the people's knowledge of qigong, I asked Master Zhao to give several lectures, which gave rise to even more enthusiasm over qigong at our university.

Oh, Those Qigong Healing Reactions!

During that year, I also experienced many healing reactions. Qigong healing is different from taking western medication. Once the qi works in the meridians, it tries very hard to push through any blockages. To break through the blocked areas is not an easy thing. The body will experience pain while the qi is working through the blockages. In Chinese medicine there is a saying, "Where there is blockage, there is pain. When the blockage is gone, the pain disappears!" In order to allow the qi to clear out the blockages, one has to endure the pain. Some people may suspect that it is qigong that brought back their pain. This is not true. But I did come to know many people who gave up their qigong practice because they could not tolerate the healing pain.

I learned that qi usually works on the most recent illness first, and then it moves on to those health problems that have been with you for a longer time. The first healing reaction I experienced was at the site of my chest wound where my whole right breast had been removed. The surgeon quickly created a skin graft using a piece of skin from the right side of my lower belly. After my mastectomy, my right arm and fingers were so numb that I was unable to handle chopsticks or even a spoon. I had to use my left hand to feed myself.

One day I felt as if the lower right of my chest were on fire. The second day, the burning pain moved upward about five inches. On the third day, my whole chest hurt badly and even made me short of breath. At the same time, the graft site on the right side of my belly became very painful. It took me a while to realize that I was experiencing severe healing reactions. Placing my complete faith in qigong helped me to endure the pain without getting too upset or depressed.

What was very interesting was that whenever I was practicing qigong, the pain was soothed away. As soon as my practice came to an end, the pain came back. So, I just put up with the pain and carried on with the things that I needed to do. Within a week, the pain in my chest was completely gone. What was more remarkable was that I could lift my arm up to reach the lower tree branches in the university's garden. I was so excited. I jumped up and down to touch the branches. It felt as if the meridian system in my chest and right arm had been restored. Even the numbness that I experienced in my right arm and fingers was gone. It was a miracle. Qigong had really worked a miracle!

Several weeks later after a morning qigong practice, I was walking upstairs to my apartment when suddenly my neck became so stiff I could not move my head. When I sat down in my apartment, the neck pain was so bad I felt I would throw up. I tried to turn my head but there was no movement. I could not lie down, either. Another healing reaction was underway.

Within the hour, my old schoolmate, Gu, Ze Qing, came to me with two tickets for a downtown art gallery and asked me if I would like to meet her there later in the afternoon. Only hesitating for a few seconds, I said yes. I assured myself that I should not be afraid and that I should live normally, despite the healing reaction. Later, I met my friend at the gate of the exhibition hall. The gallery was wonderful as there were more than a hundred beautiful oil paintings on display. However, they were hung high on the walls, and since I could not lift my head to look up at the pictures, I had to bend my body to one side and peek up at them sideways. I must have looked very peculiar, as many visitors had fixed their eyes on me instead of the artwork. Strangely enough, after the gallery visit my neck loosened up.

In a few days the pain went away completely. Out of curiosity as to what might have caused the neck healing reaction, I went to have it checked out at the university clinic. After an X-ray of my neck, the doctor told me that I had seven spurs on my cervical vertebrae and he recommended that I have surgery. My neck did sometimes feel uncomfortable before I learned qigong, but I had no idea that there was a physical problem. With my strong confidence in qigong, I of course refused to have the surgery. Instead, I continued with my daily qigong practice. Much later in 1998, I would have another X-ray taken at a large Beijing hospital. That result showed that the cervical vertebrae problem had improved. Since then, my neck basically remains flexible. Again, qigong helped to heal me!

In late summer of 1984 while doing my morning practice of spontaneous movements, I started coughing violently. My throat itched so much I simply could not stop. After a few minutes of constantly coughing, something came up out of my throat. It felt strange and I became curious, so I spit it out into my open hand. Looking at it carefully, it seemed to be the knotted end of a thread. Then, I remembered some twenty years earlier that I had gotten very sick. My tonsils became severely infected and I was sent back to Beijing for emergency medical treatment. The doctor said it was hard for him to stitch such big wounds, but a week later when the doctor was trying to take out the stitches, the end of one thread refused to come out. He said, "It doesn't really matter. It will dissolve because it is made from sheep gut. I'll just leave it there and it won't be a problem." True, it had not bothered me for twenty years. But the fact was the thread did not dissolve, and the qi would not allow something foreign to stay there any longer.

During my childhood and into adulthood, I often suffered from toothaches. At times it was so bad I would go to the dentist for an injection just to stop the pain. However, after practicing qigong, I had far fewer toothaches. Yet one night around midnight a terrible pain awakened me. The pain was very sharp and all my teeth were hurting. Of course I could not go back to sleep, so I decided to practice qigong. I was hoping the pain would go away as it had before in my other healing reactions.

As soon as I began my qigong practice, the pain completely stopped. I practiced for an entire hour. But, right after I finished the routines, the pain came back. At that time of night, I could not get a taxi to go to the Beijing Dentistry Hospital, which was far away from my home. So, the only relief available to me was to keep doing qigong. I practiced five sessions of the Five Routines and Standing Meditation in a row until dawn. Then I went to the bus terminal and boarded the first bus. The tooth pain was with me during the long two-hour journey to the hospital. It was so early when I registered to be seen at the dentistry hospital, that I was first in line. The pain was still there as I sat in the chair waiting my turn to be called into the dental clinic.

Finally when the dentist examined me, he lightly tapped on my teeth, one by one, asking which tooth was bothering me. It was so strange, but I felt no pain in any of my teeth. I felt I needed to tell the dentist the whole story. He queried, "Since you have no toothache now, and I cannot see anything wrong with your teeth, what am I going to treat?" Puzzled as well, I could not explain the strange phenomenon. Without a word, I stood up and left the dentistry hospital. Amazingly, I have never had any tooth pain again, so I called the toothache healing reaction, "A general attack!"

Throughout 1984, it seemed that I experienced one healing reaction after another. In addition, I was very happy and full of vigor. My confidence in qigong grew even greater.

A Bonus: Spiritual Growth through Qigong

While my health improved and physically I got stronger, something more important was also happening to me. A spiritual change had been taking hold. Early one morning in June of 1984, I did my qigong practice facing the east. The sun was rising and it was very quiet and peaceful in the garden at the university. When I lifted my arms in the beginning of the first routine of Soaring Crane Qigong, I found that clouds far in the distance moved upward just as my arms lifted up. When I stopped, the clouds did the same. Again I moved my arms upward and the clouds ascended as well. When lifting my arms all the way up over my shoulders, the clouds went all the way up and covered the red rising sun. Immediately, the sun disappeared behind the clouds that I had lifted up. After a few seconds, the sun revealed itself in a dark gray color that had a silver lining round it. This sun turned around clockwise and then counter-clockwise. Since I had been taught in school that the sun did not move, I began to think that surely the scientists had made a mistake.

Shortly thereafter, I saw red flames, both long and short, shooting out from the "darkened" sun. Then, a thick flow of dark smoke burst forth from the sun and I felt a strong force coming from the smoke, though I did not hear the sound of an explosion. The smoke scattered then united itself to cover the sun. A few seconds later, another plumage of smoke burst forth and repeated the same actions. Wondering if I were in a dream, I knocked on my head but found I was truly awake, standing there alone in the university garden.

Somehow, my eyes would not stay open anymore. I just had to close them. In front of me, I "saw" a spindle of colorful crystals forming and spinning out of nothing. It seemed that I could not control my body as I turned around and around following the turning spindle. This went on for more than ten minutes. Then the spindle disappeared and my body came to a stop. After regaining my balance, I opened my eyes and was surprised to see that all the different flowers in the garden had turned the same golden color. It felt like I was in a fairyland.

By then, the students began walking through the garden to their classrooms. In looking at them, they all seemed different. Observing them from the rear, I noticed a big round ball of light in everyone's upper back. In those who were walking toward me, I saw a bright-lighted triangle in each of their chests. Immediately, I understood it was their middle dantians that were shining. In qigong, it is said that everybody has three dantians that hold energy: the lower dantian located three inches below navel; the middle dantian in the middle of the chest and the upper dantian in the forehead. The qigong theory we had been taught stated that the three dantians were round spheres of energy. But, at the middle dantians, I saw circles on the back, and triangles in the front. I have never found an explanation for what I witnessed that day.

After watching people pass by for a while, I left the university garden and headed for home to have breakfast and get ready to teach. On my way home, I noticed a bicycle repairman leaning against the wall of his little repair shop. On the surface he looked quite ordinary, but I could see that his whole body was filled with light. This puzzled me. And when I encountered the little boy who lived downstairs from my apartment, he also had a brightly lit body. Other people I saw had a shining light only at their middle dantians. Amazingly, everyone looked young and beautiful to my eyes.

That morning, a visitor was to come to our class at the university; I met her at the gate. On our way to the classroom, I noticed how beautiful the sky appeared to me that day. Besides the white clouds against the blue sky that we normally see, there were intensely colorful shades of pink and light purple. At that moment, I felt as if I were in another world. Of course, I could not help but tell the visitor what I saw. While I was describing the sky, she seemed to be very interested and asked me to share it with her. So, I held her hand in mine. "Oh, my God," she exclaimed, "the sky truly looks different! How come it is so beautiful?"

I said, "Maybe the sky is always this beautiful, but our eyes are normally covered with dust making it impossible for us to see the true view of the sky." During our 20-minute break from class, the students and teachers left the classrooms and went outdoors to enjoy the spring sunshine. There were several female teachers talking together, so I went to join them. To me, they appeared to be angels and I described how beautiful each of them looked. Staring at me with some skepticism, I could tell they thought I was teasing them. Actually I was telling them what I truly saw. It seemed to me that I was seeing their original souls through layers of pollution.

From then on and for many days, I saw the ever-changing beauty of the sun. At times, the sun would cast its light in golden rays and the rays would become wider as they neared the earth. I saw myself standing in one of those sun rays, which made me think of children's drawings of the sun with the rays cast out around the golden sun exactly that way. Maybe through the eyes of children, the sun looks like that. Amazing!

Very soon after this experience, I developed the power to change the view of the sun just by moving my hand. As soon as I waved my hand over it, it would change from pink into shades of gray. Any time during the day, I could make it happen, especially when the sun was not very bright or during the time that the sun was rising or setting. Not only did I play with this power every day, but I also showed some of my colleagues what I could do by holding their hands. While they could describe the sun's changing colors, the intensity of the colors was less noticeable to them.

One day, I told qigong-teacher, Sun, Ji Xian all about it. I confessed to him that I did not practice qigong as much as I probably should because I was trying to care for my neighbor, who was suffering from late stage stomach cancer. She could not eat anything unless I fed her, so she depended on me for eating three meals a day. Teacher Sun said, "You were given a gift from the universe because of your love for your neighbor."

In ancient qigong books, I found many stories of similar phenomena that I had earlier doubted. But, after experiencing phenomena myself, I began to believe that those stories were true. Relatively new to qigong and lacking knowledge about spiritual practices, my ego began to grow. It seemed to me that I was very special; that I must be a super woman. Being able to see the activities of the sun, perhaps I would help the astronomers uncover more knowledge about the universe. Undoubtedly, I would become famous for my extrasensory power.

More and more, my ego was fueled until one day Master Zhao directly criticized me as I showed off my powers to him. Thanks to his sharp criticism, I changed my attitude toward developing extrasensory powers. Later, I would come to know that everybody has these latent potentials, and a spiritual practice like qigong, will cultivate these potentials as more and more brain cells are activated. As we humans become more intelligent and come to better understand the universe we will be able to benefit humankind. However, if a practitioner solely pursues extrasensory powers, this can become very dangerous and lead that person into a deviation.

Still my ego grew, I repeatedly ignored my teacher's advice. While I understood that I was not a trained healer, often I would offer to heal people using my qi. One day, a female student kept coughing throughout our class period. During a break, I offered to stop her cough. By moving my hands from her chest down to her waist, it only took five minutes of treatment before she stopped coughing. For the next hour, the girl did not cough at all. Both of us were happy and the rest of the class viewed me as a powerful healer.

Since I taught this class only two hours a week, I did not see this student until the following week when she came into the classroom. Immediately, I asked her if the cough had returned. She told me her cough went away right after I treated her. However, she had developed a terrible pain in her lower back. After going to the hospital for an exam, the doctor told her, "You'd better go back to the teacher who gave you the treatment. We cannot find anything wrong with your abdomen." Of course, the girl looked at me with the expectation of another treatment and another cure.

There I was, never having been instructed in how to treat people with the power of qi. I had even been warned by my teacher, Chen, De Yi not to use my qi to heal others before being taught healing techniques. In fact, my qigong teacher was adamant that I keep the qi that I had obtained for healing myself first. But, I totally ignored his advice. I had inadvertently moved the diseased qi from her chest to her lower back. My mind raced, "Now what am I going to do to help this girl get rid of the pain at her lower back?" In that moment, there was no one else I could turn to. So, I created another method to move the diseased qi from her waist down to her feet. As I knelt on the floor, I used both hands to chase the bad qi from her waist all the way down and out from her feet. I was totally exhausted after this so-called treatment, but luckily for me, the pain from her lower back disappeared.

I am embarrassed to admit that, at the time, I did not learn from this important lesson. Almost every day, I would treat my colleagues in the office. The treatments I gave were effective, yet I found myself growing weaker with much less energy overall. Teacher Sun sharply criticized me, "You have just recovered from cancer and many chronic diseases. You should not use your qi to treat others, unless it is absolutely an emergency. You must listen to me." His dire warnings, coupled with my bad experiences in healing others finally led me to stop healing people. It was fortunate that I finally listened to him. Eventually, my energy returned.

Celebrating a Western Christmas

As Christmas of 1984 approached, I was leading the university's English chorus. We planned to celebrate Christmas with our western friends living at the Beijing Friendship Hotel. After the open door policy instituted by the Chinese government in 1979, many foreigners came to work in China, especially in big cities like Beijing and Shanghai. In all twelve departments at our university, dozens of foreign experts from the United States, England, Australia, Canada, Switzerland, the Soviet Union, Japan, Vietnam, Korea, and Arabic countries were teaching our students.

In years past when Christmas or the New Year came, these experts would be invited to a banquet hosted by our university leaders. However, this particular year, some of our teachers suggested that we celebrate Christmas together with the foreigners out of respect for their tradition. Our English chorus had spent many hours practicing Christmas carols under the guidance of professional conductors. The choir members were in high spirits and they sang very well.

On Christmas Eve, with candles in hand, I led the group of carolers around the residences of the foreign experts. Through many of the windows, we observed the decorated Christmas trees in their sitting rooms. Surprised by our beautiful singing in English, many people opened their windows to look out. Their faces beamed with big smiles. Many opened their doors, threw on heavy coats and caps, and joined the choir in singing the familiar holiday tunes. People seemed truly touched by this unexpected event.

As we walked to the beautifully decorated auditorium, there were nearly one hundred people who had congregated, a merry mix of Chinese and foreigners. Our choir's hour-long performance won warm applause from the audience. Another English performance that evening was by the children's singing group, which I had organized. Among the singers was my 10-year-old daughter, Ping Ping. After the performance, there was a ball with dancing, which everyone enjoyed.

It made me very happy to see the joy that our efforts brought to our foreign friends. I just imagined how I would feel if I were abroad at the time of Chinese Spring Festival and local people set firecrackers off to pay tribute to my new year's celebration. So, it was no wonder that I had seen some foreigners weeping as they came out of their home to sing along with us that evening.

The following day, the Beijing Daily reported on this event. A foreign expert who had been working in China since 1950 said, "I have been working in this country for more than thirty years and this is the first time that the Chinese have celebrated Christmas along with us. I feel at home."

Since that first Western Christmas, all the universities that had foreign language departments tried to offer holiday performances for foreign friends staying at the Friendship Hotel. These events illustrated that China's open policy was in full swing, even though some conservative people still believed the government was going too far.

Wow—Out-of-Body Experiences!

One night during this same period, I had a very odd experience. I was lying in bed reading a story about a famous Daoist in ancient China. I was totally absorbed in his story when suddenly, a strange feeling came over me; I felt as if my body and my mind were out of control. The book I was holding dropped from my hand and my entire body felt paralyzed. A force of energy rushed out the crown of my head at the acupoint called Bai Hui. The energy shot up very quickly into the dark blue sky, which was filled with countless twinkling stars. I saw the figure of a young lady in the image of a *Fei Tian*[17]. She was dressed in a light-green silk gown with long sleeves and her long hair bound in a ponytail.

Young and pretty, she was flying freely in the dark blue sky. A sense told me, "It is you!" I was flying out in space. There were also two similar figures, flying not too far away. As I flew higher and higher, I looked down and saw a globe wrapped in two thick transparent layers of light, one layer blue and the other green. The lights were soft transparent laser lights. The globe was spinning slowly, magically. Again a sense told me, "That is the planet where you live."

Flying upward, I felt so light and comfortable. While I was enjoying my flight, several thoughts popped into my head, "I had not turned off the light and shut my mosquito net, nor had I used the bathroom." As soon as these thoughts entered my mind, my energy came quickly back into my body. I hurried to the bathroom, just as quickly turned off the light, shut my mosquito net, and lay back down on my bed. Closing my eyes tightly, I hoped to resume my flight up in the dark blue sky. But, it was not to be, nor has such a flight ever happened hence.

I would come to understand that everyone has two different minds: an intellectual mind and a spiritual mind. The spiritual mind serves as link between the universe and the individual. Only with the intellectual mind out of the way, can the spiritual mind do its work. Whenever the intellectual mind is active, the spiritual mind retreats.

In qigong, we refer to the spiritual mind as "yuan shen" or prenatal mind; the intellectual mind is the "shi shen" or postnatal mind. Meditation quiets the intellectual mind, which allows the spiritual mind

---

[17] A flying Apsaras (Hindu nymph), found in the Dunhuang Caves frescoes in China

to reveal itself. This in turn makes it easier for us to be in touch with the universe. Most people are monkey-minded–the brain never stops chattering–and they never experience a truly peaceful mind. Spiritual practice quiets the intellectual mind and helps us to obtain peace of mind.

One night a short time later, I was suddenly awakened from a deep sleep by some mysterious force. In my clear consciousness, I saw an old man headed towards me using a walking stick looking exactly like "Longevity Man" from the ancient Chinese legend. He was in a pure white gown, his long white beard hanging down onto the ground. As he stopped in front of me, he asked, "You practice qigong, right?" I answered, "Yes." Then he continued, "Your lower body is not cleansed yet. Let me help you." Upon saying this, he moved his right hand from my waist downward. As he did this, I felt a strong comfortable flow of energy moving downward.

Again he inquired, "You practice qigong, right?" Again I answered, "Yes", to which he remarked, "Your upper body is not cleansed yet. Let me help you." Upon saying this, he made a similar motion with his right hand upward from my waist. *Boom*! I heard a loud sound as the energy blew out the top of my head. Following this, I flew swiftly upward, penetrating through seven thick layers of clouds where I found myself standing on top of a landscape of clouds. As I was trying to figure out where I was, I heard a big commotion nearby. Gazing in the direction of the din, I saw countless naked infants lying in the clouds, crying, their faces looking downward. In that moment, I sensed that this was the place from which infants were sent out into the world. Their wailing grew louder and louder until I could no longer stand it.

Then, my energy rushed back into my body. What was that?! I simply did not understand what had happened to me. (Years later, I would meet a psychic in the United States who told me he had had the same experience. His story will follow later.)

On another evening, my older daughter, Sha Sha came home from her college after her final examinations, suffering the onset of a severe flu. She was running a high fever, and after making her a bed on our long couch, I gave her some medicine and asked her to rest. In order to be close by to care for her, I opened the folding bed beside the couch. At midnight, I got up, felt her head and found that she was still feverish. I lay back down on my bed and casually looked up at the ceiling. Where upon, the ceiling appeared to open up and I could see the stars in the dark blue sky.

Suddenly, I flew up through the ceiling into the starry sky. After flying for a few minutes, I found myself lying on grass at the foot of a mountain. The moon was shining very brightly as it hung high up between two big mountains. It was a very beautiful and peaceful scene. As I lay there alone looking at the moon, I had never experienced such stillness in my whole life. Happily enjoying the moment, a thought suddenly crept into my mind, "I am alone here in the wilderness. What if a wolf comes from behind that mountain?" Just as this thought arose, my body started to float downward on its return trip home.

As I floated, I heard a beautiful piece of music and even though I had listened to many of the most famous pieces of music in the world, it was unlike anything I had ever heard before. This music was not only pleasing to the ear it opened my heart and filled it with love and happiness. Accompanied by this soothing melody, my energy made its way back into my body and onto the folding bed. Conscious of my soul returning to earth, I opened my eyes and saw that the ceiling was closing up. Oh! What a wonderful out of body experience! I arose and felt my daughter's forehead. To my great surprise, the fever was gone. Sha Sha asked for a drink of water and said that she was feeling better. The following morning, she got up and cleaned the bedroom as if she had not been sick at all.

During this whole period of time, I was enchanted by qigong. I practiced at least two hours a day and wanted to talk endlessly about qigong. But, there were not many people around me with whom I could share my spiritual experiences. Still, I told some of my close friends about my wonderful encounters. Moreover, I began a quest to read every book on qigong theory and Buddhism and Daoism that I could find.

Over time, I came to understand that the goal of qigong practice is not to cultivate extrasensory powers or have out-of-body experiences, for these are only by-products of qigong or a spiritual practice. They are likened to the branches of a tree; if too many branches grow out of the tree, the trunk will not grow sturdy and straight. Instead the tree's energy will go to the branches rather than to its trunk. Should psychic phenomenon appear, just ignore them; the final goal of spiritual practice is to attain enlightenment.

I am reminded of a story about an Indian spiritual master who set off to visit a village. Since he had to cross a broad river, he boarded a small boat. Just at that time, there came a man walking out onto the water. This man was a psychic and he had spent his whole life practicing how to walk on water and now he wanted to show off his skills. He deliberately walked alongside the boat and looked at the master every now and then, as if saying, "Look, how capable I am!" The master ignored him and remained very quiet. When both the master and the psychic got to the other shore, the man asked the master, "What do you think of my powers?" The master took out a penny, handed it over to the boatman and said to the psychic, "You spent your whole life practicing to walk on water, while I only need to use a single penny."

Although I continued to have out-of-body events, I learned to appreciate them as gifts from the universe, which revealed more about me to my own self. I no longer had any doubt about the potentials of human beings and I came to believe that there are other dimensions in the universe.

A Personal Encounter with
Grand Master Zhao, Jin Xiang

During the early 1980's, many Soaring Crane Qigong practitioners had their latent potentials cultivated. The extraordinary phenomena caused some confusion among the practitioners, as well as with ordinary citizens who witnessed it. People in general lacked knowledge about qigong and extrasensory powers. As a result, much gossip circulated. Knowing there were not enough experienced Soaring Crane Qigong teachers to give guidance to all of the practitioners, the master worried and tried to keep the extrasensory powers of the practitioners under control.

When Master Zhao, Jin Xiang learned of my spiritual experiences and extrasensory powers, he asked my teacher, Sun, Ji Xian, to bring me to him. Master Zhao informed teacher Sun that he needed to monitor me. Since I was "the head sheep of the flock" at my university, he worried that there would be too many practitioners developing extrasensory powers. He explained to Sun that I was like the electric switchboard for all the qigong practitioners at the university. Turning off my extrasensory powers would help stop the other students from likewise cultivating their psychic potential.

On the morning of January 2, 1984, I was taken by teacher Sun to see Master Zhao at his home. As soon as I entered his sitting room, I saw him sitting by a table with two of his students seated beside him. At first glance, I saw that a thick layer of golden light coated his head and hands. I just stared at him without saying a word. He asked me to sit down. I sat down and said, "Master Zhao, I see a thick golden aura around your head and hands." Looking at me sternly, he said, "You have very good eyes. I invited you here, today, to tell me about your extrasensory powers."

That was all the encouragement I needed. I became very excited and told him about the many spiritual experiences I had, one after another. As I talked about my ability to share my power for seeing the sun's beautiful colors, his two students asked me to share it with them. Of course I agreed. They stood up and walked to the big glass window to join me. That day the sun was high and bright in the sky. As I took hold of their hands, they immediately witnessed what I was seeing. With great excitement, they shouted, "Oh, heavens! The sun is shimmering with color!"

At that moment, Master Zhao slammed his hand down onto his desk and shouted at me, "What are you doing? The Heavens gave a gift to *you*. It is not for you to share it with others. If you go on like this, either you are going to lose your power or you are going to shorten your life span." I stopped the experiment and we went back to our seats. After being criticized by the master, I got a bit nervous, but I did not quite understand why the master would not allow me to share my "seeing" gift with his students. My mind started racing. "My extrasensory powers had been cultivated by his form, Soaring Crane Qigong. Being the master, he should be happy about that." But, I dared not speak my mind. Then Master Zhao explained, "Everybody has great potential. Those who diligently practice qigong and have a deep root of wisdom will activate their gifts. Such gifts are given to individuals and everyone's gift may be quite different. These are called *"the secrets of the Heavens"*. The receivers should value these gifts and keep them to themselves. When students do not understand the psychic phenomena, they should turn to their teachers for an explanation and not talk about them to anybody". After his clarification, I understood how wrong I had been.

Master Zhao asked me to study with him whenever I had time. So, from then on I did. After I finished teaching my English classes at the university, I often went to his home. He took me to many places and introduced me to important people in the Beijing qigong community, such as Zhang, Zhen Huan, the Chairman of All China Association of Qigong and Sciences. These visits provided me many opportunities to witness discussions and stories of the larger qigong community.

It was a period during which the Chinese government paid great attention to the development of qigong. Instead of depending on medication, millions of people practiced qigong to maintain their health. The positive effects of qigong even reduced the expenses of the government's medical budget. (At that time in China, cadres, workers, and college students enjoyed free medical service.) Every morning before six o'clock, thousands of people headed to the parks and joined their qigong practice groups. As Qigong became a household word, fantastic stories were passed around about the positive effects.

From east to west and from south to north, people practiced qigong everywhere in China. Bookstores were filled with qigong books. Ancient philosophy books were reprinted after dozens of years' absence. One by one, institutions dedicated to the study of qigong were established as scientists shifted their research focus to qigong. Numerous qigong organizations cropped up, while national and international qigong conferences were held in many of China's big cities.

Once, Master Zhao took me to the home of Dr. Qian, Xue Sen, who was the most famous nuclear scientist in all of China. His wife, Jiang, Yun was a Soaring Crane Qigong practitioner. She was formerly a singer and had studied music in Germany. As she aged, she had lost her ability to sing the high notes she previously had sung in her many solo concerts. After practicing qigong for a few months, she regained the ability to sing the high notes, just as she had when she was young. She also told us that her husband had previously been physically weak and had to be hospitalized for several months a year. However, because she practiced qigong and shared the same bed with him, his health had improved, too.

Dr. Qian valued both Traditional Chinese Medicine and qigong. On several different occasions, he gave lectures on somatic science. He encouraged scientists to do research on how the science of the cells in our body was related to extrasensory powers. Stating that qigong would be the key to future sciences, he maintained that the cultivation of human potential would play an important part in future scientific developments. He shared a story about Joseph Stalin of the Soviet Union. During the Second World War, someone introduced Stalin to a psychic from Yugoslavia who was named Mishkin. It was said that Mishkin had the power to manipulate people's vision. Stalin doubted that, but wanted to see if he could prove his special powers. So Stalin directed Mishkin to meet him in his Kremlin office the next morning at 10 o'clock. Of course Stalin knew that the Kremlin security would not permit any stranger to go directly into his office without special permission.

Stalin had instructed his guards that no strangers would be allowed near his office that morning. However, at 10 o'clock sharp, Mishkin showed up and stood in front of Stalin inside his office. Surprised, Stalin inquired how he had passed through all the gates without being stopped by the guards. Mishkin reminded Stalin that his instruction to the guards was not to allow any strangers into his office. He had not specified that his closest friend would not be permitted. This friend was a frequent visitor to Stalin's office. So, Mishkin used his power to change himself into the image of Stalin's friend as he passed by the guards; they even saluted him as he went by. Stalin would later hire Mishkin to be his adviser.

Stalin was also a close friend of Dr. Qian, Xue Sen's mentor, a well-known physicist and professor in the United States. Stalin reported this psychic phenomenon and the experience to the physics professor and asked for an explanation. The professor was unable to answer Stalin's question. Later, in telling Dr. Qian about his conversation with Stalin, the physicist said that during his lifetime he probably would not be able to do any research on this subject. So, he encouraged Dr. Qian to do research on this kind of phenomena.

With Master Zhao, I also attended many special demonstrations presented by qigong masters and psychics. These experiences greatly increased my understanding about qigong. Master Zhao encouraged me to practice qigong even more diligently. Being around him so often, I never missed an opportunity to seek his opinion. One day, he was a bit impatient with me and said, "You intellectuals ask too many questions. I advise you to practice qigong like an idiot. Do not use your little brain to think so much." Nevertheless, I still had a lot of questions and would try in every way to find an answer. During those days, I was pre-occupied with thoughts of qigong: talking about qigong, reading about qigong or practicing qigong. Qigong became my life. I also spent a lot of time studying ancient Chinese philosophy, which not only helped me understand the foundation of qigong, but also opened my mind.

Qigong Inspirations

In the summer of 1985, I was doing my early morning practice in front of our dormitory building. First, I did the five routines of Soaring Crane Qigong, then standing meditation. While I was deep in meditation, I suddenly had a vision of Jesus standing on a cloud in the sky. While my eyes were closed, his black and white image was very clear to me and was even realistic in size. Without any movement of his mouth, he asked me, "Why did you major in English?"

I understood that the question had come to me telepathically, but I hesitated to answer. For me to respond to such a hard question would be difficult. When I joined the revolution, it had been the Chinese government that decided that my college major would be English. I did not know what to say. Jesus went on, "Use your English to spread qigong all over the world!" Having delivered his message, he disappeared into the clouds. Somewhat puzzled, I pondered, "I have never thought of that. What a good idea!"

I carried on with my regular schedule that day. Afterward, I went to study with Master Zhao. Relating my experience about what I had heard from Jesus, he remained very calm as he looked at me seriously. Then he said, "Do it!" I was expecting to hear more from him, but he said only those two words. I had been hoping that he would tell me exactly how I should "do it", since I had no idea how to spread qigong all over the world.

Professionally at that time, I was the Director of the Reading Skills Office in our English Department. An English expert, Lina Jia, came to our office one day. On learning that I had benefited a great deal from qigong, she asked me to teach it to a group of women who were visiting Beijing. These women were the wives of the staff from the Embassies of the United States, England, and Australia. They were all native English speakers, so I eagerly accepted the invitation. It would be the first time that I would teach qigong in English.

I prepared my lessons carefully and as I taught these students I learned some new English terminology. I soon grew comfortable and found that it was not at all difficult to teach qigong in English. As more and more people benefited from qigong practice, Lina continued to bring me group after group of English speakers. Maintaining constant contact with the foreign students in Beijing enriched me with the knowledge of their culture and their idiomatic ways of expressing things.

Slowly I came to understand why Jesus had sent me the message to spread qigong all over the world. I was the perfect candidate; I grew up in a Christian family. In my childhood, I had heard a lot about Jesus, and in my heart a respect and love for him had taken root. Even though I was not a Christian, I did not have any real exposure to other religions. After I joined the revolution, I was totally brainwashed by the Communist education and I accepted atheism. I even criticized myself for being influenced by Christianity. But, my love for Jesus and all the good deeds he had done to save people remained in my heart.

Qigong is Heaven's special gift to the world's people, but most people are ignorant of this. Qigong is actually a science of self-realization. It is a method to connect all human beings with the source of life. Qigong is a treasure from the East that needs to be introduced to the West in order to benefit as many people as possible. I think Jesus chose me to do the work because I benefited so greatly from qigong and because of my ability to teach English-speaking people.

Qigong Prevails in China

By the early 1980's, qigong had become a common household word in China. Every morning and every evening, millions of people practiced qigong in its different forms in public parks, by the side of the road, or on playgrounds. Many qigong masters came "out from the mountains" to share their secret skills with the general public. The people's faith in qigong increased day by day as they witnessed many friends and neighbors recovering their health.

The leading Qigong organization was called the All China Association of Qigong and Sciences. While qigong had a long history of more than 4,000 years in China, it had never been as popular as it was in the 1980's, when it reached a peak. During those years, qigong was also being introduced in the United States, Japan, Canada, and some European countries as well.

In Beijing, bi-weekly qigong lectures attracted thousands of people and I was among the most loyal of listeners. Many famous qigong

Mr. Yu, Xiao Fei was invited to lecture at our school (1985)

masters and philosophers were invited to give lectures relating to qigong. One young lecturer in particular impressed me, Mr. Yu, Xiao Fei. He was only twenty-six years old, but his knowledge and wisdom far surpassed that of the other teachers in the qigong community. He was not only a genius, but extremely well read. His lectures were both inspiring and informative. Yu, Xiao Fei explained that qigong was the cream of the Chinese culture and he encouraged practitioners to study Buddhist and Daoist teachings in order to reach a deeper level of understanding about the true meaning of qigong. He pointed out that the major goals in learning qigong were to raise the people's consciousness and quicken their spiritual growth.

Once, during a break from his lecture, I approached the stage and asked Mr. Yu if he could spare some time to visit with the qigong students of my university. He gladly accepted my invitation and came to our university. His lectures on qigong were wonderful and aroused a great deal of interest among our teachers and students.

Another master that made a lasting impression on me was Master Yan, Xin. He was from Sichuan Province and his "lectures given with qi" had a specific effect on the audience. While he lectured, he would send healing energy to the audience. This energy would evoke spontaneous movements in most people listening to him. His appearance in Beijing was a big event in the qigong community; he was highly respected and honored by the qigong practitioners. He also did a lot of scientific experiments with professors from Qinghua University to demonstrate the effectiveness of qi. These experiments had very positive results.

Among all of the qigong books I read, one that especially aroused my interest was titled: *"Who Am I?"* by Mr. Lin, Qing Chuan.

In his book, the author boldly talked about the existence of souls. He said that each person is composed of two entities: one is the physical body and the other is the soul. This kind of belief and statement may be quite common and well accepted in the West. But, at that time in China, no

With my best Qigong friends in Beijing (1985)

one dared make such a claim unless it was delivered in a church or temple. I thought Mr. Lin, Qing Chuan was very courageous. Therefore, I bought all the books he'd written and I learned a great deal from them.

I would also become acquainted with Professor Chen, Fu Yin at an international qigong conference. As one of the leaders of the Chinese Academy of Somatic Science, he was frequently mentioned in the qigong community, so I was very happy to meet him. Impressed with his lectures, we became good friends and I often went to study at his home. Later, he invited me to work in the Somatic Science Academy where I was responsible for the liaison department.

As I became well-recognized as a qigong practitioner, many people came to me with questions about qigong. I never tired of sharing what I knew. Many of them were sick and pinned great hopes on qigong for their healing. Often they asked me to introduce them to qigong healers. I was busy all day long. It pleased and excited me to see qigong become so popular.

"Practice Qigong 24 Hours a Day"

The first time when I heard the phrase, "Practice qigong 24 hours a day", I thought it sounded ridiculous. How could I practice qigong 24 hours a day? When would I have time for work, for food, or for sleep? The more I studied and listened to teachers' lectures, the more that I came to realize exactly what this sentence really meant: To be a true qigong practitioner, I should keep in mind the true meaning of life. And I should be a good human being. Whatever I thought, whatever I said, and whatever I did, should adhere to this principle.

One day as I was walking along Qianmen Street on my way to a friend's home, I saw an old man lying on the ground in front of a fruit shop. He was dirty and looked very sick. No one from the crowed shops and booths was doing anything to help him. So I went up to him and asked him where he lived. The old man pointed to the other side of the street. As I helped him get to his feet I noticed that he had wet his pants; it smelled very bad. After I got him up, two young men in the fruit shop shouted loudly at me, "You do not have to do that. He is here every day." I said, "He has wet his pants and has to change them." The young men laughed uproariously as if to say, "You silly woman!" But I held the old man by his arm and walked him slowly across the street. Then I gave him all the change I had. I was so upset with those young men; they were so cold-hearted! The elderly need help and I knew that we should offer them help. If only the young men could change their attitude towards older people.

During the summer, Ping Ping and I joined a tour organized by our university; we went to Beidaihe beach. One afternoon, after our swim, we were among many women washing off salt and sand in the public bathroom. Ping Ping and I had finished showering and were dressing in the outer room. Suddenly, we heard a loud noise as if someone had fallen and then screams filled the air. I rushed into the bathing room and saw a large woman lying on the ground; she had fainted and looked very pale. Without a second thought, I pushed through the crowd. "Step back!" I commanded and everyone stepped back. I asked two women to help flip the unconscious woman over onto her back. Remembering the qigong remedies I was taught, I first pinched her Ren Zhong acupoint between the bottom of her nose and her upper lip. Then I directed qi into her heart and lower dantian in her abdominal area. After about twenty minutes, the woman came back to consciousness, slowly stood up, and left the bathroom under her own power.

The next morning, I could not get out of bed. I realized my exhaustion was due to my giving away too much qi. Ping Ping stayed with me the whole morning and watched over me. She was swimming close-by while I lay on the beach under a big sun umbrella. Gradually, the universe gave me back sufficient qi and I felt rejuvenated. At that time, I had learned some qigong healing techniques, but I was not a professional healer. However, I acted according to the Chinese adage, "maintain an army for a thousand days to use it for an hour". In such an emergency, we should go ahead and do our best to help.

It is astounding to realize that every serious practitioner of qigong may also be able to develop healing powers. Not only to heal himself or herself, but also to emit qi in order to help others. The universe has an infinite abundance of qi. So long as you are connected to it and ask for assistance, the qi comes to help you. It was very clear that it was not just me, but that the universe was helping the woman through me; I was no more than a conduit. But, I was happy to be of some help. Many opportunities have come up during my life to help others; I have always been glad to do so. Gradually over time, I have come to fully realize just what it means to "Practice qigong 24 hours a day"

It became evident to me that the mind was the link between the universe and human beings. My thoughts were of the universe and qigong during most of my spare time. I felt that I had actually become immersed in a qigong lifestyle. While my life had more meaning and I was happier, there were still many problems that confronted me.

Morality Is the Mother of Qigong

In nearly all the qigong books that I read and at the lectures I attended by qigong teachers and Chinese philosophers, the importance of morality was emphasized. Over and over it was repeated, "No morality, no qigong." Not merely a physical exercise for health, qigong is a life-long practice to attain peace of mind; it is a lifestyle and it is a pathway to enlightenment. Many qigong practitioners may be unclear as to the true purpose of their practice and as a result, they do not benefit from it as much as they could. The very purpose of qigong practice is to achieve peace of mind. Only when the mind is at peace can qi circulate smoothly in the body. And only when qi circulates smoothly can good health be maintained. There are three different layers of life: the spiritual layer, the qi layer, and the physical layer. Symptoms in the physical layer are usually a result of some imbalance for an extended time at the qi layer. When there is some dis-ease manifesting at the level of qi, there most likely is something wrong on the spiritual level. Therefore, a focus on the spiritual aspect of life serves to root out disease.

There have been many suggestions put forward on how to achieve peace of mind. First, become aware of the purpose of life. We are all spiritual beings on a human journey. We all come to this planet to learn about life through our experiences; we are likened to a rock that contains gold. If you want to be tempered into pure gold, you have to burn in a furnace. The fire of the furnace will burn off the stone, turning it into ash and leaving only the pure gold. Once you are tempered into pure gold, you will never again be like an ordinary mineral. Life itself is the blaze of the furnace. Problems in life arise and present opportunities that will do us good. Be they financial problems, health problems, or emotional problems. If your life problems are perceived as tests to go through, one can be content and deal with them with great patience and a light heart.

Qigong practitioners come to know that qi is both healing power and consciousness. When qi moves smoothly along the meridians, blood follows. In turn, good blood circulation guarantees good health. Qi is also consciousness. It is spiritual light that can shine within and illuminate the dark parts of one's self. In this way qi can lead us to know ourselves better and help us overcome our own shortcomings. Accepting that the purpose of life is to contribute to society and to purify your soul, we aid society in whatever ways we can. While occupations vary, as long as you have done your best, we can say that you have made a great contribution. It's one's attitude that really matters.

Purifying your soul is more difficult. The most challenging thing is to observe one's self, and recognize what needs to be corrected or improved. To remain humble at heart, and not just on the surface is not an easy thing to do. Everyone likes to receive compliments. But, to accept criticism with sincere humility seems difficult for most of us. Many cannot accept opinions differing from their own. Even when other methods and tactics may be helpful, they are unable to accept them because emotional problems in their life disturbs the heart and hardens their stubborn resolve.

From my own experience with qigong practice, the qi truly opened my mind and increased my awareness of the real meaning of life. It helped me to understand that life itself is a blessing. For no matter what happens in my life, it is to my advantage. It became clear to me that how I looked at my life problems determined how I experienced life itself. This was a big change for me. In the past, I would often blame fate for my problems. I complained a lot about the misfortunes that happened to me. I was angry. I was miserable. I was depressed. After practicing qigong, I changed my way of looking at my experiences. I began to be thankful for all the misfortunes that had occurred. For instance, if it were not for the cancer, I would not have learned qigong.

Cancer truly was the turning point of my life. Before I had cancer, I never paid any attention to my health. I was a workaholic, often hot-tempered and depressed. As a result of not addressing my symptoms, I developed all kinds of chronic diseases. What topped them all was that diagnosis of stage four cancer. With regular qigong practice, I slowed down and became more positive about life. As the qi became more balanced in my body, it changed my temperament; I seldom lost my temper. Thus, my health improved with each passing day. I realized that if it were to be a long-term effort, I would need much more training in the time to come. Qigong would become my lifestyle. The reality was that life continued to give me tests. As the old Chinese saying goes, "The trees want to be still, but the wind never stops blowing."

One day, I received a phone call from a very close friend of mine. He began with some advice, "Hui Xian, do not sabotage other people's marriages." I was shocked upon hearing this but managed to ask, "What are you talking about?" He said, "Fu told me that you are having a romance with her husband." Naturally I got upset and demanded that he tell me the details of what he had heard from Fu. He said, "Fu told me that you taught her husband qigong and that you two go to the woods at 4 o'clock every morning to practice together. She said, 'God knows what they do there in the dark.' Fu said she had requested her violinist husband to make more money by teaching kids to play the violin. But, he only wants to practice qigong and does not want to make extra money. She said,' He's spent a lot of money on books about qigong and Chinese philosophy. This trouble is all because of Chen; he only listens to Chen.' So, Fu suspects that you two are having a romance."

I was very angry when I heard this. An hour later, I got another phone call from a friend. She told me the same thing and reported that Fu was going to write a big Chinese character poster to hang up at our university. That made me furious. I wanted to confront Fu with the truth and clear up the matter immediately. Her rumors were going to ruin my name. Apparently, all of this happened because I had criticized her the day before. She had used a kitchen knife to pry open her husband's bookcase with the intent of burning all of his spiritual books. When he tried to protect his books, she almost sliced into his fingers with the knife. I learned all this because Fu's husband had come to me to relate the story. Obviously, she was crazy.

Just as I was about to leave to find Fu, one of my qigong teachers stopped by to see me. After listening to the whole story, he said, "You should thank Fu. No demon, no Buddha!" His words snapped me out of my rage and calmed me down. I decided not go to argue with Fu and later, she simply stopped spreading the rumors. It turned out that nobody really believed her anyway. With regularity, I kept up my practice, doing qigong every day with much more focus on the spiritual aspect. This served to quicken my spiritual progress.

Predictions from a Fortuneteller

During 1985, I was busy teaching English, heading up the Chinese Language Training Center, studying with Master Zhao and translating his Soaring Crane Qigong book into English. Meanwhile I was cooking for my family, attending to Ping Ping's studies, going to weekly qigong lectures, and assisting whoever turned to me for help. Life became very meaningful and my daily qigong practice kept my health in excellent condition.

Then, my husband separated from me and, against my will, asked me for a divorce. Not knowing what would happen made me very anxious. One day, a qigong friend recommended I visit a very good fortuneteller. I had never really believed in fortune-telling but as I was of two minds about my marriage, off I went.

The fortuneteller was blind and lived in a small house on an old lane in downtown Beijing. The first thing he asked me was my birth date. I only knew the day and year, not the exact hour. "It is important," he responded, "to know the hour of your birth. However, since you do not know, I will guess. In a family, if there are a row of sisters, from six to ten of them, then you would have been born between 5 and 7 o'clock in the evening." I was shocked at this accuracy, as I had eight sisters! After that he began to talk about my parents, what they did and how successful they had been in their careers.

When it came time to talk about me, he said, "You have married twice. You have a daughter from the first husband and you have another daughter with the second one. Two years ago, you got very sick and had an operation on your chest where the disease was located. Your husband now wants to divorce you." I interrupted him, "Yes, you are right. But, I do not want a divorce. Don't you think there is hope that I can maintain my family?" He shook his head as he said, "Your husband will insist on the divorce and there is no way to convince him otherwise. Better just to leave him." He went on, "Very soon, you will go abroad to the United States to spread Chinese culture. You will bring honor to your ancestors. And many foreigners will travel with you to China in order to learn about our Chinese culture. But, when you come back to Beijing, please do not forget to bring me some cakes." He laughed and continued," Your fate is very good. Let's have you draw a fortune *lot*[18] for me to read." He went to a corner of his room and took out a bamboo tube and told me to shake it. Accordingly, I shook the tube and one of the lots dropped onto the floor. I picked it up and handed it over to him. As he held the lot, he explained, "This lot says that you are a 'winter sweet'[19]. You do not attract attention in spring among peach and plum blossoms. Instead, you stand out attractively in the cold snowy winter. That means that when you get older, you will have a wonderful career."

The blind man continued, "You and your older daughter will have opportunities to go abroad next spring, but somehow neither of you will go. However, when fall comes, both of you will go to the United States, one following the other. Congratulations! Unfortunately, before you leave Beijing, there will be a number of misfortunes which will happen to you."

Honestly, I was a bit afraid of him because he knew so much about me. I timidly asked him, "Are you psychic? How can you know so much about my past and future?" He responded, "No, I am not psychic. When I was seven years old, I was struck with a high fever. Because my family was poor, my parents could not send me to the hospital to treat the fever. I thus became blind. My father sent me to a famous fortuneteller so I could learn from him. But he only taught me to memorize an ancient fortune-telling book. Now I ask Dao to guide my fortunetelling. This is how I make a living." My curiosity aroused. I asked him, "Who takes care of you?" He pointed to a small kitchen in the yard, where I saw an old woman cooking at a coal stove. "She is my Mother. She takes care of me." I waved to greet her through the window. After I left the blind man, I could thoroughly believe what he said about my past; he had been one hundred percent correct. However, I was not too sure about his prediction for my future.

My older daughter Sha Sha graduated from college in the summer of 1984 and was assigned to work as a translator in the Ministry of Forestry. In 1985, she applied for further studies in the United States after passing her Test of English as a Foreign Language. We were attempting to get financial sponsorship for her but it was difficult to find someone living in the USA who could do that.

---

[18] A bamboo slip used for divination with a message carved in the bamboo
[19] An ornamental shrub bearing sweet yellow flowers in winter

Earlier in 1984, Sha Sha became acquainted with an American tourist named Mrs. Judith Haber, who was traveling in Beijing with her friend Evelyne. They kept in touch by writing to each other after Mrs. Haber returned home. One day, Sha Sha got a letter from Mrs. Haber inviting her to visit her in the States. Sha Sha did not take the invitation seriously, but when she mentioned this news to me, I thought why not ask Mrs. Haber to sponsor her studies in the USA instead of just going for a visit. Upon receiving our request, this kind-hearted woman agreed to sponsor Sha Sha and sent her all the necessary documents. So, it was just a matter of waiting for the letter of admission from South Dakota State University where she had applied.

The following spring of 1986, Sha Sha called me to say that the Ministry of Forestry had asked her to serve as a translator for a group that was going to the United States to purchase computers. However, the ministry was granting her permission only on the condition that she sign a five-year contract promising to work only for the ministry. Since Sha Sha had already prepared to go to the United States for her master's degree, she could hardly agree to sign such a contract. Continuing her studies was far more important to her.

Around the same time, the head of my university's English Department talked to me, "Now that you have recovered from cancer, we want to send you to Switzerland to serve as an interpreter for a United Nations' organization." I said, "Thank you very much for giving me this opportunity to go abroad. I imagine that teachers in our university might only have one chance to go abroad before retirement. However, I have been separated from my fourth sister for over forty years as she lives in Taiwan. Among all of my brothers and sisters, I am the only one who may have an opportunity to see her. Just now she is visiting her daughter in San Francisco. If I go to the United States, she and I will have a good chance of meeting there. So, I'd rather wait for another chance to serve." The leader nodded his understanding. The fortuneteller had been right. Both my older daughter and I gave up great opportunities to go abroad that spring.

One Saturday in late July, I went to Sha Sha's dormitory and she told me she had been admitted to South Dakota State University and was required to register before September 1, 1986. At almost the same time, my department head informed me that they had decided to send me to

Arizona to the American Graduate School of International Management as a visiting scholar to teach Chinese. Hearing this, the girls in Sha Sha's dormitory laughed as if I were telling them a joke. I said, "I did not make it up. It is true. I remember that the fortuneteller said Sha Sha and I would go to the United States one following the other. Now, if both of us go on the very same plane, I will be doing something against my fate." Sha Sha agreed and said, "I can wait for you as long as I am not late for registration."

The Foreign Affairs office was applying for a visa for me and asked me to be prepared to arrive at AGSIM before September 1st. Since we needed to shop for all the necessities for the trip, on Sunday, Sha Sha, Ping Ping and I made our way downtown. I brought along all the money that my university gave me for supplies; it was a lot—ten times my monthly salary. Finding a backpack at one shop, I reached into my purse ready to pay, only to find that all my money was gone! It must have been a pickpocket who stole my money while I was shopping. What a big loss!

Sha Sha had received her visa from the American Embassy. The Foreign Affairs office would get my visa for me, so I did not have to do anything but wait. And wait I did, for there was no news. As it got closer to the September 1st deadline for Sha Sha to register at the university, it did not seem possible that we would take the same plane. Instead, Sha Sha left on August 16th with Ping Ping and me seeing her off at the airport.

It was around noon when I returned to the university from the airport. On my way to my office, I met a young teacher from my department. He stopped me and said, "Oh it's so good to see you. I have been looking for you. Your visa has been in my pocket for two days. The Foreign Affairs office asked me to pick it up when I went to the Ministry. Here, take it."

Gratefully, I took my passport from him, but I thought life must be playing a joke on me. I had missed going on the same plane with Sha Sha because my visa was being carried around in a colleague's pants pocket. The next morning, I went to meet an old friend who worked at the airport and bought a ticket for the following day. Then I called San Francisco to tell my niece, Ellen Chan and her mother, my fourth sister, Yi Xian the time of my arrival. They had been very happy to greet Sha Sha who had arrived safely and was staying at Ellen's home. Since I would be arriving there the next day, Sha Sha decided to wait for me one more day before she headed for the university in South Dakota.

The morning of August 17th, many colleagues and friends came to my home to see me off. The departure time as printed on my ticket was 2:00 pm. When I got to the airport at 12:00 to check in, I was told that the plane had already left. So I had to go to my friend who sold me the ticket. After looking it over, he covered his face with his hands and said, "I am terribly sorry! It is my mistake. I wrote the wrong time of departure. I will give you another ticket for tomorrow." I did not complain; I thanked him as I left. Once I returned home, I called Ellen to explain the mix-up.

My colleagues and friends laughed a lot when they heard about the mistake but they said, "It's good that we have you one more day." That fortuneteller was a mischievous person! I did have a lot of misfortunes before I left China for the United States.

I Arrive in the United States of America

After the long flight, the first impression I had when I arrived at San Francisco airport and walked off of the plane was how very quiet and peaceful this piece of land was. While there were many passengers moving around, I heard almost no noise. Civilization!

As I left Customs pushing my luggage cart, the flash of a camera caught my attention. A beautifully dressed woman ran up to me. I immediately recognized my fourth sister, Yi Xian. We hugged tightly

Reunion with my sister after 40 years of separation

and tears of joy ran down our cheeks. Forty years' separation! People around us sensed our meeting was something special and smiled their happiness at our reunion. Ellen, her husband Walter, and my daughter Sha Sha were all there to greet me. Sha Sha was especially happy to see me before she went off to study in South Dakota. When Ellen left our hometown of Jiaxing forty years before, she was a little girl and now she had grown into a mature attractive woman. Her big smile expressed her warm hospitality and Walter politely greeted me, too. Both Ellen and Walter were very kind to us.

It was a warm sunny day, so Walter drove our group to Golden Gate Park in San Francisco. On our way, the amazing city views made me excited and happy. In the park, a couple was having their wedding celebration. I had never seen a bride in her wedding gown out among real trees and flowers in a park setting. The sky was clear with some thin white clouds floating overhead. The scene to me was more like a movie picture than reality. Later, as we drove along the streets, I saw one little house after another, each house a different style and painted a different color with gorgeous flower gardens in the front yard. I felt as if I were in fairyland.

Ellen's house was not too far from the airport. It was not a large house, but the furnishings in it showed that the couple loved antiques, both Chinese and Western. There was a hot tub in their backyard. My sister Yi Xian, Sha Sha and I soaked and enjoyed the warm water tub for the rest of the day. In the evening, the whole family gathered round the dinner table and talked about what had occurred in each of our lives during our separation. Sister Yi Xian and her family left our hometown for Taiwan in 1948, before the Communist Party took over the power and established the People's Republic of China. After that time, no communication was allowed between Taiwan and Mainland China. Before my parents died, they both missed my sister Yi Xian, her husband Yao, Yi Fu and their two children, Yao, Zhi Qing (Ellen's Chinese name) and her older brother Yao, Zhi Bai. After the family got to Taiwan, they had one more daughter and one more son. Later my sister Yi Xian and her husband divorced. Yi Xian remarried and had two sons with her second husband. Everyone lived in Taiwan until Yao, Yi Fu and his four children moved to the United States. How lucky for me that my sister Yi Xian was visiting her children at the same time I arrived in California. During my short stay in San Francisco, I was also able to meet with my sister's ex-husband Yao, Yi Fu. He was a good man and still cared about all my brothers and sisters. We had so much to talk about; I filled him in on the details about the whole family in Mainland China.

Sha Sha spent only a couple of days with me in San Francisco and then left, with a little pocket money, to begin her new life as a graduate student at South Dakota State University.

A New Life in America

After staying in Ellen's home for a few days, I was off for Arizona. The dean of the American Graduate School of International Management (AGSIM) greeted me at the airport and drove me to the school. Tropical trees lined the streets and the weather was extremely hot. The tall, thick cactus stood like giants in the desert sand. I had never seen a huge saquaro cactus before, except once in a vision during a sitting

Visiting the Grand Canyon (1986)

meditation. It had happened in Beijing a few months before my coming to the United States. I realize that the vision might have been a premonition.

The apartment the AGSIM provided for me was very spacious and comfortable. From my bedroom window, I could see the vast desert covered with dry grass and wild tropical flowers. I was enchanted by the exotic view.

That first night I had a strange dream. I dreamt that I was walking towards a rocky mountain in the desert. I saw a big cave and went into it. With a thundering loud noise, a gate closed behind me. A Chinese voice came from nowhere saying, "You are led through this gate by your master. It will depend on you alone to wake up spiritually." I awoke from the dream and knew it was a message encouraging me to overcome the many difficulties and hardships I would encounter in order to carry out the inspiration from Jesus to spread qigong throughout the world. I could not go back to sleep again and lay there until daybreak. Then I got up and went out to the area covered with dry grass and wild flowers. The sun was about to rise from behind the hills. As I felt its heat, the faint fragrance of the flowers overlapped the uneasy feeling I felt from the heat and I began to practice my qigong as usual, enjoying the desert qi.

Assigned to teach Mandarin, I had a small class of ten graduate students. Having been a language teacher for almost 30 years, I was quite used to teaching, even though it was in a different environment and, in English. The students liked me and I tried my best to improve my communication skills to quicken their progress.

Professor Andrew Chang, the head of the Chinese Language Department, and I already knew each other from Beijing when one summer he brought a group of students from AGSIM to our university in Beijing to study Chinese. Originally from Taiwan, he had been teaching Chinese at AGSIM for many years. His wife Mary and their three children lived close to the school's campus in a very large, impressive house. They took good care to make me feel at home in Arizona. Over the first dinner they invited me to, I talked about qigong. Immediately, Professor and Mrs. Chang expressed their desire to learn this new skill. They became my very first qigong students in America.

Every morning, we three gathered together to practice qigong; this caught the attention of other teachers and students at the school. More and more people showed an interest in the art of Soaring Crane Qigong, so I offered to teach whoever was willing to learn. Very soon, I had dozens of students. One day, a local newspaperman came and interviewed me and took many pictures, which appeared in the local paper along with an article based on our interview. A few days later, I was invited to talk about qigong on a Phoenix radio station. There I met the most famous Daoist master in Arizona, Kaiti, who

Published in Phoenix newspaper (1986)

would become a very good friend of mine in later years. Kaiti was a very knowledgeable spiritual master. He would come to see me often at the school and would invite me to join him for meals and conversation at various restaurants. Each time we went out to eat, many people would

218

greet him or even hand him a slip of paper expressing their admiration. One day, my curiosity was aroused, I asked him why he was so popular. He smiled and said, "I teach Daoist philosophy on TV. Also I am an actor and have played several roles in different movies." Since I was unfamiliar with current American movies, I did not know any actors in America.

He often took me to his home; it was there that he explained how he celebrated the death of his wife. It was the first time in my life that I met somebody who did things like that. He told me he was sad about her death, but he believed that her soul had left this planet to ascend to a higher plane and for this, he should celebrate. His manner of experiencing death opened my mind.

During my time teaching at AGSIM, I was a frequent visitor to Professor Chang's home. His wife Mary was a good cook and always prepared delicious food to nourish me. On weekends, they took me shopping and sightseeing. We visited the Grand Canyon, Sedona, the Native American reservations, and many other places in the southwest. These trips were just the beginning. There was so much for my eyes to absorb and my mind to grasp. America was such a rich country with so many different cultures.

Celebrating the Moon Festival

August 15th of the lunar year is the date for the traditional Chinese Moon Festival. The moon is very round and bright that night if the weather is not cloudy. In China it is a day for families to gather together, have dinner and share moon cakes. There were more than fifty Chinese teachers and students at AGSIM. Almost half came from Mainland China and the other half were from Taiwan. In 1986, the relations between Mainland China and Taiwan were tense. Being a teacher, I thought it was my responsibility to gather all the Chinese together to celebrate the Festival even though we might not politically be in agreement. So I put out a proposal to hold a party on the school playground on August 15th. Chinese students from both Mainland China and Taiwan responded enthusiastically. Since moon cakes were not available in the local shops, at the party I could only share the box of moon cakes my niece Ellen had mailed to me from San Francisco. There were only four moon cakes so we cut them into tiny bits so that each person could have a taste. Everyone ate their little bite with great pleasure.

Then I suggested that we have a singing contest between a Mainland Chinese team and a Taiwan team. First, both teams sang the most popular songs in China before the Communist took over the state power from Kuomingtang, such as "Man Jiang Hong", "Ye Lai Xiang", "Graduation Song" and so on. After singing more than ten songs, we found we had run out of the songs both teams knew. After that, the Mainland Chinese team sang a song in praise of Mao, Ze Dong, "The East Is Red" while the Taiwan team sang their national anthem. Because of dozens of years of political separation, the songs circulating in the two places were not the same. The two teams sang their popular songs from the 50's, the 60's, then the 70's. One after another, we sang more than twenty different songs simultaneously, which sounded so chaotic, we laughed a lot while we sang. Then, when it came time to sing the popular songs from the 80's, the two teams sang the same school campus songs that had been introduced to Mainland China by Taiwan singers. We were all very happy to be able to be singing the same songs together again. Everyone present was touched that this singing contest had brought harmony and unity between the Mainland Chinese students and the

Taiwanese students. From that time on, the Chinese students often held activities together.

AGSIM also held an "Asian Night" once a semester. Students from different countries cooked their authentic food and made some pocket money selling it. Once, there was a fashion show at the Asian Night celebration. We Chinese dressed up in our traditional costumes. I even wore a Qipao, a lady's long gown, and as I walked on the stage, I held a little Taiwanese girl's hand as we pretended to be mother and daughter. That was the first time and the only time in my life that I was in a fashion show. It was so much fun! In winter when the oranges were ripe, they fell to the ground in the orchard. And, since the students had no time to pick them up, I went with an American friend to gather the oranges. When we got back to the campus, I called all the Chinese students to come and take some fruit. Later, you could hardly tell who was from Mainland China and who was from Taiwan. We treated each other like brothers and sisters!

A Special Man

One of the Taiwanese students invited us to her home to make Jiaozi, Chinese dumplings. More than ten students and teachers from our school came to this event. Most of us were Chinese so we chatted excitedly in our own language and laughed while making dumplings around her big dining table. Her American husband, Charles, had come to AGSIM to visit her and when he saw the piles of dumplings, he said, "I'm sorry I don't know how to make dumplings, but I'm sure I can cook dumplings." He then went to the stove and turned on the burner under a big pot of water. When it was boiling, he dumped two trays of dumplings into it and started to stir the dumplings quickly back and forth with a ladle. After seeing how he planned to "cook" the dumplings, I stopped him. "Charles, you should not stir the dumplings like that. You should push them gently with the ladle in one direction." As I said it, I took the ladle from his hand and showed him how to do it. Suddenly he shouted, "Oh, my God! I dreamed of this exact scene last week." His voice was so loud that it caught everybody's attention. He continued, "I dreamed that a Chinese woman was teaching me how to cook Jiaozi exactly like this." Everybody had a good laugh.

A week later, I got a call from Charles asking me to meet his father who was visiting from the east coast. Charles told me that he had called his father and explained to him what had happened at the Jiaozi party. At once his father decided to make a trip to Arizona to meet me, the woman who had been in his son's dream. I had no idea why he wanted to see me, but I agreed to go to their home that night. Since I couldn't drive, I asked Professor Chang to take me there.

As soon as we entered the sitting room, I saw a solemn-looking man in a priest's attire, sitting upright in an armchair. Politely, I greeted him, first introducing Professor Chang and then myself. He, in turn, introduced himself to us. He went on, "I hear you have been practicing qigong for a long time. I would love to hear some of your stories." Never had I talked about my qigong experiences with a priest before, to say nothing of an American priest. I was a bit nervous and did not know exactly how to start. As I usually did, I began with my story of having cancer and how I healed through practicing qigong. After listening for a few minutes, he interrupted me by saying, "I am not interested in your healing stories. I want to hear about some of your spiritual experiences during your qigong practice."

Per his request, I began to relate some of my out-of-body experiences. I told him how it had felt when my soul flew into the night sky and I saw myself in a green silk gong like the Chinese ancient Apsaras. As I was telling him about being brought up into the sky by Longevity Man, he motioned for me to stop talking, and he began to speak, "Then you were brought to the top layer of the clouds and you heard the loud noise of babies crying. And, you saw hundreds of naked babies lying in the clouds facing downward." I was taken by surprise and asked, "How do you know about all this?" He smiled and said calmly, "I too have been there a couple of times." He continued, "Ever since I was a child, I often had out-of-body experiences. The many places I have visited and the strange things I have seen do not exist on this planet; I knew that I had special gifts. I entered a theological seminary and I became a priest, after graduation. My superior in the church directed me to different families to pray for people that were dying. Each time, when the person's soul was leaving the dying body, I always saw the soul leave at the corner of the room waving good-bye with a smile. Whenever I saw this, I would speak to the tearful family gathered around the loved one, 'Do not cry. Look! He or she is leaving, waving good-bye to you with a smile.' I would point to the corner of the room and describe to the family what I witnessed.

"In my married life, there were more out-of-body experiences and my wife would not be surprised when she saw my face turn pale and my body became motionless. Before disturbing me she would wait until my soul came back into my body."

At this moment, I silently recalled my father's passing and the story my family told me. My father's last words were about the angels he saw in the corner of the room—it sounded so familiar now. He continued, "People listened to me, but none of them had seen what I saw. Several months later, I was accused by my superior of telling lies and then I was fired." Charles's father said sarcastically to me, "They talk about souls all the time, but they don't believe in the existence of souls. Certain clergy are not to be trusted." He told me he was very happy to meet me, someone who understood this sort of phenomenon. When it came time for us to part, he opened my hand, looked at it carefully and held it for a while. Then he said, "We are friends! I am coming to your school to watch you teach qigong tomorrow afternoon."

The next day around five o'clock, he showed up at the playground along with his son, Charles. I greeted them and began to teach. For the whole hour, they watched us. When I was accompanying them out of the playground, Charles's father put his arm round my neck and whispered to me, "I tell you a miracle happened to me last night. I've suffered terrible back pain for more than forty years and I've tried every way to cure it in vain. Yesterday after I held your hand, the pain disappeared. I am free from the back pain. Thank you!"

Once again, I was taken aback. How could this have happened? I was not a healer and I did not have any clue about his health condition. Later, I wrote a letter to Master Zhao asking him to explain this phenomenon to me. He answered that it was because I had the type of element in my body that he needed to heal his back pain.

Later, I returned to China and lost contact with Charles's father. I only know that he became a peace activist, traveling all over the world working for world peace. Meeting this special man was an important event. For the first time in my spiritual practice, I had found someone to validate the places that I had been to in my out-of-body experiences, for he had visited them, too.

My Pleasure in Meeting Judith Haber

As soon as I arrived in Arizona, I called Judy. I could not thank her enough for having sponsored my daughter to study in the United States. But, she said, "When I was young, my father helped me a lot. In thanking him, I said, 'How can I repay you?' To which my father answered, 'Don't repay me. Remember during your lifetime, if anybody needs your help, just do it.'" I was deeply touched by Judy's words.

During the winter vacation of 1986, Sha Sha and I–from two different states, South Dakota and Arizona–went to New York to visit Judy. It was close to Christmas, but Judy and Evelyne were visiting Paris and would not be back until the day after Christmas. In their place, a friend of Judy's received us and we spent the night at Judy's home. That night we were taken to a big church to celebrate Christmas Eve. I was overwhelmed by the beautiful performance of the choir; it was a mixed group of children under ten and adult singers over seventy. What an unforgettable evening!

Early Christmas morning, I was headed off to Central Park to practice qigong. On my way, I saw a little pine tree lying in the gutter along with many gift boxes and bits of colorful wrapping paper. Suddenly an idea came into my mind and I rushed back to wake up Sha Sha. I told her that we could make a wonderful Christmas tree for Judy's home with all these discarded items. So, we collected all that we needed and dragged the little pine tree back to Judy's apartment. Both of us were good at handicrafts, so we spent the whole day creating

Christmas tree decorated with items we found on the street (1986)

ornaments. We made flowers out of the colorful paper and cut pictures out of the gift boxes. To finish it off we scattered some white plastic foam drops onto the branches. The Christmas tree was done and it was the most beautiful Christmas tree I had ever made in my life. Then we put all the gifts we had brought for Judy and Evelyne under the tree. The next day when they came home, our Christmas tree immediately caught their eye. After hearing the story of how we had come to find and decorate the tree, they laughed and said we had become real New Yorkers.

Judy was a very kind lady. She treated us warmly, just like old friends. But I could not figure out what I could do for her in return. The only and best gift I could offer her was to teach her qigong. After listening to my introduction about the spiritual part of the practice, she said she wanted to learn Master Zhao's qigong form. Judy began calling some friends to join us in a workshop and very soon a group of ten people gathered in her home. I began to teach them Chinese Soaring Crane Qigong every evening. Our time together for learning and practicing was very successful and the result of their study was positive. At the closing day of the workshop, Judy presented me a flower basket and in tears, she said to me, "Now, I know why we met Linda (Sha Sha's English name) in Beijing. It was meant to bring you to me."

Judy presenting me flowers at my first Qigong workshop – New York (1987)

While I was in New York, I read a small advertisement in a Chinese newspaper that Mr. Wu, Yi and his wife, Shen, Rong Er were teaching Soaring Crane Qigong in the city. I was very happy to know that and invited them to come to meet Judy and me. They came to Judy's home and we talked almost the whole night through, deciding to establish the Soaring Crane Qigong Association of the United States.

A week later, I paid a visit to my former schoolmate Professor Charles Wu and his wife Diane Ma in Andover, Massachusetts where they taught at Phillips Academy. Charles invited people from his school to listen to me talk about qigong. Showing a great interest in qigong, Charles was willing to help with spreading qigong in this country. I also connected Charles and Diane with Mr. Wu, Yi and Shen, Rong Er from whom Charles later learned Soaring Crane Qigong.

My assignment as a Chinese instructor at AGSIM in Arizona soon was completed. I was excited to return to China with the newly formed mission of bringing Master Zhao and Soaring Crane Qigong to the United States.

Preparing for Master Zhao's Visit to America

The second day after I returned to Beijing, I went to visit Master Zhao at his home. He was out, but his wife told me where I could find him. During that period of time, the Master was writing his Soaring Crane Qigong book with the help of a female writer. With too many people coming to visit him every day, they had taken to hiding out in a new building under construction to do their work. When I arrived there, I only found the woman whom I had met once at a qigong conference. Master Zhao was taking a break and had gone to the street to buy something. Somewhat mysteriously, the co-writer told me, "I tell you that I am experiencing something very strange. I am here to assist Master Zhao in writing his book. He has not written a word. What he does is just sit meditating with his legs crossed and his eyes closed. He channels and I take dictation of whatever comes out of his mouth. You know I am a Communist and would never believe such kinds of things were possible if I were not experiencing them personally. While he was channeling the theory portion of the book, he spoke so fluently that I was very rushed taking dictation. Now, look! Here is all that I have written down." She handed a thick notebook full of the channeled information over to me. After the master came back, he said to me, "When the book is finished, I will authorize you to translate it into English and we will use it when we go to the United States."

Not long after that day, Master Zhao authorized me to translate his first book titled *Chinese Soaring Crane Qigong*. At that time, I was very busy. Apart from teaching English 12 hours per week, I also taught qigong. But, since I practiced qigong every day, I was full of energy. Still, I did not have much spare time to translate his book, so I had to seize every minute at home to get the work done. I had my typewriter open all the time and whenever I had some time, I would sit down and do his translation even though I could only translate one or two sentences at a time. Gradually, I finished the draft translation, and later I asked Judy to edit it. Thanks to Judy Haber, the English version of Master Zhao's *Chinese Soaring Crane Qigong* book was completed.

In order to understand more about qigong, Judy paid a special visit to China and participated in the National Conference of Soaring Crane

Qigong in Beijing. She was warmly welcomed as an honored guest and was invited to give a lecture at the conference for which she won loud applause. Qigong people were excited to learn that even Americans were interested in qigong. Judy's presence was the highlight of the conference and later news of her visit became widely known among thousands of Soaring Crane Qigong practitioners.

I Am Appointed Director
of the Chinese Language Training Center

One day in 1987, President Sun, Wei Yan called me to his home and told me that the leading group at the university had made the decision to establish a Chinese Language Training Center. They were appointing me to be the director of the center. Upon hearing this, I said, "Oh, no. I do not think I am suitable to be the director. I am not a Chinese language teacher and I do not have much experience in leadership." President Sun smiled and said, "We consider you to be the right person for this job and your experience in teaching English will help you in accomplishing your work. We trust you. Have confidence in yourself." There was no sense in arguing, so I accepted the appointment.

Very soon, I was given an office, and along with two other people, we began preparations for the program. We put advertisements in the *China Daily* and some foreign language magazines that were circulated in other countries. Several months later, our efforts paid off as a large number of foreign students enrolled in the program. Some moved onto the university campus and some stayed in hotels in the neighborhood. At the opening ceremony, I presented the welcome speech in English and close to the end of my speech, I remembered my mission and asked the foreign students if they would like to learn qigong during their spare time. The response was unexpectedly enthusiastic. All the students stood and cheered. At once I realized what a great opportunity I had been given in spreading the knowledge of qigong. At six o'clock the next morning, I began to teach dozens of foreign students Soaring Crane Qigong in English! Every morning after their Chinese lessons were complete, we practiced together.

The university provided the best Chinese language professors and teachers to teach at the center. Apart from their regular studies, the students went on field trips organized by the center to visit different places of interest such as the Summer Palace, the Great Wall, and the Forbidden City, among others. In the evenings, they often attended various performances at different theaters. We tried our best to make their stay a meaningful one. But, still, some students were not happy with the facilities at their hotels. One day when there was no hot water for a shower, a student became very angry and broke the door of his hotel

230

room. Some students did not want to walk from their hotel to the classroom on a muddy road when it was raining. Others were not quite used to the food and refused to eat it. There were many problems that had to be dealt with; I was kept very busy all day long. But, we managed to make the language program work.

As group after group of foreign students came, the center expanded. Our Chinese Language Training Center was one of the earliest Chinese language programs in China. For their part the students learned a lot and most were very happy to have had such a life experience in China.

A Divorce–I Had to Agree

My second marriage never went well. Life was dull and I was miserable. I only focused on my work. In 1983, my husband asked for a divorce. Though I did not have much love for him, I still wished to keep the family together for the sake of our daughter Ping Ping. She was a lovely girl and I did not want her to suffer from losing her father. I begged him not to divorce me, but he insisted on it. We lived in separate rooms and seldom talked to one another even though we ate our meals at the same table. I advised him not to divorce and that he might regret his decision. But, he said he would never regret such a decision. We did not argue any more but stayed in a "cold war" relationship for a long time.

Another failure in marriage. Had I learned nothing from my first failed marriage? Had I not learned that marrying a man with no love for me would end badly? One day, I found Ping Ping reading a magazine filled with legal articles. I was surprised that at her young age she showed such an interest in the law. I asked her why she was interested in reading that magazine. She said, "I cannot bear seeing you and dad so unhappy. After reading some articles about marriage and divorce, I have come to realize that if there are no stable families, the society will not be stable. If you want to keep this abnormal relationship for me, please do not do that. I am not happy to be in this kind of family." Her words relieved me from the struggles I had been having between two minds. So, I agreed to the divorce. The only condition to the divorce that I made was that custody of my dear daughter Ping Ping must belong to me. My husband agreed and the divorce was final in May 1988. My love for my daughters has always surpassed my love for my husbands.

Master Zhao, Jin Xiang Visits the USA

At the beginning of 1988, Judy Haber sent an invitation to Master Zhao and me. With the support of the University of International Business and Economics, Master Zhao and I went to teach qigong in New York in July of that year.

On the very first evening of our arrival at Judy's home in Germantown in upstate New York, Master Zhao called me into his room and motioned for me to sit on the floor opposite him. He asked me, "Have you ever suspected that Soaring Crane Qigong was not my invention?" I stared at him and shook my head, "How could I suspect a great master like you?" "It is time," he said, "to tell you the truth. When I was very young, I became very sick and was sent to Beidaihe Sanitarium for convalesce. I was given Chinese medical treatments and was taught a very simple qigong sitting meditation. Day by day, I got better. Then one day, I took a train and went to my hometown to visit my family. On the train, a poorly-dressed old man was sitting on the seat opposite me. The old man kept his eyes on me for a long time and then he said, 'Young man, you are very good at qigong.' I smiled and said, 'No, not at all. I only learned a kind of simple sitting meditation and practiced for less than a year.' The old man said, 'You are gifted at qigong. Do you want to learn more?' Out of curiosity, I said, 'Oh, yes.' Then the old man told me to hold the corner of his shabby outfit and prepare for an adventure. I simply did not understand what he meant and reached out my hand. He pushed my hand away and said, 'Stupid! I mean to hold the corner of my outfit with your mind when I take you off with me. Now, close your eyes and do not be afraid.' All of a sudden, I felt that I left my seat and flew out of the compartment. I was flying after the old man high above the train. I saw the trees passing by us and the train running very fast below us. Then, I became nervous and afraid. So I again held the corner of his outfit with my mind. Suddenly we came back to our seats. The old man said, 'This is advanced qigong; I only gave you a bit of a taste. I tell you that you have a big mission in this lifetime. Listen, after visiting your family, I want you to go to the places I direct you to and to study with the masters there.' He then named several mountains where I should go to study. He gave me the passwords and the names of the masters. But he did not give me permission to let his name be known to anyone. So I cannot tell you who he was.

"After visiting my family, I did as this mysterious master had instructed. I visited all the masters he referred me to, but they did not teach me anything. Maybe, they all initiated me but at the time I did not realize it. After I returned to Beijing, I felt strongly that I should invent a qigong form for sick people to practice. Every evening, I would sit at my table with a piece of paper and a pencil trying to write something. But, always, I fell asleep. A few days later, as I felt sleepy, I went into a trance. I would see a person standing in front of me teaching me a routine. When I woke I could remember all the details of the routine. The next morning, I drew the movements on a piece of paper. My sketches looked like a stickman doing funny movements. The next evening, the same person taught me another routine. Then I learned another routine and another. I learned all the five routines this way and even now, I do not know who taught them to me. After that, I practiced the five routines everyday and found myself getting healthier and healthier. One day, I received a message from out of nowhere telling me to teach the five routines to the public. I did not know how to teach or where I would find students. I begged not to make me teach and said that I was afraid. But the message told me that everything would be well taken care of and encouraged me to go out and teach.

"So, I went to the park looking for students. Observing several people who looked very sick, I offered to teach them qigong and they all agreed to study with me. I found nine students and I taught them bit-by-bit until they learned all five routines. The routines worked wonders and all nine students recovered from their sickness in a couple of months. It so happened that

The Soaring Crane Qigong Association of USA is established (1988)

one of them was the chief editor of the most popular newspaper *People's Daily* in China. The paper reached into every corner of the country. The editor had been diagnosed with late stage lung cancer and nobody in his office ever expected to see him back at work. When he showed up at his office and told his colleagues about me and the qigong routines, he was encouraged to write stories about each of the nine students as well as me and to publish these stories in their newspaper. So he did. In the following days, letters and phone calls from the readers came to the newspaper like snowflakes. In almost every letter, they asked for information about qigong studies and where they could find a teacher. I was at a loss and did not know what to do. With the help of the All China Trade Union, I began to train my first nine students to be teachers and we began to teach the form that I named Chinese Soaring Crane Qigong. In a few years, Soaring Crane Qigong reached almost every province in China. Millions of people benefited from this form." I listened to his story with great interest and promised to help him accomplish his mission in spreading Soaring Crane Qigong in the West.

With the English version of the book *"Chinese Soaring Crane Qigong"* complete, plans to bring qigong to New York were set in motion. While I was back in China, Judy along with Wu, Yi and Shen, Rong Er established the Soaring Crane Qigong Association of the United States. Judy had arranged a 10-day workshop for Master Zhao and me to teach near her home in upstate New York. The workshop was scheduled at a local high school. Wu, Yi and Shen, Rong Er prepared another workshop for the master to teach during his remaining days in New York. Since it was during my summer vacation and I was not teaching, I was able to accompany Master Zhao, serving as the translator and his teaching assistant.

Judy had prepared everything for the workshops from her manor in Germantown. Her home was huge with one major two-story building, a flat that could hold twenty people and another smaller building for guests. There was a very spacious yard with tall leafy trees surrounding it and down the slope of lawn, there was a swimming pool. Many people stayed in her large home, including Master Zhao and me. But most of the students stayed in motels downtown. Altogether there were more than 60 students when we all gathered at Judy's place. While most of them were beginners, some were ready for advanced training as they had already learned the form from Wu, Yi and Shen, Rong Er. It was exciting for me to see so many enthusiastic "foreign" students. They came from different places in America and some even came from Europe.

Among the students, there were many who were sick. Judy gave them special care. A man who suffered from AIDS did not feel comfortable sharing the same room with other students. When he came to tell Judy about his health condition, Judy offered her own sitting room and made a bed for him to sleep on. Judy's love and generosity touched my heart.

Master Elie Hien

The day before the workshop began, a group of Judy's spiritual friends gathered in her sitting room to talk about publishing Master Zhao's book. In the middle of the meeting, an honorable guest, a black man, arrived accompanied by Ms. Evelyne Jankowski. At the sight of him, Master Zhao turned over a used envelope and wrote to me in Chinese, "He is from 'Yan Wang Xing'!" I was astonished and a flow of heat rushed to my head. "What does that mean?!" After Evelyne introduced Master Elie Hien to Master Zhao and the group, Master Zhao asked. "Are you from Yan Wang Xing?" I had no idea how to translate this into English, as I had never heard of this planet, even in Chinese. So, first I apologized for not being able to translate the academic name of the

Posting a sign for the Qigong workshop in Germantown, NY
(L to R) Master Elie Hien, me and Master Zhao (1988)

planet and then I had to translate it into Chinese English, "Are you from the Swallow King planet?" After Evelyne translated it into French for the African master, he solemnly smiled and answered, "Yes, I am. My planet is full of swallows and swallow fish." I then gave a literal translation of this sentence into Chinese. At that moment, I felt as if I were in the clouds. Never had I heard any conversation like this before and I didn't know what to believe. Master Elie Hien respectfully said, "I come from another planet to meet a great master from China." The two masters sat face-to-face and talked about the future of the world. It felt to me as if they were the presidents of the United States and the Soviet Union talking about the big changes coming to the world. Master Elie Hien advised Master Zhao to work hard to spread qigong and said, "In future, the ancient philosophy of China–the Daoist philosophy–will prevail in the whole world and will be universally accepted. People will look for natural ways of healing instead of depending on modern medicines." I was really impressed by his words. And his presence at the workshop was a highlight of the whole event.

As we started the qigong workshop, everyone was excited and happy. But in July, the weather in Germantown was very hot. Master Elie Hien said he was going to help. He then began to meditate in his small room in order to manipulate the weather. I had heard and read many stories about psychic people changing the weather, but I had never seen it happen with my own eyes. Watching very carefully, I was really curious as to what Elie was going to do with the blazing hot weather. To our great surprise, we soon had rain and it kept raining for two days. The temperature dropped making it much easier to be at the workshop. Then the students asked Master Elie if he could make it rain at night and bring out the sun during daytime. Elie promised to do so and also guaranteed that nobody would get sick and that there would be no traffic accidents during those days. From that point on, we enjoyed very pleasant cool weather. It was so comfortable and everyone was full of energy and our skin felt cool and smooth. At night, around bedtime, it started to pour and before daybreak, the rain stopped and the sun was out smiling. As unbelievable as it may sound, it was true!

Master Elie Hien told us he was originally from a small village in West Africa and used to be the head of a tribe. He did spiritual practice all his life and had greatly cultivated his latent psychic potential. He made predictions and he could maneuver the weather. Later, he left his hometown and resided in Paris. Judy and Evelyne had studied with him before and had thought to invite him to join us during Master Zhao's visit to New York. He had promised to help Master Zhao with the qigong workshop. After the 10-day workshop and before his return to Paris, he suggested that we hold a ceremony in West African style as he foretold the coming of a storm. More than twenty people stood in a circle on Judy's lawn with a bonfire in the center. Each of us had prepared something edible to throw into the bonfire along with a wish for world peace and for compromise between families or individuals. Before everybody stood in their place, Elie had us paint our faces according to our birth time, day and year. Elie said that he was going to elevate our souls into the sky and when our souls came back we should be able to recognize our own bodies. Everyone painted their faces carefully with different seasonal colors and we laughed a lot at our funny appearance.

As we stood in our places, we all followed Elie in singing and dancing. He was beating his African drum, sending out beautiful rhythms. Some participants took out their cameras, ready to take pictures. The master stopped them saying, "If you take pictures of this ceremony, your camera will be ruined, so don't blame me for that." All cameras were put away. At that time, the sun was high in the blue sky and the weather became as hot as before. About two o'clock, dark clouds suddenly gathered above us. The ceremony began! Very soon, the sky darkened as it threatened rain. According to Elie's instruction, when the person standing in the south walked towards the bonfire, a deafening thunderclap broke the silence. A lightning flash almost hit the lawn and I felt it pass by me. I was scared! Along with the thunder, big drops of rain began to fall. One after another as scheduled, each of us walked up to throw the food in our hands into the bonfire and recite our wishes mentally. In a few minutes, we were all soaked to the skin. When all of us had finished, Elie asked us to sing our own folk songs. Since we came from different countries, we all sang different folk songs in different languages. As the songs echoed in the air, our sound became the most touching chorus of love, beauty and peace. Tears flowed from our eyes mixing with the raindrops as we hugged each other joyfully. In the middle of our excitement, Master Zhao tearfully grabbed me by the hand and urged me to go with him to Master Elie Hien. Evelyne immediately came to translate for us. Master Zhao cried like a baby and could not speak his mind. Elie held him in his arms and said, "Oh! I totally understand you. It is hard to spread qigong because people still do not understand what qigong really means to them. But, do not worry. The day will come when qigong is welcomed by all people." Master Zhao only nodded. It was the first time that I saw Master Zhao cry like that.

When the ceremony was over, Master Zhao asked me, "Did you go up, did you see anything during the ceremony?" Actually I was so completely absorbed in the activities that nothing special had happened to me. So I answered, "No." Master Zhao said, "Elie Hien is very powerful. When the storm was about to come, I saw him riding on the middle part of a long log with two other black men riding at either end of the log; they were flying very fast from the north in the sky to the space over our heads. Elie was manipulating the rain." "But, he was standing in

239

the circle with us at that time," I replied. Master Zhao looked at me. "The one in the sky was his higher self!" It was truly the most amazing and unbelievable event I had ever experienced in my life.

A Prophecy

One morning during our time with Master Elie Hien, he had Evelyne come to tell me that he wanted to give me a consultation. I was both surprised and overjoyed to have such good fortune, so I quickly followed Evelyne back to Elie's little room. Master Elie Hien was already in a meditative posture, seated on the floor in the middle of the room. Next to him was the stick that had dozens of silver spots dotting the wood. He had explained to us that each spot represented one of his ancestors, so it had been treasured by his family. On the floor in front of him were countless shells and small stones. As we entered his room, he motioned for me to sit down opposite him. Then he started channeling and the god he called the Oracle began to talk through Elie. The first thing the Oracle said was, "This lady does not love money." He went on to say that I had a great mission this lifetime, but I had remained unconscious for a long while. I had been given cancer to change all that; the cancer was a turning point.

Just at that moment, Master Zhao knocked at the door. Once he entered the room, his interruption changed the subject of our conversation. Elie suddenly looked very serious and he began to discuss the future of China and the whole world. He predicted that there would be a big event happening in China during the early summer of 1989. He said thousands and thousands of people would pour into the streets of Beijing demanding democracy and freedom. There would be an uprising of the people. However, he said, the demonstration would not be successful.

To me it seemed impossible. For during those years, China was flourishing. Many foreigners came to China to do business and to establish joint enterprises. China was opening up, everything was developing so fast, and people were doing well. I did not understand how there could be an uprising. Elie spoke to me, "It is not your duty to participate in the demonstration." Truth be told I did not believe what Elie was telling us. Then he paused for a while before saying, "The Socialist Camp will collapse. There will also be big changes in the Soviet Union and some of the other Eastern European countries in the years to come."

My Consultation with Master Elie Hien Continues

The following day, Master Elie again sent Evelyne to bring me to his room. He explained that he wanted me to be clear about my life's mission. First, he asked me why I thought I had gotten cancer. I said, "Maybe it was because I worked too hard and never took care of myself." He shook his head and said, "No. You were meant to be a spiritual teacher in this lifetime, but you were never aware of this. Therefore, you were given cancer to change things. After you practiced qigong faithfully, you recovered very quickly and you enthusiastically began to spread qigong. You should know that your mission is even greater than that of your master." I was frightened by these words, for I would not even dare to think that way. He said, "You are going to live in the United States and teach qigong. You will teach in a medical school and train many qigong instructors. Do not be afraid. You are blessed, so just do your best. You will have a great influence on people in the West. After seeing me, there will be a big change in your life and in your work. Also, you need to get your younger daughter to the United States. It will influence your work if she stays alone in China." Then Master Elie Hien asked me to go to Paris to study with him. I told him it would be impossible, for I held a Chinese passport with a visa permitting me to visit only the United States. I would not be allowed to go to another country directly from the United States.

As we neared the end of our consultation, he reminded me that I should not participate in the demonstration that would happen in Beijing the following year. He said that if I did, I would be punished. He repeated the message; "Your mission will take place in the future. Later, you will return to China. At that time, China will be as lovely as a newborn baby, and you will contribute more to your country in your older age."

Master Elie Hien concluded our time together by telling me that Soaring Crane Qigong's origins were from the Blue Star. As a qigong form, he said it was very powerful and effective. This was the first time that I had ever heard mention of the Blue Star, so I had no idea as to what the Blue Star was. Later, I asked Master Zhao if he knew, and he too was unaware of the Blue Star.

Powerful Qigong Healings

Many of the students asked Master Zhao to give them qigong treatments, so he did. We spent one whole day with him treating the sick; they had many different kinds of disease. There was one woman who had a very peculiar health condition. Ever since birth, her body was half warm and half cold. She had never felt what others described as normal temperature. While she had visited many doctors in several different countries, there had been no cure. After she explained her case to Master Zhao, he explained to me, "This kind of condition is termed 'yin yang person' in Chinese." Never before had I heard of this term. Then the Master asked the woman to lie face down on the massage table. First he felt the qi from both sides of her back and told me to feel the different temperature of the two sides. It was so obvious that one side of her body was cold and the other was warm to the touch. The Master used his hand to 'chase' the qi from the right side to the left side and did the same from the left to the right. The patient was very sensitive to the qi and said that she could feel the cold side was becoming warmer, bit-by-bit. After moving his hand across her body for about ten minutes, the Master then pressed his thumbs along her spine and said, "Now I am sealing the spine with my qi so that the cold side will not return to cold again." When the patient got off the table, she hugged Master Zhao and said, "I have never felt so comfortable in my life. Thank you, Master!"

The students were amazed to see the effectiveness of the healing and hoped that someday they could do the same. Master Zhao encouraged them saying, "Everybody has healing power. You can heal yourself through constant practice of qigong and you can cultivate your ability to heal others through qigong practice as well. When you have accumulated enough energy and have learned the healing techniques, you can treat others. But, in Chinese, we have a saying, 'Train the soldiers for a thousand days, but use them only one hour.' It means that you should not use your qi to heal others unless it is absolutely necessary. Qi is a treasure of the body. A good circulation of qi leads to a good circulation of blood; a good circulation of blood guarantees good health." Master Zhao had been very sick in his youth and had healed himself with diligent qigong practice. And now as an adult he had proven to be a very good healer of others.

These healing treatments were the first opportunity for me to watch Master Zhao giving qi treatments to patients. As his translator I was standing close to him all the time. I was very curious about qi healing and I focused intently on what he was doing throughout the day. By the end of the treatments, I was feeling nauseous and quite dizzy. One evening, after the qigong treatments, we were invited by the patients out to a restaurant for dinner. But, I was feeling too sick and I excused myself from joining them. They left, and that was when it occurred to me that I must have absorbed the diseased qi from the patients. As a remedy, I began to do the standing meditation of Level 2 of Soaring Crane Qigong. Oh, my god! The spontaneous movements that came up seemed violent and uncontrollable. I jumped high; I rolled on the floor; I kicked my legs; and I swung my arms like crazy. I never had that kind of strong movements before, in all the years of my qigong practice. Half an hour later, the movements came to a stop. I was myself again; I felt that all the diseased qi had left me. I was light and happy, but also very hungry. Alas, no one was around to take me to the restaurant! But, I had resolved to go to bed on an empty stomach: once in a while would be good for my health. So I did.

The New York City Workshop

The ten days in Germantown went by quickly and all the students were very happy with the workshop. Master Zhao certified some of the advanced students to be teachers of Soaring Crane Qigong, making them the first group of instructors trained in the United States. Students and teachers wore specially designed light blue T-shirts with 'Soaring Crane Qigong' in bright red lettering on the front. There was singing and dancing at the farewell party. And everyone was very thankful for Judy's wonderful efforts as the organizer.

Master Zhao and I headed off to New York City to stay with Wu, Yi and Shen, Rong Er at their home in Queens. There was a big welcome meeting planned with hundreds of people scheduled to participate. But before then, we had one day free for sightseeing. Shen, Rong Er and her student named Michael Oruch took Master Zhao and I to visit the Statue of Liberty. Shen, Rong Er was sitting opposite Master Zhao on the ferry and Michael sat facing me. We were happy and delighted to be talking so freely to one another. In the midst of our conversation, Master Zhao suddenly said loudly, "Stop talking! Receive message!" We were at a loss and could not understand what he meant. Quickly he took a small notebook and a pen from his pocket and started to write as if he were receiving dictation. As I sat next to him, I just stared at his face not knowing what to do. During the whole process, I felt a strong vibration coming into the top of my head, but I did not hear anything. About five minutes later, Master Zhao stopped writing and said in relief, "That's it!" We asked him in unison, "What is *it*?" He said with a broad smile, "The Statue of Liberty sent me a message." We all turned at once to look at the statue off in distance. Then he continued, "The message is a draft of the speech I am to deliver at the welcome meeting tomorrow." He read it out to us in Mandarin, of course, and asked me to get the translation prepared. The major theme was: "I am from China; I am an ordinary Chinese man. And I have come to this country to teach qigong, which is both old and new. It is very beneficial to both health and spirituality. Qigong is a most advanced science. People have not realized the importance of qigong yet, but they will in future. We should bring together as many people as possible to promote qigong. Additionally, we hope scientists and medical doctors will pay attention to this new science. Qigong will help raise people's consciousness. There may be difficulties in spreading qigong but all difficulties will be overcome!" The next day, Master Zhao read his "received" message word for word without changing anything. It was a very powerful short speech that won warm applause at the meeting in New York City.

This "receiving" event led me into deep thought. The Statue of Liberty was made of bronze, so how could she talk? I thought, maybe she had been standing in the water with her crown pointing to the heavens for more than two hundred years and had become an antenna. Master Zhao said the voice came from a high intelligence that chose the Statue of Liberty to channel the message. That made sense. I once had a similar experience back in China while I was sitting under a tree. But, that message was about an illegal affair between a girl and a married man. At first I felt strong vibrations coming into my head like telegram signals and then a voice telling me his name. Also, I had many people telling me that they had received messages, seemingly from nowhere. Master Zhao explained that not all messages were useful; some of them were helpful and some were not. He had advised me to ignore those that might bring me trouble–such as the one I got while sitting under the tree.

The workshops in New York City were very challenging. There were just too many people. In one of the workshops, the organizer had to call the police to come so they could keep order. It made for very difficult teaching conditions and the participants were not happy with the results. However, the word "qigong" had begun to circulate among the residents in the neighborhood.

Off to Alaska

Following the workshops in New York, we flew to Fairbanks, Alaska on a trip scheduled by Judith Haber. It was summertime. As we flew over Alaska, I saw chains of snow-covered mountains with glaciers between them. There were small ponds and lakes on some of the mountaintops, even a few swans swimming peacefully in the clear blue water. It was a heavenly sight! My heart was filled with joy. When I was a child, I read a lot about Alaska and the Eskimos. I had always hoped that at some time in my life I could visit Alaska. And here I was, heading into this wonderful and mysterious land.

A very kind couple, Gland and Sat Dharam, hosted Master Zhao and me. Their house sat atop a mountain with lots of trees surrounding it. During the summer, there were 22 hours of daylight with only two hours of night time where the sky was dark gray, never getting fully dark outside. We had to draw the window curtains in order to sleep during the night.

Master Zhao lecturing in Fairbanks, Alaska (1988)

On the first morning of our arrival, I got up very early and went out into the woods. It was silent as I stood on the edge of the hill and looked far down to the city of Fairbanks. Green trees and colorful wild flowers surrounded me. Down the valley, there were a few houses scattered here and there. It seemed to me that I was far removed from the real world. Suddenly, I heard the howling of an animal. Since the sound came from far away, I was not terrified at what sounded like the crying call of a wolf. Instead I felt lucky that I had actually heard the voice of a wild wolf. As I ran through the woods, I picked beautiful wild flowers and made a wreath, which I wore on my head. It felt as if I had returned to my childhood.

The Fairbanks workshop began with just eight students. We practiced in the front yard of the couple's house. Most of the students had done spiritual practice for a long time and therefore it was very easy for them to learn qigong. As a result, the teaching went smoothly.

Jeff, one of the students, was very knowledgeable. On the first day after the workshop, he took us to visit the gold mine where he worked. It was an unforgettable trip. Then after the workshop on the second day, he gave us the special treat of flying us to the North Pole in his small plane. What a fantastic experience! I had never ridden in such a small plane; it held four people, including the pilot. We flew low so that we could see the snow very clearly. As he flew the plane Jeff, acting as our tour guide, pointed to a gaping hole in the side of a snow-covered mountain and said, "See that big hole there? Nobody knows what's inside. Nobody dares to enter it." Out of curiosity, and without telling us, Master Zhao used his extrasensory power and "went into it". All of a sudden, I found that his head was lowered and he had fallen asleep. I wondered what was happening to him so I patted him hard on the shoulder to wake him up. I thought it would be a pity for him to miss all the beautiful views. He woke up with a start and said with a deep sigh, "Oh, thank you! You know what? I sent energy out of my body into that hole trying to discover what might be inside. But, a strong force took hold of me and I was terrified and could not pull myself back. When you gave me a hard pat, it brought me back. You saved me! I can hardly imagine what would have happened to me, if I had been dragged deeper into that black hole. I really do not know what that force was."

On the third day of our visit, during our nap-time, I was meditating in my room when I heard a loud nervous call, "Chen, Hui Xian, come here!" The call came from Master Zhao's room across the corridor. I rushed into his room and asked, "What happened?" He asked me, "Who is Kazan?" He had pronounced the word Kazan in perfect English. I answered without thinking, "He was a god in Greek Mythology." I had no idea how I had gotten this information.

Then, pointing his hand at the sky above the hill outside he said, "He came to me a moment ago. He has blonde hair and a beard; a very handsome man in his late thirties. He was standing in the clouds and asked me, 'Who are you?' I answered, 'I am Zhao, Jin Xiang.' Sternly he asked me, 'What are you doing here?' 'I am here to teach qigong.' I replied. Then he quizzed me again, 'What is qigong for?' I answered, 'Qigong is for health.' Kazan shook his head and said, 'No.' So, I quickly added, 'Also, it is for the spirit.' Kazan nodded and said, 'Right! Now, listen! Alaska is a sacred place. You should spread qigong from here to the whole world. Therefore, you should choose five of the students from your class, now, to be your disciples and to establish a qigong organization here.' He also told me the names of the five students." Then Master Zhao repeated their names in English. It was only the third day of our workshop and in the past Master Zhao had never bothered to memorize the names of the American students. Since he did not know any English at all, I was very surprised that he could tell me the five names in perfect English. Then Master Zhao asked me, "What am I going to do? I have never taken beginners as my disciples before, and Kazan wants me to take these five students out of eight?!" My advice to Master Zhao was, "Just do it."

Before the workshop came to an end, Master Zhao had individual talks with each of the five selected students and had accepted them as his disciples. While some individuals felt they were not quite ready at first, eventually they all agreed.

One afternoon, Master Zhao channeled for the five disciples all that they needed to do. He told us that some information was from Guan Yin Bodhisattva, the Buddhist God of Compassion, and some was from a god whom he did not know. Master Zhao described this god as wearing a loose white gong with a rope tied around his waist. He had long blonde hair and a beard; he was barefoot." We agreed it must have been Jesus.

After seeing the snowy mountains and glaciers, I still wanted to see the northern lights. So, I asked our host to wake me up if the northern lights were out. He understood my curiosity and purposely stayed up late. On the third night he woke me up and I covered myself with a thick overcoat and ran out into the front yard. Wow! In the darkness, I saw a large pale light moving slowly across the sky. It was the first time in my life that I witnessed the northern lights. It was fantastic! Two nights later, I was awakened again and the sky was even more beautifully lit up.

There were two very large sections of different colored lights–pink, light blue and faint yellow. For a long time, they looked like light angels floating in the night sky. I was so excited and happy! My childhood dreams of seeing Alaska had been fulfilled.

One evening after teaching, I was taken to a local fair. To my delight, I saw Eskimos for the first time. I also learned that the people I call Eskimos are actually called Inuit. Of course, I had imagined that all Inuit would look like what I saw in books. They were wearing fur hats, thick fur coats, and large fur gloves in the pictures. But, the Inuit I saw at the fair that day wore very fancy dresses and hats. They were so polite and kind to me, some of them even said that I looked very much like them. Yes, it was true. A student had given me an Inuit dress and a pair of shoes during my visit to Alaska. I immediately put them on and everybody around said that I looked just like a native.

Another unusual thing that I saw in Alaska was the many small planes that were parked out in the open. People said that planes were more convenient to use in Alaska than cars because of the mountains and the lack of roads. While it was a short visit in Alaska, it left such a deep impression that I decided I would come back again. Actually, Alaska was the most beautiful among all the places that we had visited during our trip to America. Before we left for home, Master Zhao told the Alaska students to establish a qigong association. And I asked Jeff, "Could you do me a favor and get more information about Kazan?" "I'll try," Jeff replied.

A Visit from Guan Yin Boddhisattva

On our way back to Beijing, we had a layover at the Tokyo airport. Both Master Zhao and I felt happy and relaxed after the month-long visit in the United States. The time spent there had been very successful and fruitful. A large number of students had learned Soaring Crane Qigong, and we had helped many sick people recover with qigong healing. It was a bonus for us to have visited so many wonderful places in such a beautiful country.

After sharing a delicious Japanese dinner together, we talked a while and then went to our rooms to rest. I was really tired, so I went to bed early. At midnight, I suddenly awoke for no reason. I could not open my eyes; it seemed as if they were being forced shut. Suddenly, I saw Guan Yin Bodhisattva[20] flying towards me. Her pure white silk gong was accented with beautiful jewels encircling her hair, which was knotted on top of her head. She was radiant with a loving light. Her right hand shaped a *mudra*[21] with the index finger pointing up, the little finger stretched out, and the other fingers joined together. Her left hand, also in a *mudra*, was placed under the right elbow, with the palm facing up. It was not just one Bodhisattva. There was a long row of the same figure, each smaller than the previous one. My sense was that Guan Yin Bodhisattva had come to teach me something. However, at the same time, I was aware that I was lying in bed. It occurred to me that it was not proper for me to meet Guan Yin Bodhisattva in this disrespectful manner. I sat up and threw a jacket over my shoulders. Alas! The vision was gone. I had no idea why she left so suddenly.

The next morning, I told Master Zhao about my late night event. He cast a very stern look at me and said, "Stupid! You should not move when you receive a spiritual message." I murmured, "I never knew that!" Master Zhao told me. "Guan Yin Bodhisattva did come last night. She gave me a 'pearl'." I understood that he meant to say he received an "energy ball" from Guan Yin. I believed that Guan Yin must be happy with what we had done during our visit in the United States. Since that unforgettable night, the image of the beautiful Guan Yin Bodhisattva remains in my mind; I believe she will forever.

---

[20] A Hindu Goddess of Compassion
[21] A symbolic gesture of deep meaning

Soaring Crane Qigong Pioneers the Way

Upon our return to Beijing, there were many large meetings held to welcome us as we reported to the qigong community about our wonderful experiences. Many articles about our visit appeared in the newspapers and magazines both in China and abroad. The following is an excerpt that was published in the November 1988 issue of Qigong Magazine in the United States.

SOARING CRANES BRING
PEACE & PROSPERITY
by Wang, Ning

In the early 1980s, the sunspots exploded and substances of high energy were produced, making a tremendous force that brought about some significant changes in the universe. Nine hundred soaring cranes, the biggest flock ever seen in the world, landed and settled down in China. This is symbolic of the upcoming peace and prosperity of mankind at large. Chinese Soaring Crane Qigong, now in maturity, made its emergence on November 19, 1980.

Included in Chinese Soaring Crane Qigong are Five Routines, Eight Remedy Routines, Standing Meditation, Sitting Meditation and Crane Walking Steps. When it was brought to light, Chinese Soaring Crane Qigong became popular and highly esteemed by people from all walks of life because it is easy to learn. In a short time, one could gain the energy, clean the channels and bring about the latent powers from the brain.

In China and abroad, Chinese Soaring Crane Qigong soon came to be a good approach for people to get rid of their diseases, better their health, and tap their wisdom.

ZHAO, JIN XIANG
AND CHINESE SOARING CRAIN QIGONG

The creation and widespread of Chinese Soaring Crane Qigong are inseparable from its originator, Master Zhao, Jin Xiang. Master Zhao was born into a peasant family at Ling County, Hebei Province. His kinfolks and neighbors were good at Qigong and martial arts and his father could give treatment by acupuncture and point pressure. Gifted as he was and influenced by traditional culture, Zhao had unswerving belief in Qigong since his childhood.

When he had a job in 1953, Zhao began to suffer from chronic infiltrative pulmonary tuberculosis due to overwork. Later, his suffering worsened to chronic fibro-cavitative tuberculosis and no medicine whatsoever could heal him. Master Zhao, at his weakest, was sent to Beidaihe Sanatorium for recovery. Apart from conventional medical care, he was taught some kind of sitting meditation. In addition, he threw himself into the study of traditional Chinese medicine and even prescribed for himself. As a result, his TB was gone.

On his way home in 1971, the Master happened to meet an old man on the train who initiated him and taught him some mysterious qigong. This senior had attained a high degree of perfection in Qigong. Guided by the forerunner, Zhao brushed himself up to a high level of Integral Qigong.

Having been told about his mission and at the sight of the painful sufferers and helpless relatives, the survived Master, sympathetic to their sufferings, felt it his duty to help them. As he was deep in the study of China's ancient qigong and the theory of traditional Chinese medicine, he was encouraged to do his best to promote qigong and bring it into full swing.

Soon, Master Zhao created the Chinese Soaring Crane Qigong–a set of movements that embodies the movements of the sacred cranes with a basis of ancient and modern qigong and traditional Chinese medicine.

To make it a widespread exercise in China, Zhao dedicated every bit of his hard-working life. During the years after the birth of the unique exercises, the originator could often be seen sharing his experiences here and there, south and north of the Yang Tze River, or in almost every province of the country.

Thanks to his teachings and strict demand, a large number of accomplished coaches are at work laying a sound foundation for the popularization of Chinese Soaring Crane Qigong. Under his guidance, coaching centers and research institutions have been set up in many of the cities and provinces in China for promoting qigong in general, and Chinese Soaring Crane Qigong in particular.

In April 1986, the book Chinese Soaring Crane Qigong by Zhao, Jin Xiang was among the best sellers in China. His books standardized Soaring Crane routines, telling how one's disease is replaced with sound health

Requested by the Association of Soaring Crane Qigong of America, Zhao, Jin Xiang went to the United States for a short visit in July 1988. During his visit, classes were held in New York, Alaska and San Francisco, and lectures followed by performances were given in answer to the invitation of the U.N. Research Institute of Qigong, Institute on Yoga, and Institute of Telepathy. Chinese Soaring Crane Qigong, treasure of oriental culture, now began to send off its splendors in a foreign land.

Experience was exchanged between Masters from different countries and friendships promoted among different nationalities. This paved the way for unity among qigong researchers and routine originators of different countries.

Master Zhao, Jin Xiang, presently a faculty member of the University of International Business and Economics in Beijing, is making strenuous efforts for peace and prosperity so that someday his wish will come true: "The cranes are soaring into the sky for the happiness of mankind."

Integral Qigong

Chinese Soaring Crane Qigong, belonging to the scope of Life Gong, is step one of integral qigong. Integral qigong is the type of qigong that will enable one, after years spent doing it, to possess the sort of qi that results in health improvement, wisdom tapping and enabling the human body to communicate with the universe. Integral qi passes through each of the veins, arteries and internal organs thus cleansing all the channels and the internal organs. Soaring Crane Qigong has been proven, through the practice of millions of people, to be very effective in curing diseases and maintaining the balance of Yin and Yang qi in the human body, the microcosm.

In the scope of Life Gong, Chinese Soaring Crane Qigong helps bring about good health by way of opening and closing the vital points, cleaning the channels, enriching the vital energy and combing the two qi, Yin and Yang, in the human body so that the vital energy travels through the body freely, laying a solid foundation for communication between the human body and the universe.

The same Qigong Magazine also carried my article published in a Chinese magazine, which was then translated by Mr. Wang, Ning. You might find it interesting.

CHINA'S QIGONG BENEFITS AMERICA
by Chen, Hui Xian

There is a call from America. At the request of the Soaring Crane Qigong Association of the United States, the University of International Business and Economics in Beijing sent Master Zhao, Jin Xiang and me to the U.S. for the flow of information and culture between the two countries.

At 4:30 pm on June 30 1988, the Japanese airliner, carrying the two of us among its passengers, rose into the sky. Master Zhao, in tears, was looking out of the window and I could not calm down because of the waving hands and cheerful faces minutes earlier.

The following day, we were on our way to New York. On the plane, Master Zhao handed me a sheet of paper that said:

These points should be made clear during our visit:

1. *Qigong is a top skill in modern science.*
2. *Originators and researchers of qigong all over the world should work together for its improvement.*
3. *Qigong benefits mankind by defeating diseases.*

"Wonderful!" I said, "Let's do a good job."

It was midday on July 1 when we arrived in New York. At the airport to meet us were Mrs. Judith Haber, the president of Soaring Crane Qigong Association of the United States, Mr. Wu, Yi, head of the Association, Madam Shen, Rong Er, a qigong teacher and some others. They came up to meet us shaking hands and hugging us: "You are here at last! Welcome to New York!" Large bouquets of flowers were presented and photos were taken.

After a while, Mrs. Judith Haber drove us to Germantown, a beautiful little town in the suburb where we stayed and taught qigong. Mrs. Judith Haber's mansion was huge with a two-story house and several flats for guests on the sides of a spacious green lawn surrounded by tall old walnut trees. Down the slope, there was a swimming pool.

Around 60 students had already arrived. Some stayed in the guest rooms and some rented rooms in town. Most of them were from different parts of the United States, but some were from Germany, Belgium and France.

The next day, we began our first class. Mr. Wu, Yi and his wife Shen, Rong Er, had already trained the students. They were there for advanced training. At noontime, a special guest came from Paris. Mrs. Judith Haber and Ms. Evelyne Jankovsky had invited him. His name is Elie Hien. He is a master from West Africa. He said he could be a good help to Master Zhao and wanted to learn Chinese qigong in order to teach his country folks. He believes that the ancient Chinese culture will convince the world philosophically in the days to come.

As it was too hot for training, the African master spent the whole afternoon in his room meditating to manipulate the weather, and to our great surprise, he maneuvered a rain that evening. He promised that it would be getting cool and we would be free from traffic accidents. For ten days he defined himself as a weather manipulator and we had a pleasant cool time: rainy nights and shiny days.

To celebrate the close of our first class, the warm-hearted Elie Hien held a ceremony of West African style and foretold a coming rain. He is as true as sunrise. From doubt to belief, the happy dancers and singers around the bonfires were showered by a sudden thunderstorm amid the highlights of the celebration and they knew they had a Master who maneuvers the weather.

After we waved our goodbye to our dear admired African Master, we began our second class. As most of the students work in medicine, they believe qigong is an approach to keeping fit and refreshing one's mind. Unlike those in the first class who are healthy as a result of their past training, some trainees in the second class suffer from chronic diseases.

Actually some were also there for treatment. For instance, a girl, named Eva, suffered from uneven temperatures in the body. Half of it is warm, while the other half, cold. She had been to many famous doctors the world over, but none of them could relieve her of this trouble and she was in despair.

When she came to Master Zhao for help, she was told that the Yin qi and Yang qi in her body were out of balance, and it was difficult to put them in order. Then the master raised his hands as if to get a sort of force from the air and in a peculiar gesture, he transferred it into the troubled body as if to mix up the different qi within.

Soon after, he began to feel along the junction line between the two halves of her body, left and right, to make up for the strip of crack, it seemed. Before long, Eva exclaimed, "Good heavens! I feel warm all over now." There was no one happier in the whole of America.

Another student, Maureen, had a story that may interest you all the more. On the plane heading for New York, Master Zhao told me that he would see a slim, good-looking woman in his class. Yet, she never appeared. On the third day, however, the foreseen woman came up because of a message sent to her by telepathy from the master. She said she would have given it up had it not been for a dream that led her there. For months, she said, there seemed to be a sort of force that made her write for a couple of hours each morning. She was writing about the relationship between the human body and the universe, and how it could be interpreted in physics and chemistry. What interested Maureen more was the broad light belt she saw flowing from the master to herself during his treatment on her. She felt fresh and relaxed. Never before had she had a better feeling.

Many students covered thousands of miles to reach us for a gleam of hope. They did not come in vain; training or treatment improved their health and depression gave way to optimism. When they left, some could not control their tears.

At the United Nations, Master Zhao made a speech on Integral qigong. The listeners were from America, England, Canada, India and other countries. I was also asked to give a talk on the benefits I gained through qigong practice. When I told them that I had survived my deadly disease through qigong, applause resounded the hall.

The master was requested to show some of his extrasensory abilities, he said that it is not the major thing to achieve through qigong practice, but for fun he demonstrated before the public: "Odor removal." First, he brought strong sandalwood smell from a sandalwood Buddha in the Lama temple in Beijing. The people present cheered when they smelt it. Then he was asked to bring the rose smell from a rose garden in Paris. Everyone was astonished when the master waved his hands and the room was filled with sweet rose fragrance! The master had never heard of any rose garden in Paris, to say nothing of having been there. He told the publisher that he only used his imagination.

But, that is not all. When everyone was too sleepy to follow the talk in the hot afternoon, the master joked, "Let me bring some cool air from the North Pole." Yes, after a few movements of his hands towards the north, the crowd cheered for the cool room. They were delighted to hear there is potential in every one and qigong can help bring it out.

When we were about to leave New York, we had a long-distance call from Howard, a student of the second class, saying that he happened to find out there is the International Crane Foundation in Wisconsin. Howard invited us to go see the farm with him, and we would not miss it for the world.

During the break between trainings, we flew to our Wisconsin destination. We were driven to the farm and greeted by Mr. Archibald, the director of the foundation. In his youth, Mr. Archibald learned that the world's rare cranes faced the danger of extinction. As if by instinct, the bird lover began to save the poor cranes by raising them with one of his fellow students on the farm offered by the latter's father. Year in and year out, the two helped their cause by collecting all the 15 species of cranes in the world for breeding, or hatching the young ones. Afterwards, they returned the grownups in pairs to their homelands for more breeding. Thus, they won support from institutions of various countries and developed their business further. When we learned all the stories, we could not help but nod admirably. After a while, Mr. Archibald went on to introduce the origin and character of each of his dear cranes and we listened with great interest.

To remember his day in a world of sacred birds, Master Zhao had a few photos taken in his movement, "crane touching the water," before a big beautiful bird with its fellow companions. When we turned our eyes to the rest of them, the remaining 14 species, we seemed to be in a picture of colorful cranes.

Those in light gray with a red crown looked attractive, and the ones with a white-neck leading a gray body are a fascination because of a piece of pink skin on the upper part of their bills. A few of those cranes, black-billed and white feathered, attracted my special attention. Those in light blue color kept their visitors in forgetful silence. The more we enjoyed looking at them, the more we were reluctant to leave.

A few steps onward, we were almost struck by the sight of a few pheasants in bright colors moving about in the world of cranes. To match the miscellaneous colors of the feather that covered the body, each of the beautiful birds had a red neck, and a black forehead heading a gold-colored fan-like crest. Surely they stayed at a wrong home!

Our observant host quickly put us at ease by saying that they were cranes of a small species, the most beautiful of all the species. Then some loud calls from among them pleased us so much that Master Zhao had them recorded for listening pleasure.

Also, you may find it interesting to learn about a pair of cranes from cold Siberia, who lived together for years in the same cage without ever mating. Everyone's curiosity was aroused, from the director to his colleagues. They made a special trip to the homeland of these two birds and found out that they were brother and sister. The curious people could only marvel at the loftiness of the heavenly birds.

After 40 busy days on the outskirts and inside New York City, August 10th saw us at Fairbanks in Alaska, one third of America's territory. People often think that

Alaska is a snow-clad land all year round. True, you can have a splendid view of the icy rivers and snowy mountain chains up and down from a passing plane, but flowers come into bloom and green willows can be seen along the roadside from May to September.

On either side of the Fairbanks airport, a huge specimen greets you to the cold town. The polar bear suggests that the North Pole is not far off and the reindeer, ten times larger, is a prey of the Inuit. The prey, often in crowds 200 miles off town, can be hunted legally only by the Inuit, provided that prayers are said before hunting and ceremony is held before eating.

Among those at the airport to meet us was Sat Dharam, our landlady, who lived in a two-story house enclosed by forest up on the mountains. When we looked out at the far side of the mountains from her home, the beauty of nature overwhelmed us. Next morning, I exercised out of the house. Mountain air and hollow echo relieved me of my bustling urban life, whereas the picturesque scenery around accompanied by occasional roars of distant animals told me of Mother Nature, into whose embrace I fell.

In Alaska, we had eight clever hard-working students, most of whom had studied some ancient philosophy and basic Chinese medicine. They came to feed themselves with more Chinese exercise and they all made fast progress.

Often during training, the hospitable native cranes flew across calling aloud and flapping their wings to beckon us to follow them home. When we went for a visit at a reaped wheat field one day, hundreds of small brown cranes greeted their guests. We loved Fairbanks; Fairbanks is a crane town.

A student named Jeff impressed us greatly. He is a shareholder in a gold mine and contributed a large sum to a sanatorium, while leading a simple life himself. That is an example to follow. To enrich our tour, Jeff flew us in his private 4-seat airplane to places in Alaska where no human being has ever set foot. Down below in full view were the petroleum pumping stations and the missile base; miles of marshes serve as paradise for pairs and pairs of lovemaking swans. But how are animals able to live in the wilderness! When we were within the North Pole circle, a day to remember, gleaming glaciers in the valleys between the silent snow-covered mountains looked up towards us.

The daylight keeps North Poler's awake for a long time, from 4 am to 11 pm and the gray night leads them into dream in the few remaining hours. In the daytime, the Northern lights appear from October to April, almost a span of long nights, that you do not believe your eyes before the prodigy of the universe.

All eight of the students worked perfectly well. The Chinese Master, for his part, looked into every little improvement they made, gave talks on the theory, discipline and merits that a trainee should be qualified with. At the end of the class, they all expressed that qigong was a turning point in their lives. Upon leaving, tears rolled down the cheeks of the women. The qigong spark is there and a prairie fire of qigong will roar across Alaska in no time.

The famous city of San Francisco did not keep us for more than a few days. The visit to the United States was during our summer vacation, but the master had no time to see a museum or tour around New York. The only spot of interest that will remind him of his USA days is the Statue of Liberty. His days there can be counted but his merit, not.

Now, it is time to say goodbye to the 60 and more trainees, to the audience of 400 listeners who attended the talks by Master Zhao during our stay, to the lovely cranes on the marshes in Fairbanks, and to the United States of America.

Let us say goodbye once again to the hospitable land along with all who treated us as their best friends. Let us expect that the day will come when more cranes will soar all over the world from America to bring about a longer healthier life for mankind.

I Was Introduced to Master Liang, Guang Hua

In China there were a large number of qigong magazines and articles printed in the late 1980's, and I read almost all of them. One day, I came across an article about a master from Harbin, which is in northeast China. I was fascinated by the stories. His name was Liang, Guang Hua, and he was the originator of Awakening Light Gong. Master Liang and his form were new to me, but I was very much touched by his virtue and the good deeds he had done for people.

Master Liang, Guang Hua

It was reported in the qigong magazine that there was a boy about ten years old who was a deaf-mute. Frequently the boy begged by the side of the road in the city of Harbin. One day, Master Liang happened to pass by. When he saw the little boy, he immediately gave him all of the coins that he had. The boy thanked him by making gestures with his hands. Master Liang realized that this boy could neither hear nor speak, so he gave him a treatment right away. The next day, Master Liang came again and gave him another treatment. After several days and several treatments, the boy could hear a few sounds and then later he could hear people talking.

Since this boy had been born deaf and mute, he was very much surprised to experience the new phenomena of sounds. He got so excited that he wanted to express his joy to everyone he saw. People who often passed by noticed the change in him and began to ask him what had happened. Because he had never been able to speak, he could not explain it to them. Master Liang continued to visit this boy and began to teach him some simple words. Word that the deaf-mute boy could speak was surprising and the news spread very fast in the neighborhood. Newspaper reporters interviewed Master Liang, but he did not say much about it, just that it was what he needed to do. Many people were not really surprised by the great power of the master because many Awakening Light Gong practitioners had already experienced it. People were very much touched by his love and compassion for the boy. In Harbin as talk about Master

Liang's virtues increased, more people went to listen to the Master's lectures and to learn Awakening Light Gong.

After I read this story, I talked a lot about this master to my qigong students at the University of International Business and Economics in Beijing. At that time, we had a qigong office at the university and many university students studied qigong. One afternoon, when I was again sharing the story with students, one postgraduate student named Liu, Yu asked me, "Are you talking about Master Liang, Guang Hua in Harbin?" Excitedly I replied, "Yes, do you know him?" Liu, Yu smiled sweetly and said, "He is my father-in-law!"

Hearing this, I was overjoyed and asked her to introduce me to Master Liang. Very soon, she connected me with the master and we began to communicate by phone. I found Master Liang very humble and patient. He never tired of answering my many questions, and we established a good friendship. However, I did not have the time to go to visit him in Harbin. Instead Master Liang sent me materials about Awakening Light Gong so I spent a lot of time reading them. Strongly sensing that Awakening Light Gong was a good form, I was determined to study with him when the right time came.

A Letter Arrives from Alaska

A year after Master Zhao and I had returned to China, I was in the qigong office when I was handed a letter that had been sent from Alaska. It was from Kay J. Kennedy who was a friend of Jeff's. In her late eighties, she was among the very first newspaper reporters in Alaska, and she was very knowledgeable and wise. She had sent me information, which she had researched about Kazan.

KA-SAN—KA-ZAN—KI-ZEN

Each indigenous society has recorded its own unique legend and pronunciation of Ka-San. However, as so often happens, the story behind the legend seems to have common ground. From the tombs of ancient Egypt to the Mayan ruins, evidence of Ka-San has been unearthed.

From the steppes of Russia through Siberia to the high reaches of Himalaya's, the same legend is contributed to Ka-Zan. In China's most ancient records Ki-Zen played a significant role. Historians have failed to give any significance to these legends, allowing this rich source of ancient knowledge to be entwined in moldy cobwebs, only to be resurrected through the psyche.

Some of the legendary meanings that come to mind:

KA	SAN
Cosmic	*Nature (natural)*
Male	*Female*
Light	*Life Force*
Spiritual Force	*Fertility*
Dormant	*Growing*
Winter	*Summer*

A pre-Zarathustrian, Sumerian legend has KA coming from one planetary system, SAN from another. They meet to materialize on earth in cultures, which had lost the secret of soil fertility (light) and right living.

A book found mostly in archives entitled, "The Kazonian Period" (unknown author, printed source) deals with the rejuvenation of the earth after the Last cataclysmic event.

Currently a number of spiritualists and psychics claim to have received messages from Ka Zan who takes care of the areas from the Himalayan ranges to the Alps.

Excitedly reading the information, I immediately translated it into Chinese for Master Zhao who was also in the qigong office. After he read the translation, he was very happy and said, "You see, Kazan is a god; he did come to me."

All the spiritual events that happened during our visit to the United States put me deep in thought. From a doubter to a believer, gradually I came to understand that I had been blind about the true face of the universe. Owing to my Chinese education, my ignorant mind always rejected this kind of phenomena, it was all "just superstition".

Born in a Christian family, I often went to the Bible school on Sundays when I was very young. After listening to the stories about Jesus, I loved him because he sacrificed his life for other people's benefit. But, I never really believed the priest's description that an all-powerful God created the universe. I thought the universe just existed forever on its own. After the Communists took over the state power, I stopped going to the church and accepted Marxism. However, by nature, I loved mythology. I read many fairy tales, both Chinese and foreign. I liked to relate them to friends because children's fairy tales all carry good messages. When I became a teacher, I often selected fairy tales as teaching materials. It was my thought that religions and their teachings were to educate people to be good, to be compassionate, to be generous and to be helpful so that this world will become a place of harmony and happiness. During my life, I have tried hard to be a good person. I never believed that a soul would exist forever or there would be any other planes existing in the universe. But the experiences I have had since I started qigong practice, have opened my mind and given me great encouragement along my spiritual path. The fantastic experiences I have had were glimpses of the spiritual world that truly exists. Apart from purifying my thoughts, overcoming my shortcomings and doing good things for others, I was also interested in the discoveries of unknown secrets in the universe. I even read reports about UFO's, as I am by nature a person full of imagination and curiosity; I want to know more about the universe and I try to always keep an open mind to new experiences.

Science is a very small part in discovering the universe's secrets, for science has a very short history. How long is the history of the universe? How much more is there in the universe that mankind does not know? Religions have been dealing with the spiritual part of life by teaching people how to be good and science has been dealing with the material part of life. It seems high time that these two combine to benefit the world's people both physically and spiritually.

A Scheme to Punish Me

A few days later, as I was preparing for my flight to the United States in spring, 1990 to see my daughter Sha Sha in California, I was suddenly summoned to an office at the university. When I entered the room, there sat three leaders looking very serious. "What's up?" I asked. One of them showed me a piece of paper as he said, "We have received a letter from the American Graduate School of International Management in Arizona. The letter says you cheated their school out of two thousand dollars." Upon hearing this, I burst into tears as I shouted, "What!? I never did anything like that. I worked very hard to foster the relationship between our university and their school. Why would they wrong me that way?"

One of the leaders, a man who had retired from the People's Liberation Army and worked in our Personnel Department shouted back at me, "If you do not admit your mistake, you will not be permitted to go abroad." Grabbing my purse, I took out my passport and the plane ticket and threw them in front of him. "I am a good citizen of China; I have never done anything criminal. You think you dare to stop me from going abroad? Here is my plane ticket for the day after tomorrow; you take care of returning the ticket." Letting the door bang behind me, I was furious as I left the office. I was especially angry with the People's Liberation Army retiree. His attitude strongly suggested that they were punishing me in a round-about way as if they thought of me as a reactionary.

Directly from the office, I went to President Sun's home to complain about what had happened. The president remained very calm as he spoke, "I have seen this letter from AGSIM. Truly they said that Professor Chen cheated their school out of two thousand dollars." I said, "Then you should have done some investigation before you talked to me. I do not even have a clue what they meant by their letter."

That night, I was so upset that I lay in bed crying. I was not only angry with them about this whole thing, I was angry over the whole political situation. It was ten months after the Tian An Men Event in 1989. Yet again, we intellectuals were treated badly. The next morning, I wanted to do my qigong but I could not even stand still. I felt very sick as if there was something wrong with my heart. Many of my colleagues came by to show their great concern for me and to comfort me saying, "They definitely wronged you. Nobody would believe that you would steal money. We all believe you." Then my qigong teacher, Master Zhang, Yu Lin, came to visit. He said severely. "I've heard about it; it is all your fault! You are angry because you are afraid of getting a bad name. You care too much about your fame. If you do not just think of yourself, what is there to worry about? Truth is truth. It will speak for itself." His sharp words woke me up, and I calmed down. But, I felt so bad. I could not fly to America so the ticket was returned and my visa was canceled. I had to stay home.

A week later, while I was out for a walk in the university garden, three leaders of our university approached me–the People's Liberation Army retiree was not with them. They stopped and said, "Professor Chen, we are sorry, we made a mistake. During our communication with AGSIM about this, they said it was not Professor Chen, Hui Xian. It was another Professor Chen who really did cheat their school out of two thousand dollars. The school also said, 'Professor Chen, Hui Xian's work was so good while she was here four years ago, that we would like to invite her back.' By this time, I was no longer angry, so I merely said, "Let by-gones be by-gones."

Spiritual Tests—One after Another

During those days, I became very depressed. On one occasion, I met a qigong friend of mine on campus, Pan, Jian Rong. He was much younger than me but he was spiritually very mature. He acknowledged me as a very devoted qigong practitioner and said that I had done much to spread qigong. But, he pointed out that I still lacked peace of mind. Both angry and jealous, I had gone through an unwanted divorce and to top it off, my ex-husband had a girlfriend. It was still very easy for me to get upset, even though I practiced qigong every single day. Jian Rong came almost every day to talk to me about the importance of tempering my heart. Even though the practice of qigong tempers the heart, the world is full of difficulties and hardships. Life is full of ups and downs. We are all spiritual beings on a human path. To be able to temper the heart while out in the real world is the very essence of qigong practice. Many Chinese qigong masters say we need to practice qigong 24 hours a day. What they mean is to keep a peaceful mind and heart all the time, no matter what happens. If we come to understand that our mission on this planet is to learn from life's challenges, we will face them with a smile. Together with Jian Rong, I studied a lot of spiritual teachings and he helped me greatly. As I poured out all the thoughts in my mind, he helped me analyze the problems, so that gradually, I learned how to maintain a peaceful mind.

It was during this time, that I had many visions. Prior to being fully awake one morning, an image appeared in written form stating, "For this week, you are not supposed to read anything, neither should you watch TV, or listen to the radio." Then before daybreak the next morning, another vision appeared. I saw my ex-husband holding his girlfriend as they stood on the Great Wall. When I saw them, I became furious and said to my ex-husband, "You told me that you divorced me because we have different personalities. Actually, you just wanted to find a younger woman." He cast a contemptuous glance my way and said, "So what!" That made me even angrier and suddenly the vision disappeared.

Later that day, I had a long talk with Jian Rong and he helped me realize that my anger came from my strong self-esteem. It was my belief that I was much better than many other women. Why should he have divorced me? After coming to understand the cause of my anger, I gradually calmed down.

At almost the same time the following morning, I had yet another vision. In it, I saw my first ex-husband and his wife together with my second ex-husband with his girlfriend, all were standing at the Great Wall. When they saw me, they all smiled. But, I did not become angry at all. This time my mind remained calm. I even assured myself in the vision, "You all go your way and I will go mine." As that vision ended, I felt completely free of the old emotions. Strange… there was no anger, no jealousy!

The spiritual tests continued though. A young man, Xiao Liu, was a very close disciple of Master Zhao. He came to me one day and asked if I would meditate with him in our university garden. My friend Professor Jiang was also there, so the three of us meditated together. In the middle of our deep meditation, Xiao Liu broke the silence by speaking in some kind of cosmic language. Then in Chinese he said out loud, "Chen, Hui Xian listen, I now speak in the name of the Buddha. You are being too proud. You should realize that you are only a layman wandering around the gate of Dao, yet you dared to criticize your master." So I spoke up and asked, "Could I talk back?" He responded, "Yes." I queried, "If a master has made some mistakes, could his disciple criticize him for the sake of helping him?" He stated, "You do not know him well enough." Then I said, "I did criticize him because I love qigong; I care about the master." To which he said, "I say that you are not qualified to criticize him. Think it over!" With that the meditation ended. Professor Jiang was frightened and condemned me, "How did you dare to talk to the Buddha like that?" I answered, "If the Heaven has no equality, I'd rather go to the Hell!" I added, "I don't care what happens to me. I will do whatever is right!"

Several weeks later, Xiao Liu returned to our university and requested that Professor Jiang and I go to the qigong office for a talk. First, he demonstrated some of his extrasensory powers, like collecting 'Healing powders' from the air. After that he said he wanted to talk to us individually. When my turn came, he was very serious as he spoke, "Professor Chen, do you know that the reason that I have come here frequently is especially to help you. You have a big mission to accomplish. But you should know that in this lifetime you alone cannot free yourself from the sea of bitterness. However, Master Zhao and I can do that for you. Therefore, you need to find ways for us to teach qigong in foreign countries."

270

Upon hearing this, a flow of blood rushed to my head. Emphatically, I responded, "No one can save me but myself. If you want me to help you, just say so frankly. In fact, I have been frank with you all the time." He was not prepared for such a sharp response. His face turned red and angrily he responded, "What a revolt!" It became obvious that he intended to use me. I forgave him though, for he was young, not highly educated and in a way, superstitious.

Several months later, I learned that Xiao Liu had had a recurrence of cancer. Previously, he had been diagnosed with stomach cancer. After practicing qigong, he got well and became very psychic, so Master Zhao had taken him as a disciple. Then Xiao Liu had gone back home to the countryside. When he became very sick, he returned to Beijing. Professor Jiang and I met him at the railway station and helped him get into a good hospital. We offered him money and brought him good food while he was hospitalized. One day when I was visiting him, he held my hand and said tearfully, "Professor Chen, I am sorry I tricked you before. I know I was wrong but I was told to do that to you." I responded, "I fully believe that there is the Buddha. There are thousands of super intelligent beings that are helping out humans and this planet. But, if someone misuses the faith to achieve an evil intention, it is a big mistake. Every person should always listen to his or her own conscience for our own conscience is our true master. Everybody has a conscience. Buddha was a conscious man." To our dismay, several months later, Xiao Liu died of cancer.

There was a heated debate among the qigong devotees during those days. Some said it was important to continue to spread qigong, because people needed it. Others said we should purify ourselves first, believing that only when we achieve enlightenment could we help others. Even some of my old friends criticized me for teaching qigong, saying that I was taking the wrong path. They advised me to stay at home and practice qigong. My belief was that our mission was to help other people, as well as to purify ourselves while doing work on our life journey. I told myself, "Go ahead and help others. Learn from all the people you contact while you temper your heart out in the real world."

It would comfort me to recall what Master Zhang, Yu Lin said, "We are all like rocks made up of minerals, including gold. We are thrown into the furnace; the furnace is the reality of this world. The flames are the problems we encounter in life. After being tempered by the flames, the rock and other minerals are burnt to ashes. What remains is pure gold. The gold will not change back to a rock again." I held on to my point of view and continued to teach qigong. I lost a couple of my old friends because of my convictions.

After studying and meditating a great deal, I came to realize all living beings or souls come from Emptiness. Despite its small size, the human body is one particle of the whole universe. It is a microcosm. Therefore, the human being's mind is capable of communicating with the universe. The problem is that we humans are "polluted". The souls, through long years of existence as life forms, have been coated with "dust". The "dust" is karma that has been created by the person's own actions and thoughts during their many lifetimes. People who remain in the dark do not know the truth of the universe; they are ignorant. People who are conscious of the truth, are working hard to purify their souls. Qigong is a means to teach people about the consequences of their actions. Qi is both healing power and consciousness. Qigong is only one of the thousands of ways to lead people to Dao, the law of the universe. As I kept teaching qigong, I kept learning. That's why I believe what I am doing is the right path.

Masters teach people to be kind, to be good, to be generous and to be selfless. But, why do they say that again and again? Finally, I understand that kindness, goodness, generosity and selflessness are the elements of the universe. The true nature of human beings has the same qualities. People have strayed far from their essential nature. That's why there is so much crime, conflict, and unhappiness. There is a way to go back to our true nature; that is to purify our souls. Qigong is surely one of the foremost approaches to purify the soul.

In the past, I was a very proud person; I seldom admitted my own mistakes. After I learned qigong, I would look at myself with a critical eye. It was as if the qi I had gathered from the universe had formed a mirror of light. In this mirror, I can see myself clearly. I see my shortcomings as well as my good points. Nobody asks me to check myself every day, but I do. While I still have a long way to go to perfect myself, I am trying. I also believe that if you are good to others, they are good to you, too. When you are selfless, people will give you more love. You will feel happy when you live in harmony with other people. Love itself is the highest energy. When people think good of you, you receive good energy.

On the contrary, when people do not like you, or even hate you, you receive negative energy that will end up having a bad effect on you. When you are in good relations with people, you live in peace and maintain a peaceful mind. To maintain a peaceful mind is the guarantee of good health. A peaceful mind is like still water in the pond. When the water in a pond is as still as glass, it will reflect the things above it and around it. The sky, the clouds, the flying birds and the trees will reflect themselves in the still water. If our minds are as calm as still water, we can think clearly. The true nature of the universe will be seen. Then we will know the truth of the universe and of our higher selves. However, life is full of ups and downs like waves of the ocean. Our minds are disrupted all the time by problems of daily living, making it truly difficult to maintain a peaceful mind.

In general it is easier to be good and to be kind to people, but to deal with your own problems is more difficult. You have to be honest with yourself and see your own weak points. To purify our soul is the destination of our life. Another purpose in life is to make whatever contributions you can to others. We are lucky to have a human embodiment, for to be a human being is one step away from Buddha. Do not waste your lifetime. Seize every moment and use every opportunity to improve yourself. Temper yourself in the sea of bitterness. We are on our way home.

If we have the right attitude towards problems and take them as tests, we will not be frustrated or angry. On the contrary, if we deal with the problems patiently and conscientiously, our minds will always remain peaceful. The great sages who tempered themselves in the real world achieved Enlightenment. The Dao is right under your feet. The Dao is in real life.

Meeting Master Yan, Xin in San Francisco

In May, 1990, I made another trip to the United States. It was a happy occasion–I would see my first granddaughter, Rena. She was such a cute little baby, only two months old, and healthy. I stayed in Vacaville, California with my daughter Sha Sha's family. Every morning, I would push little Rena in the baby stroller as we enjoyed our walks along the streets of their neighborhood. It was very relaxing and I enjoyed being with the baby. Vacaville was not a big city and it seemed very quiet. Retired from the Beijing University, I again thought about fulfilling my dream of teaching qigong in the United States.

One day I got a phone call from a former Chinese student working in New York who asked me if I would like to translate for Master Yan, Xin. My student said that he had attended Master Yan, Xin's qigong lectures in New York and learned that he was seeking a translator. I said I would be happy to be Master Yan, Xin's translator and would fly to New York at my own expense and work for the master free of charge. The student was so happy, he promised to talk to the master's sponsors and said he would call back soon. Two days later, the student called and told me that the sponsors were suspicious of my motivations for working for Yan, Xin. They did not believe that anyone would work for free. So, they refused to have me.

A few weeks later, I heard that Master Yan, Xin was going to give a lecture at a Chinese restaurant in San Francisco. Loon, my son-in-law, bought a ticket for me and drove the whole family to San Francisco. After they dropped me off at the entrance of the restaurant, I went in and sat down at one of the tables. The banquet room was spacious and there were more than twenty tables crowded with people waiting for Master Yan, Xin. At my table, a woman of about sixty years of age sat in a wheelchair facing me. She looked at me for a while and finally asked, "Do you know Master Yan, Xin? Is he capable of healing me?" She told me that she became paralyzed after giving birth to her baby forty years before and she had been in a wheelchair ever since. I told her that I did not know the master personally, but I knew he was very powerful and he might be able to heal her if she had confidence in him. As I was talking, I saw Master Yan, Xin enter the banquet room. I left my seat and ran up to him.

I greeted the master and introduced myself as the person who had been the potential volunteer translator for him. He looked at me and said in a strong Sichuan accent, "Oh, you are the one who wanted to help me. I heard about you, but my sponsors refused you, so I cannot do anything about it." So, I said, "If you need me in the future, just call me. Here is some information about me in this envelope." And I handed over an envelope, which I had prepared for him. Just at that time, people began to recognize him as the master and many left their seats to surround him. Returning to my seat, I realized that if I had not taken quick action, I would not have had a chance to talk to him, or pass him the envelope. Even though I only had a few seconds of close contact with the master, I felt his qi strongly and my heart was beating rapidly. It was not because I was shy or nervous. His vibration frequency was much higher than mine, so I got a healing adjustment from him just being in his presence.

As the banquet began, the first thing Master Yan, Xin did was to walk from table to table proposing toasts to the people in attendance. He made the suggestion that we all drink tea instead of wine, which made for a harmonious atmosphere. In a low voice I suggested to the people at my table that when the master came to our table, we should give the paralyzed woman the opportunity to talk. Everyone agreed.

When Master Yan, Xin came to our table, we all stood up except for the woman. After we toasted him with our tea, the woman said, "Master Yan, Xin, I..." The master interrupted her saying, "Do not call me master. Call me doctor. Just tell me what you want. Do not talk about your problem." The paralyzed woman said earnestly, "I want to stand up." The master motioned for her to stand up and she stood up. This caused loud gasps of surprise. Tears ran down the woman's face. Then the master asked, "What else do you want?" She said excitedly in a loud voice, "I want to walk!" The master reached out his arms and said, "Now, walk!" As she started to walk, the person who had been attending her tried to protect her. But she pushed away his hands and bravely walked out into the room. Everyone in the banquet hall stood cheering and clapping their hands. Newspaper reporters were busy snapping pictures and a video camera team was recording what the woman said as she walked.

Standing by the master, I saw how he was supporting the woman with his qi. He was sending qi from his eyes and mind to help her. What a miracle! The woman walked around the big banquet room without any physical help from others. When she came back to her seat, she sat down on a regular chair, instead of her wheelchair. Then the master said to her, "After today's lecture, please wait for me. I will give you a treatment and prescribe some Chinese medicine for you." The woman was so happy that the master had helped her walk again after 40 years of being bound to her wheelchair. The master began to deliver his lecture, along with healing qi. The woman sat up straight in her chair, listening to the master talk for five hours straight–except for two restroom breaks which she took without assistance.

As the master lectured, he urged us to eat while we listened to him. People who did not know much about qigong did not get the hint from the master that he was inserting qi into the food on the table. At our table, only a young man from Beijing and I understood why the master kept urging us to eat. So we kept putting food into our mouths. Obviously, the flavor of the food had been changed because it tasted really awful. Many people put down their chopsticks and even stopped eating all together. The master kept encouraging us saying that it would be beneficial to eat even though the flavor had been changed. What most of the people did not know was that the master was testing them to see if they had confidence in him. The young man and I kept eating and no doubt looked a bit silly to others. Continuing to talk, the master told us that he thought the admission ticket was too expensive. He said that the organizers charged too much, "$150 for each person was too expensive for my lecture," He went on, "$150 is enough to buy one person's food for a month. Therefore, I will talk more so that you get your money's worth." His lecture ended at 1:00 a.m. in the morning!

There were some people who experienced spontaneous movements as a result of Master Yan's healing qi. I benefited a lot from his lecture and his healing energy. Master Yan, Xin's great spirit deeply touched me and I hoped that I would have an opportunity to work for him. But, during my time in California, I never received a phone call from him. I also wanted to follow-up and speak to the woman who was healed and see if she was still able to walk, but I lost her contact information. A few weeks later, I was on my way to New York.

Once settled in New York, I began to teach Soaring Crane Qigong. When I saw a notice about a local lecture given by Master Yan, Xin, I eagerly went to listen, even though I had given up hope on translating for him. But, I did have ulterior purpose in mind as I had a question for the master about an idea I had. I thought it was important that the most popular book in China, *The Grand Qigong Masters* written by Mr. Ke, Yun Lu, be translated into English. In the book, the author paid tribute to many great qigong masters. And Master Yan, Xin was one of the grand masters the author focused on. At the lecture, I found an opportunity to have a few moments with Master Yan, Xin and asked him if he would give me permission to organize some people to translate the book into English. The master said, "The copyright of this book is not mine. Even though he wrote a lot about me, you will have to seek permission from the author, Mr. Ke, Yun Lu." His words furthered my respect of Master Yan, Xin. But, I never got the chance to study with him or to work with him.

A few days later, I composed a letter to Mr. Ke, Yun Lu expressing my wish to get permission to translate his book, *The Grand Qigong Masters*. I requested a meeting with him in person when I returned to China from the United States. Very soon, I received an answer from him in which he asked me to contact him when I arrived back in Beijing.

Another Test

When I was in New York City, I received a phone call from a former qigong student warning me that the book I had translated into English, "*Chinese Soaring Crane Qigong*", was being sold in New York under another translator's name, not mine. As soon as I heard this, a flow of blood rushed up into my head. The student continued that the translator had sold my book to a qigong student for two thousand US dollars and that copies were being sold in the qigong community of America. It turned out to be the translator that I had recommended to work for Master Zhao on his second visit to the United States. Before the translator left Beijing for this trip I had given him a copy of my translation, which was already in print. Never did I expect he would do such an ugly thing. I was very upset. But, I kept quiet and did not accuse him right away.

That night as I was deep in thought, I asked myself, "Why am I so upset? Obviously he was wrong, but why should I be so angry?" I tried to see myself in a spiritual light and found that I cared a great deal about my own name. Recognizing my problem, I tried to calm down. Even though the man was in New York and I knew his phone number, I decided to keep quiet and wait until he realized his own mistake. It took me three days to completely calm down. All of the spiritual teachings I had learned and the meditations I did during those previous months truly helped me. I took this as another spiritual test. I thought, "Some day when he recognizes his mistake, he will talk to me about this matter and the results will be much better."

Approximately one month later, my phone rang at midnight. With his voice trembling, the translator said, "Professor Chen, I am terribly sorry. I have made a terrible mistake. I know I was wrong and I have been on pins and needles since then. At the time, I needed money badly. I apologize for what I did. I am going to give you the two thousand dollars." Then I interrupted him saying, "I am glad that you know your mistake. What I want to tell you is this. You are still young. Only make honest money the rest of your life. I know things are financially difficult for you so do not give me the two thousand dollars!" He burst into tears. I was really happy about the results, and the fact that I had grown spiritually from this event.

Being Robbed Shocks Us

Returning to California, I flew into Los Angeles. There, my daughter Sha Sha, her husband Loon, and little Rena met me. From the airport we headed off for our scheduled trip to Disneyland. It was the first time I had visited such an amazing place. As we were leaving–all of us in a happy mood– my son-in-law suggested we pay a visit to the Disney Hotel nearby. He parked the van along the street not far from the hotel. He said, "You can leave everything in the van, because it will be a very short visit." So, we only took our camera and left everything else in the van, even our purses. After about twenty minutes of walking around, we returned to our van where we found the front door window smashed and the ground covered with pieces of glass.

When we looked into the van, everything was gone. Missing were my two suitcases, packed with all the gifts I had purchased for my family and my purse, which contained my passport and money. Gone were my daughter's purse and new purchases, along with her husband's wallet– all stolen! Nothing was left except the baby's stroller. As I realized what had happened, I remained very calm. But, my daughter flew into a rage and blamed her husband for having asked us to leave everything in the van. Loon did not say a word. I tried to calm my daughter down saying, "Since our things have already been stolen, there is nothing we can do. Look, the four of us are unharmed. We are lucky."

We looked around and saw a big truck about twenty feet away. Four big men were standing by it looking at us. But, we did not even dare to ask them if they had seen what had happened. Instead, Loon started the van and headed to the police station which was close by. When we reported the case, a policeman examined the broken window, shrugged his shoulders and said, "Sorry! Every day, we have cases like yours reported to us, almost one every ten minutes. Here is a form for you to fill out and we will provide you with a report stating that the theft is real." With that, we left the police station. Fortunately for us, my daughter still had $40 in her pocket, so we could get enough gas to get home. Loon found a thick piece of cardboard from the roadside and fixed it to the window to stop the cold wind from blowing in. On our way home, we did not complain about our misfortune. We joked a lot. Loon said, "The thief only left the stroller because it is not useful to him."

Sha Sha quipped, "Maybe he has a baby, too. He knows how important a stroller is if you have a baby. So maybe that's why he did not take it away." I remarked, "There is a Chinese saying: You lose a fortune to avoid a disaster."

It was getting dark and the winter wind was blowing hard as we were driving to Vacaville. Eight hours later, we got home but none of us felt frustrated. I was happy that I had passed another spiritual test. Thanks to the problems I'd had before I left Beijing, along with the spiritual teachings, I found that I had progressed a great deal spiritually. In reality it took me quite a long time to have a new passport issued in San Francisco, which delayed my return to China. I truly had learned to temper my heart in some real-life situations.

After I finally obtained my passport and visa, I began to plan my return trip to China. That is when an idea seized me and I decided to go home via Arizona. I contacted Professor Andrew Chang to request permission to present a seminar on the Lozanov methodology at AGSIM. Many language teachers from AGSIM came to listen to my lecture. To my great surprise, President Sun, Wei Yan of our University of International Business and Economics in Beijing was visiting AGSIM at that time. He attended my talk and afterward he came over to me. He said that he was interested in learning more about this methodology. So, I had a long talk with President Sun about the Lozanov methodology and he listened intently. At the conclusion, he said, "You should bring this methodology back to our university, too." Overjoyed, I said, "Yes, of course. I am just on my way back to Beijing."

An Accelerated Learning Methodology
Is Introduced in Beijing

During the summer of 1990 while I was in New York, I had the opportunity to learn about an accelerated learning methodology. Dr. George Lozanov was a famous scientist from Bulgaria. After long years of studying the human brain, he came to understand that the right hemisphere of most people's brain had not been cultivated, or even tapped into. He developed a method to increase the activity of brain cells by using Baroque music, an ancient Oriental relaxation method and many other activities to enable students to learn faster. According to his experience, one can basically learn to use a newly acquired language within a month. A friend of Judith Haber had applied this methodology in the foreign language studies at her school. As soon as I heard about it, I wanted to know more. She gave me the opportunity to learn this new methodology by working at her school and attending all the classes being held there. Even though I had been a language teacher for many years, I had never seen a happier classroom atmosphere or a more congenial relationship between the teachers and students. I fell in love with the methodology. As a qigong practitioner, I knew the importance of cultivating the potentials of the human brain. This methodology was definitely a unique way to transform the three-dimensional aspect of humans into a higher level. During my learning process, bit-by-bit I came to realize the close connection between the teaching technique and qigong. The final goal is the same, but the approaches were different. I studied hard and worked at the school for a few months. Believing it would be a very acceptable teaching method in China, I decided to introduce this methodology to Chinese students.

I felt that I needed to acquire more experiences in teaching this methodology, before formally implementing it at my university. So, I decided to hold an experimental class at my home. I discussed my idea with a close friend of mine, Wang, Li and she gathered together ten fifth-grade elementary students from among our colleagues' families. They were all very excited to have been invited to this experimental class. None of the children had learned any English at school or at home. Within a few days, I had prepared the materials I would need for instruction.

According to this system, the kids should be able to learn simple English from scratch and be able to express themselves both orally and in written form within ten days. The program schedule that I devised was to train the students for ten days in a row, with three hours of instruction and three hours of review per day. I began my teaching with phonetics and the alphabet. The class was held in the sitting room of my apartment. The students were very disciplined and the program went along smoothly. I was full of enthusiasm and energy.

The progress they made not only encouraged the students, but also surprised me. I had been teaching English for about thirty years and never had I seen such rapid progress made. The chief characteristic of this methodology was to cultivate the latent potentials of the brain, by using specific music, meditation and various kinds of games. In turn this would stimulate and enliven the brain cells so that the students could learn things much faster and retain what they have learned. Our classes were filled with laughter; everyone was happy with the program.

On the last day of the experimental class, I invited President Sun and a few other teachers to see the presentations of the students. Short plays, dialogues, cross talk, recitations of poems, songs, etc. were presented all in English. The visitors were very happy to see the wonderful results of the program. President Sun said, "It is amazing that they could master such a big vocabulary." Another professor said, "It is almost unbelievable that the students could have learned so much within only ten days. It is truly a wonderful methodology."

The news about this methodology spread very fast in our university. Most people showed great interest in it. But, some did not understand this system so they talked a lot about it with a negative attitude. Some said it was nonsense. Others said that I was just fooling the kids by playing games in class. And some gossiped that I introduced this methodology to win great fame. I was even condemned for having applied qigong in the language instruction that I put together. No matter what they said, I knew what I was doing was right.

Soon after witnessing the students' presentations, President Sun wrote a report to the Minister of International Business and Economics about the excellent results. The Minister replied by requesting that our university teach English to the leaders of the ministry. That required a lot of English teachers partaking in the preparation. A very smart and gifted female teacher was assigned to be my teaching assistant. Her name was

Liu, Yu. She was a sweet young lady and had been a soloist in the English singing group at our university. I liked her a lot and we worked well together.

The students we had from the ministry were all over 50 years old. Only a few of them had learned another foreign language, such as Spanish, French or Italian. But, none of them had learned English. They were given this opportunity to study and had been given rooms in the hotel of our university. Basically, they were not allowed to go back home unless some crisis occurred. They even ate in our university's dining room. These "old" students were very happy to come back to school again. Their program was 15 days long with three hours of instruction and three hours of review per day. Even the teaching materials had been especially prepared for them; the content focused on international business.

Many people got involved in the program. My focus was only on the teaching, which was the most demanding aspect, because I had to create a game or an activity for each day's class. In order to remain creative, I meditated every evening. It was truly incredible that after a few minutes' meditation, a new idea that would perfectly serve the purpose would pop into my head. I was really blessed! Liu, Yu and I worked so well together, that the results of our first class were very successful.

At the completion of the program, the leaders of our university held a farewell banquet for the ministry students in the university's dining room. The most surprising thing at the banquet was the English speech given by one of the students in the group. Everyone applauded and I was almost touched to tears! The Lozanov methodology had worked wonders.

Then the ministry organized two more classes for us to teach. With the exception of a few students, most of them learned very well. English presentations were given to many leaders from the ministry as well as to some professors at our university. One of the visitors was in charge of adult education in the State Council of the Central Government. After watching the presentations, she said, "I have been in charge of adult education for decades and it is the first time I have observed such a remarkable teaching method." Later, she said to me, "How about having me organize English teachers in China, so that you can pass this teaching method on to them." Her comments made me a bit nervous because I knew if I undertook such a big job, I would never be able to accomplish *my* mission "to spread qigong all over the world".

We found that this methodology not only enabled students to learn faster but also helped them improve their health. In all the experimental classes, the students said that they never felt tired. They were full of energy and became healthier and happier. One of the girls in the first class held at my home woke up at midnight and asked her mother to bring her to me, "Mom, I want to go to Grandma Chen's home to study. I am so happy every day to study there. I wish our school had this teaching in all our classes."

One of my "old students" had suffered some hearing loss from the bombs dropped during the Liberation War. After taking the program, he said, "At the very beginning, I sometimes could not hear the teacher very well. Later, I found my hearing improving and now I can hear very well." Another "old student" was tearing during each sitting meditation in class. I could tell that he must have liver problems (because in Chinese medicine troubles with the eyes are related to the liver). After the program, he said he was feeling much better and I encouraged him to continue meditating at home. Two more "old students" related that they saw the image of Guan Yin Buddha during one meditation and wondered why. I explained to them that, "There is a great deal of mysterious phenomena that human beings are simply unable to explain today."

Later, President Sun asked me and Liu, Yu to apply this methodology to the English studies for the Russian Department's students at our university. The students learned fast and well. Later, when I moved to the United States, Liu, Yu continued to teach it and I heard about the excellent results from her teaching. After they graduated from the university, instead of using their major of Russian in their work, they used their English instead. It turned out that English was more useful to them.

President Sun and other leaders of our university wanted to promote this accelerated program. So, they organized all the language teachers from different departments of our university and asked me to introduce the basic principles of this methodology. The big classroom was packed with teachers and department leaders. During my talk, a young teacher from the English department stood up and said, excitedly, that he had never heard of this kind of effective methodology, but that he would like to learn. At the end of the presentation, the head of the Russian department stood up and said, "It seems to me that this is a good methodology. But, it would take a lot of time and energy to prepare for the actual teaching. Unless you, President Sun, pay us double for the extra time, we are not going to try it." Of course, his words set off quite a fuss in the room. Although the teachers wanted to improve their teaching skills, during those years the teachers' pay was very low. This meant they needed to save time and energy in order to earn extra money in other ways to improve their life.

For the remainder of 1991, I continued to work with the Lozanov methodology. Since our young people are the pillars of the future, it seemed important that their brain potential should be cultivated. Qigong provides an effective way to get vital energy into the body to help cleanse the channels so no disease can invade the body. Also, bringing the vital energy into the brain clears out disturbances, so that peace-of-mind can be obtained. In China, Qigong had proven to be very effective when applied to certain fields, such as music, calligraphy and art. If Qigong could be combined with this program for the students, it would make a significant contribution to their education. However, it seemed to me that there would be many obstacles to overcome in order to gain the Chinese educational community's acceptance of this methodology.

A Visit with Mr. Ke, Yun Lu

Though work at the university kept me busy, I never forgot my major mission was to spread the influence of qigong. So, one day, I called Mr. Ke, Yun Lu and made an appointment to visit him at his home. Since he lived in the suburbs of Beijing, it took me a couple of hours to find his home. When I reached his building, I saw a middle-aged man out front, standing under a small tree. Although I guessed that it might be Mr. Ke, I pretended not to have seen him and walked straight up to his apartment on the third floor. As soon as I knocked at his door, a voice from behind me said, "Are you looking for Ke, Yun Lu?" I turned and saw the man who had been standing in front of the building. He introduced himself, "I am Ke, Yun Lu." Just as I was politely greeting him, his wife opened their door. Together with big smiles, they invited me into their home.

After tea was served, Mr. Ke asked me to tell him who I was and what kind of work I did. Having given him a brief account of myself, he replied, "It is so good that you love and practice qigong. You know qigong is the future. No matter what happens in your life, never give up your qigong practice and never give up working for qigong." Then I had a question for him, "You are a very famous writer and you have written many books regarding social problems. People love your books and also the films and TV dramas that have been made, based on your books. Why is it that you suddenly took up the subject of qigong?" I told him that several of my friends had raised the same question and they asked me to try to get an answer from him.

He pointed his right index finger upward to the heavens and with a smile, he said, "When you are told to do it, you just do it. I'll bet you understand what I mean." I nodded in agreement. A very sweet lady and a famous poet in China, his wife, Xue Ke, sat by his side. Mr. Ke continued, "In the letter you sent from New York, you asked me if you could organize translators for an English edition of my book, *The Grand Qigong Masters*. Of course, I would say yes. You just go ahead, get my book translated into English. There is no need to discuss anything concerning publishing or anything else. My motivation has been to let more people know about qigong and get them involved in it."

To which I replied, "It is true that more people sought out qigong instruction after reading *The Grand Qigong Masters*." He nodded and said, "Many readers who previously had doubts about qigong wrote to me saying just that. After reading the book their doubts went away and they believed that qigong would really benefit them, so they started it because they trusted me. I am happy that I have contributed something to the development of qigong."

I also told him that I had been teaching Chinese Soaring Crane Qigong while in the United States. He said, "Oh, good, Soaring Crane Qigong is a very powerful form." I was very encouraged by the pleasant visit with Mr. Ke, Yun Lu and his wife Xue Ke. It had given me even more confidence about spreading qigong.

My Role Model–Master Liang, Guang Hua

It was during this time in Beijing that I decided to make a special trip to Harbin to study with Master Liang, Guang Hua. Master Liang was the originator of Awakening Light Gong, which was practiced by millions of people in China. I read all the material I had been sent and found that Master Liang had practiced Zen Meditation and had studied Buddhist teachings for more than 50 years before he began to teach his form to the public. Awakening Light Gong, though simple in form, has very powerful outcomes. Taking care of the practitioner's physical body and spirit, it combines the teachings of Tibetan Secret Buddhism, Daoism, and Traditional Chinese Medicine. Practitioners of this form recovered from many diseases and remained in good health. The form also aided its practitioners in their spiritual growth, since it is an advanced type of gong. While practitioners do the form, chant the mantra and visualize with spiritual music, they are connected to the spiritual light in the universe. Dao manifests in light; light manifests in qi. That is why Light Gong is a higher form than qigong. And Master Liang enjoyed a reputation for excellence within the qigong community. And, at the same time, he served as a role model to all his students and friends.

The master sent his wife, Li, Ning to greet me at the Harbin railway station. Her warmth immediately touched my heart. Even though the master and his wife had never met me before, they welcomed me like a sister. Master Liang invited me to stay in his home, as it would be more convenient to teach me privately. Because of his tight public teaching schedule, he would have more time at home to spend with me. I was very grateful for his kindness.

Since they lived in a one-bedroom apartment, I wondered where they would put me for the night. Right after our dinner together, he started to teach me Awakening Light Gong. When night came, he pointed to their queen size bed and told me to share the bed with his wife. Then, he unfolded a small bed for himself in the same room. Never had I seen such an easy-going master like him.

As I got to know him, I was very much moved by the simplicity of his life. The Master had been a vegetarian all his life. At each meal, he only ate vegetables and some egg. Worried about a lack of nutrition, his wife often advised him to try some meat, but he denied; he would never do anything against his Buddhist devotion. During one meal a few days later, Master Liang asked me seriously, "Hui Xian, would you please do me a favor?" Of course I replied, "Oh, yes. What is it?" He looked straight into my eyes and said, "Someday, if I am in a coma before I die, be sure that Li, Ning does not feed me chicken broth. That will ruin the whole thing!" Li, Ning laughed and said, "Do not worry. I promise I am not going to do that to you." Master Liang smiled in relief.

Every day the master took me to the group practice sites for the Awakening Light Gong; some were indoors and some were outdoors. With the groups, the energy was so strong that I felt as if my whole body, especially my fingers, were wrapped with a thick layer of qi. Master Liang gave a lecture one day to as many as one thousand people. During their practice, the whole hall was filled with spiritual lights and the participants had all kinds of amazing spontaneous movements. Many young people danced beautifully like fairies, especially the girls. Men and women, old and young, displayed spontaneous T'ai Chi movements. Some elders bent their bodies backwards reaching very low; others turned continuously head over heels and many gave spontaneous treatments to others who were sick. The movements were incredible.

While people were doing their spontaneous movements, Master Liang stood on the stage channeling light from the universe and sending it to the participants. He would sweat heavily all over when he was doing this; sometimes, I saw his shirt would be wet, drenched with sweat. I respected the selfless master so much, but I also worried that he was giving out too much. One day, I said to him, "Master Liang, it is good that you take care of these people, but I think you overwork yourself." He looked at me for a while and then said, "I know that my time on earth is limited. I just want to help as many people as possible while I am here." I looked into his sparkling eyes, which shone with sincerity, and said nothing more.

One evening, Master Liang asked me if I knew where Zu Qiao, the ancestral cavity, was located. I pointed to the spot on my forehead. He quizzed me as to who had taught me this, remarking that most teachers would rarely give out this knowledge. I answered, "Nobody taught me. I figured it out for myself during meditation." Upon hearing this, cheerful tears ran down his cheeks. He was happy that I had experienced my Zu Qiao.

While I was with him, he never missed a chance to teach me. He also gave me a great opportunity to speak to his students and another time to speak to one thousand in a huge auditorium. I felt greatly honored, but I also realized that this was also part of my training from him. During the time of my studying there, what I learned most was not verbal teachings, but the lessons that came from his actions. He worked from morning until night: practicing with students; verbally answering their many questions; writing out answers to others; giving lectures once or twice a day; conferring with the Awakening Light Gong instructors and giving healings to those who badly needed help. But, I worried about his health for he was thin, looked very pale and he would sweat all the time; he just gave too much of himself. However, no one could stop him. He just wanted to use every minute of the remaining days of his life to help as many people as possible. What a noble man, a shining example and a great spiritual teacher!

Before I left his Harbin home, he talked to me alone. He said, "It is your mission to spread Awakening Light Gong in the West. It is not my mission. You have invited me to teach in the United States, but I will not go. I want you to teach. However, you will have to wait until the time is right, in about ten years. In the meantime, practice Awakening Light Gong and be ready to teach." And with that, he formally presented me with copies of the spiritual music that would be needed for my future teaching. I promised him that I would teach the Awakening Light Gong in the United States when the right time came.

"Genuine Qigong" with Master Zhang, Yu Lin

Master Zhang, Yu Lin was another master that I studied with in Beijing. Master Zhang told us that he had not been a good student when he was in elementary school. His scores were always the lowest. His father, who was a carpenter, decided to teach his son carpentry skills instead of keeping him in school so that in the future he would have the means to make a living. At the age of twelve, his father was hired on a carpentry project at a Buddhist temple in the northeast of China. Young Zhang, Yu Lin went along with his father as an assistant on the project. The old monk of the temple noticed Yu Lin and offered to teach him to recite Buddhist teachings. Once they began, the monks were all surprised to find that the boy had a wonderful memory. Later, the old monk took him on as a student to learn about Buddhism, This training served him well, for as an adult, Master Zhang was pretty good at explaining Buddhist teachings. At the same time, the monk taught him Chinese Genuine Qigong. Having practiced for dozens of years, Zhang, Yu Lin became very healthy. When he moved to Beijing with his own family, he only wore thin clothes in the winter and would practice qigong early in the morning in the snow with a bare upper body. Many people observed him as he practiced and sought him out for instruction.

After he retired from a factory job in the 1980's, he decided to introduce Genuine Qigong to the general public. Qigong was at its peak at that time in China and thousands of people were attracted to his teachings. In a very short time, he became famous among the qigong communities. You could see hundreds of people practicing Genuine Qigong in the parks, not only in Beijing but also in many other cities, as well as in the countryside. The Master toured many places giving lectures and was even invited by a Beijing television program to lecture on a regular basis. Once I heard his talk, I was attracted to his teachings. A close qigong friend introduced me to him and I took up the study of Genuine Qigong.

Basically, there were no movement forms to learn in this type of qigong. Master Zhang taught that the major aspect of Genuine Qigong was to understand the relationship between the universe and the human heart and the importance of tempering the heart in daily life. The dynamic element to Genuine Qigong was simply spontaneous movement. Once the practitioner understands the importance of keeping a calm mind, the energy from the universe would mingle with the energy in the body, causing the body to make spontaneous movements. The energy might push one back and forth, cause the arms to swing, roll the person on the ground, or stabilize one on the ground to meditate. Whatever happens is just right. It not only provides physical benefits, but also helps mental and spiritual growth.

In 1990, I began to attend Master Zhang's lectures and I also joined the practice group at Beijing's Di Tan–the Temple-of-Earth Park. Having practiced Soaring Crane Qigong for eight years, the involuntary movements came easily to me. The master observed me closely and offered me personal coaching at his home. I was very grateful for his help.

After studying with him, I more fully understood that in order to cleanse the meridians qigong movements require a connection of energy with the universe. But, what is most important is to purify the soul by checking one's thoughts, speech and everyday actions, to determine whether one is a good and honest human being. Many times, thanks to Master Zhang's teachings and his personal help, I passed calmly through the spiritual tests that came up in my life. With this deep sense of gratitude I thought it would be very important to introduce his teachings to students in America.

Therefore, in 1992, again with Judith Haber's assistance as sponsor, Master Zhang and I spent six months in the United States where he taught in New York and Alaska. I served as his translator and teaching assistant at the workshops. We started in New York where the sessions were attended by many of the students who had previously learned Soaring Crane Qigong. But, other participants who had never studied any type of qigong found it very difficult to embrace Genuine Qigong. They were not able to calm their minds while in the standing meditation position. That, in turn, left them without any spontaneous movements, which made them very frustrated.

Master Zhang accepted invitations to speak at many places such as the American and Chinese Association and at a few Buddhist temples. Our final stop was in Alaska, where he taught a few more workshops. It was clear that he had truly made a contribution to the development of qigong with his particular teaching designed to temper the heart. This vital aspect in learning qigong made a big impact on the qigong practitioners, both in China and in the United States.

Teaching Qigong in Portland, Oregon

When I was in New York during the winter of 1992, my former university classmate, Professor Charles Wu, called me from Portland, Oregon. He suggested that I make a trip to Portland to visit him and his wife, Diane Ma. I told him frankly that I could not afford the trip. So, he suggested that I offer a qigong workshop at Reed College where he was teaching. The students were on winter vacation and he would request that Reed's Student Union cover my airfare. Happily, I agreed and flew to Portland, a city I found very impressive. It seemed that there were flowers in the front yard of almost every house and an abundance of evergreen trees filled the city with a fresh evergreen scent. I was very happy to see my old friends again. At their welcoming invitation, I stayed in their home.

Of the attendees at the workshop, there were ten students who were from Reed College and two others who were Charles' friends—one of whom was a teacher at Oregon College of Oriental Medicine (OCOM). His name was John Allee. Having previously learned a form of qigong, he was very much interested in my offering of Chinese Soaring Crane Qigong. For ten days, I taught every evening. The students were all very attentive and practiced hard on their own during the day. Everyone said that Chinese Soaring Crane Qigong was a very powerful form.

That is when the universe stepped in and John recommended me to the president of OCOM, Elizabeth Goldblatt, who was presently searching for a qigong instructor for the college. Before I left Portland to go to California, the president invited me to do a qigong workshop at OCOM the following month.

OCOM must have done a lot of publicity for my workshop because more than 70 people showed up. I was shocked by the number of attendees and really did not know how I could manage so many people. However, no one wanted to leave, so I had to do my best to teach all of them. In order for everyone to see me, they had me stand on a ping-pong table, which was a bit shaky. Even with so many people, in two days I was able to teach them the five routines and the sitting meditation. My goodness, I don't know how I managed to teach so many people in one workshop. I resolved that future workshops would be limited to 30 students.

But, something very special happened during the sitting meditation. The students were sitting in a big circle; we were all very crowded and I sat among them. The meditation begins with the mantra "Yao, yao, yao, jiu; jiu, jiu, jiu, yao" being chanted seven times. So, I began to lead the chant. When I said it for the third time, I suddenly felt a very strong flow of qi come down from the sky like a shower. I could not help but ask the students if they felt it, and they all nodded in agreement. It was a very powerful meditation.

After we finished the meditation, a woman came up to me and said, "Professor Chen, there is a young lady crying over there in the corner." She pointed to the other end of the room. Immediately I followed her to the woman who was trembling and sobbing. "What has happened?" I asked. She did not lift her head but said, "I don't want to tell you. I am afraid!" I tried to calm her and said, "Please tell me so I can help you."

Then she stopped sobbing and said in a very timid voice, "While you were leading us in the chant, I saw a very bright flow of light coming down from a blue star in the southeast that covered you and the students who sat around you. A voice came to me saying, 'Those who are practicing Soaring Crane Qigong here will help save this planet!' Never have I had this kind of experience before, so it really frightened me." Upon hearing this, I was very happy. In explaining what it meant, I told her, "Thank you for receiving this message." Then, with her consent, I passed this message on to the whole class. I realized that the flow of energy that I felt while leading the mantra, was indeed from the Blue Star.

That reminded me of something that happened in July 1988 while Master Zhao and I were in Germantown, New York. Master Elie Hien, a visiting master from France had asked Master Zhao, "Do you know where you got your Soaring Crane Qigong?" Shocked at his question, I had been a bit annoyed, thinking, 'How dare you ask my master this question?' It sounded a bit insulting. But Master Zhao remained calm and shook his head after which Master Elie Hien told him it came from the Blue Star. That had been the first time I heard of the Blue Star. Master Elie Hien explained that when Master Zhao's mother was pregnant with him, she had eaten the energy of the Blue Star. Master Zhao nodded his head as he told Master Elie Hien that at that time his mother was so poor that she had to eat wild vegetables to fill her stomach. Master Elie Hien said, "She ate the wild vegetables with dew containing the energy from the Blue Star." Then, Master Elie Hien suggested to Master Zhao that all Soaring Crane Qigong students wear a badge with the symbol of the Blue Star.

It also provoked another memory from back in Beijing when Master Zhao and I were teaching qigong at the University of International Business and Economics. One Saturday afternoon after teaching a class, we both came back to the Qigong Office to get ready to go home. All of a sudden, both of us felt very sick. Master Zhao said, "What's happening? I feel very sick." I felt very sick, too. Without discovering the reason for our illness, we said good-bye and headed to our homes. The bad feeling stayed with me for the whole night and into Sunday morning. Around two o'clock in the afternoon, I did sitting meditation to heal myself. Suddenly, the sickness disappeared; I was myself again.

On Monday morning as soon as I saw Master Zhao, he asked me, "How do you feel now?" I replied. "Great!" He then asked, "When did that bad feeling leave you?" I said, "Around two o'clock yesterday, Sunday." He smiled and said, "Yes, you are right. You know what happened. I was on a train heading for Shijiazhuang to give a lecture. All of sudden, I finally received a message that had been trying to get through to me. The message told me that all Soaring Crane Qigong practitioners must chant 'Yao, yao, yao, jiu; jiu, jiu, jiu, yao' at the beginning of the sitting meditation. Chant seven times, while taking a breath in between. After the message got through, the sick feeling left me completely." I realized that the message meant for him, had affected me too since we worked so closely at the university. When the message got through to Master Zhao, I, too, was freed of the sick feeling. Master Zhao explained to me that the vibration, which carried the message, was so high that our bodies could not tolerate it and caused us to feel sick. He also explained to me that the mantra was like a telephone connection to the source of Soaring Crane Qigong.

Over time, since that first workshop in Portland, many of my students and I have seen the Blue Star during our meditations.

A Career at OCOM

Not long after that workshop at OCOM, the president invited me to teach an evening workshop for ten nights. Again, I flew to Portland. This time I was invited to stay with Jane Gao, a Taiwanese woman, whose husband, John, was very sick with late stage cancer. While she took good care of me, I tried my best to help John. We got along very well. I had met them through Dean Johnson and his wife Yanling. Dean was an acupuncturist in Corvallis, Oregon and had invited me to teach a few workshops there. The Johnson's even expressed their hopes that I would move to Corvallis and work in their clinic.

At the OCOM workshop, Liza, the president, often appeared in the classroom and always greeted me politely. One evening after my teaching, she asked me if I would like to teach qigong at OCOM. I told her that Dean Johnson would like to have me teach in Corvallis. The president asked, "Why can't we share?" Very soon, I left California and moved into an apartment in Portland across the street from the college and joined the faculty of OCOM.

The atmosphere at the college was harmonious. Many students had done some spiritual practice before they enrolled at the college. Therefore, they readily accepted qigong. The staff and faculty were all very friendly and I felt at home, happy to work there. The board of directors, and especially the president, were very supportive of my work. However, at the very beginning of my teaching, some of students were not very disciplined in class. While I lectured, some individuals would lie down on the floor, some would eat their snacks and some would chat with each other. I was not used to such an undisciplined class. So I created a list of rules and announced them to each class:

Chen's Rules
1. Students should not be late for class.
2. Students should be attentive.
3. No snacks are allowed during class.
4. No one is allowed to lie down
   during the teacher's lectures.

Very soon, all my classes became disciplined and the students were well behaved. Some students even told me that they appreciated being told what I expected from them during class; otherwise, they would not have known. The president heard about it and one day she said to me with a big smile, "Chen, it's good you discipline the students. Very good!"

Once the first semester was over, I felt satisfied with the results. The students benefited considerably from qigong; their health improved and they were happier. In order to carry out my mission to spread qigong all over the world, I had always wanted to train qigong teachers in America. So, I submitted a proposal for a teacher-training program at OCOM. One day, I was asked to attend a board meeting to present the details of why I had written such a proposal. I explained that in order for more people to benefit from qigong, we would need a lot more teachers. I felt that the Chinese medicine students would be the best choice to be trained as qigong instructors, because qigong was so closely related to Traditional Chinese Medicine.

Later, the board accepted my proposal. It was then that Liza jokingly said to me, "Chen, have you ever thought that when you train more qigong teachers, you will have fewer students?" I replied, "No, I will have more and more students." She then asked me, "Why are you so confident about qigong?" I said, "Qigong is a gift from the universe and I am sure that qigong will spread widely".

At OCOM, there was another very special person who was supportive of my work. Apart from the regular classes at the college, I often taught weekend workshops for the general public. Registrar Carol Acheson was in charge of registration for my workshops and of acquiring whatever I needed at the front office. It was a complicated job to organize these workshops, but Carol efficiently performed the administrative work. Her memory was extraordinary; she remembered all the names of the students and even most of their telephone numbers. It seemed to me that her mind was like a computer, both in accuracy and efficiency. And more importantly, she was very kind and patient with everyone. Everyone at the college liked and respected her.

The Chinese medicine faculty at OCOM was a well-selected team. Most of them were from Mainland China and they specialized in different subjects. We treated each other like brothers and sisters. Dr. Jin, Hong, and Dr. Li, Wei were my closest friends and they took good care of me. The Chinese faculty celebrated together with Chinese New Year parties at each other's home. Every semester, the college organized different activities that strengthened the relationship between teachers and students.

I really enjoyed teaching the students at OCOM. They loved the qigong class and requested that they have more than a one two-hour class each week. Most of the students were very sensitive to qi and they learned qigong quickly. It seemed that their conscious level was high, too. Apart from practicing the forms, I also selected stories from ancient Chinese philosophers such as Lao Zi, Zhuang Zi, as well as other readings on Daoism and spiritual practice. At the beginning of each class period, I would present two philosophical stories with pictures I had drawn on poster board with a magic marker that I copied from the books. Students would discuss the inspirations they got from the stories, and they told me that they really loved our "story time".

Some of the students cultivated their latent potentials. In one evening class, I was teaching qi healing techniques. I told them I was channeling qi from the moon and I reached out my hand. Just at that moment, I noticed that the sun was setting outdoors and my mind somehow switched to thoughts of the sun for a few seconds. One student immediately said, "Professor Chen, you were first channeling qi from the moon and then you channeled qi from the sun." I smiled and asked, "How do you know that?" He said, "First, the qi you channeled was light blue and then suddenly the color of the qi changed to orange, like the sun." I praised the student saying, "Wonderful! You caught me red-handed."

The Passing of Master Liang, Guang Hua

In November, 1993, I received a letter from Germany. It was from Master Liang's daughter-in-law, my good friend and English teaching partner, Liu, Yu. She wrote to tell me the sad news that Master Liang had died of a stroke. I grieved that I had lost the teacher I most respected.

His wife, Li, Ning, wrote in loving memory of him. "I lived with Guang Hua for more than 40 years. His kindness, forgiveness and generosity have left a deep impression on me, which will serve as a model for me, the rest of my life. He was a noble man; he always put other people's interest ahead of his own. Over the years, he worked heart-and-soul, never asking for anything extra in return for his work. He always remained humble, not caring about money or fame. All he thought about was how he could help more people recover their health. Guang Hua truly lived a meaningful life."

Master Liang's son wrote, "My father treated everyone equally well, and gave all his love to other people. My mother often told my brother and me, 'Your father is like a cow, eating grass, but providing milk.' Father lived a life of diligence, sincerity, honesty, selflessness, generosity and love. The countless selfless things he did for others proved him to be a true Buddhist through his actions. In my memory, I have seen few people that were as kind and nice as he was. Moreover, whatever happened in his life, he would never lose faith. He always remained calm and optimistic when confronted with difficulties. Having won such a great reputation, more than ten thousand people attended his funeral in the park. Many cried over his death as if they had lost their dearest family member."

One practitioner wrote on behalf of all her fellow students, "Master Liang saved thousands of lives, but thousands of people could not save his life! He used up every bit of his energy to help others. Master Liang's death is a great loss to the people, as well as to the country. His great spirit of selfless contribution touched every heart. His wisdom and good deeds will serve as a torchlight to us all, forever. We will do everything we can to spread Awakening Light Gong to benefit even more people."

On the day of Master Liang's funeral, the heavens seemed to be crying too, for there was a heavy snowfall. But, within the snow were big drops of rain, which mixed with the tears on peoples' faces and blurred their vision. As the coffin was being carried to the crematorium, many rushed to cling to it screaming, "Master Liang, you should not go!" The air was filled with the sounds of misery and grief.

Right at that moment, someone opened a birdcage and ten small birds flew out and sat quietly on the branches of a nearby tree. Suddenly, as if by some miracle, the snow and rain stopped. The sun shone upon the mourners out in the snow. Out of the silence at the crematorium echoed the beautiful song, "Returning to Nature" by the Irish spiritual singer, Enya. The birds took off with their wings a flutter; they soared high as if carrying aloft the soul of the great Master Liang, Guang Hua!

Alone in the United States I grieved over Master Liang's death. I vowed to the Master's memory that I would follow his example and be a good qigong teacher for the rest of my life. I was determined to spread his Awakening Light Gong when the time was right.

A year later, something very special happened. One evening as I was teaching a qigong class at OCOM, a female student who was not very disciplined began to dance around after I had already started the qigong practice tape. I motioned for her to stop, but she ignored me. So I said, "It is time to practice." Again she pretended not to hear me. I was a bit upset as I repeated, "It is time to practice Soaring Crane Qigong." Still she continued to dance. I could hardly control myself as I said with some anger in my voice, "If anyone does not want to practice, please leave the room." Never before had I been so impatient in a qigong class. However, it worked and the woman stopped dancing and the whole class began to follow me in the practice.

During the break, a student came up to me and said, "Professor Chen, your teacher came when you were upset earlier." Surprised, I asked, "Oh!? What did he look like?" Her face shone as she described what she had seen, "Your teacher is an old man with pure gray hair. He looked very handsome and kind and he was wearing a golden robe with a belt around his waist. When you were feeling upset with that student, he appeared at your left side. Smiling, he looked at you as if saying you should not get upset for such a small thing. From his expression, I could tell that he was your teacher and that he liked you a lot. Standing at your side, he put his left hand in front of your body and his right hand behind your back while he moved both hands downward to calm you."

Immediately, I thought of Master Liang who had died a year before. "It must be Master Liang!" I exclaimed and I thanked her for telling me. Actually, she had practiced yoga for more than five years prior to her study of qigong with me. Her spiritual practice had already opened her third eye, that's why she could see Master Liang when he appeared.

As soon as I got home, I wrote a letter to Master Liang's wife, Li, Ning telling her about the event and asked if she would mail me a picture of Master Liang. Three weeks later, I received a book from Li, Ning. The title of which was *Liang, Guang Hua and Awakening Light Gong*; it had been published in China just a month earlier. She wrote me a long letter in which she related similar stories that had happened in Harbin. On the seventh day after Master Liang's death, as per tradition, another memorial service was held. On that occasion, many students saw Master Liang standing in the front of the hall high in the air. He was wearing a golden robe with a belt around his waist, the same image that my student had seen.

The next day, I showed the picture to the OCOM student who had seen Master Liang. She pointed to Master Liang in the group picture and

Master Liang's wife, Li, Ning with me and his son He Ping (2005)

said, "It was him! The only difference was that his hair was pure silver." I smiled and revealed that sometimes he colored his hair black.

A year later when I went back to Beijing, I paid a special visit to Master Liang's son, He Ping. He played for me the videotape he had made during his father's illness and at his funeral. When I saw Master Liang, in a coma, with his fade eyes wide open moving his head as if searching for something, I burst into tears. It seemed to me that he was still worrying about his students. I told him silently, "Master Liang, you have already done more than enough for your students. You should rest in peace!" In the videotape, thousands of people were crying bitterly over his death; the scene touched my heart deeply. He was truly a great spiritual teacher and a grand qigong master.

Later, his students donated money and built a pavilion in his memory; they named it "Guang Hua Pavilion." Often his students met there and discussed Master Liang's many merits. The China National

Qigong Association recognized Master Liang, Guang Hua as an enlightened qigong master and called upon all the qigong practitioners in China to learn from his example. After his cremation, many relics–the crystallized energy of selfless spiritual practitioners–were found among his ashes. Nowadays they are rarely found. But, on the videotape I could see large and small pearl-like spheres of blue, purple, yellow, white, black, and red crystals. At the request of the China National Buddhist Association, some of the relics are displayed at temples in memory of Master Liang, Guang Hua. He had truly lived a holy life and he will live forever in the hearts of the Chinese people. Master Liang had proven to be a true spiritual practitioner.

I Am Granted a Green Card

One Friday during the summer of 1994, OCOM's president Liza invited me to dinner at a restaurant downtown. The tables were lit with candlelight. I was not quite used to eating under such dim light. But, I knew it must be an expensive restaurant and that to dine with candlelight was considered fashionable. After we were seated, Liza said, "Congratulations, Chen! We have received your H-1 Visa. That means you can work here for three years. And if you like, after that we can extend your visa. Also, did you know that OCOM is working to get your green card?"

I was very surprised by this news. I had worked at OCOM for about a year and the college was already working for my green card! So far as I knew, in America, one normally worked at an organization for three years before being considered for a green card and that was only if the organization was satisfied with him/her. So I said, "Thank you, Liza. I am happy to learn that OCOM is already working for my green card, however, I myself do not need a green card right away. But my daughter, Ping Ping, is going to be 21 years old. I know that if I get a green card before she is 21, then she will be able to get her green card more easily." Liza then told me to call the college's attorney in order to prepare all the documents needed for my green card application.

In my meeting with Master Elie Hien a few years back, he had advised me to get Ping Ping to America as soon as possible. He believed that if she was left alone in China for too long, I would worry about her and that would negatively affect my work abroad, or make me want to return to China to be with her. It was my hope that in August, I would get my green card because Ping Ping's 21st birthday would be in November. So, I collected all the necessary paperwork for my green card from all the different places where I studied and worked throughout China and faxed them to OCOM's attorney.

In July, through OCOM's sponsorship, Ping Ping got her visa to visit me in America. About two months later, I received a call from the attorney for OCOM. I hurried off to see him. The attorney greeted me with a big smile, and as I entered his office he asked me, "Who *are* you?!" I did not understand what he meant since he and I had already met. So, I smiled back and answered, "I am Chen, Hui Xian." He went on, "In all my forty years of work, I have never had an immigration case go as smoothly as yours. They said 'yes' right away to your green card. However, you will have to be interviewed by the American Consulate in Canton, China. I am going to make the appointment for you, but it probably means that you will have to wait for a couple of months."

Oh-oh, it was already September! I was worried that the appointment might be too late for Ping Ping to get her green card before her November birthday. After expressing the urgency to the attorney, he was very nice and told me that he would do his best to arrange the earliest possible appointment. He promised to inform me just as soon as he heard from the consulate.

Around mid-October, the attorney called to tell me that Ping Ping and I had to be in Canton for the interview regarding our green cards on October 19th. I hurriedly bought two plane tickets and we flew off to Canton. Ping Ping had a friend there who was able to find us a place to stay in an empty, unfurnished room in a new building.

Early in the morning, before the interview, I had a vision during my meditation. In it, a gray-haired man with a thick beard welcomed us and asked me several questions. He asked me why I wanted to live in the United States and how much I liked the country. The man also asked Ping Ping a couple of questions that she was able to answer in English. His warm attitude made me very happy and lighthearted. After the meditation, I told Ping Ping and her friend about my vision. When we got to the consulate, the man that interviewed us was almost identical to the image in my vision and moreover, the questions he asked were nearly the same as they had been in my meditation!

Our return flight to the United States was on October 20th. Since we had an 8am departure, we had to be at the airport before 6:00am, and the Canton airport was a long way from the place where we were staying. For me, it was mostly a sleepless night, because I was afraid if we weren't able to get a taxi, we would miss our early flight. Before dawn, we got up and took our bags downstairs to the street. To our great surprise, there was a taxi parked just around the corner from our building. The driver was leaning against the car smoking as if he was just waiting for us. Excitedly, I asked him if he would take us to the airport. He said, "Yes!"

At that moment, I truly felt the universe had taken care of us and I knew why. I had vowed to the Heavens in my heart that I would do my best to accomplish my mission to spread qigong all over the world. I understood very well that, "When you are with the Dao, the Dao takes good care of you". We arrived at the airport without issue and flew back to the United States on time. The customs officer said, "Congratulations!" to us as he stamped his seal on our passports. October 21st, a full month before Ping Ping's 21st birthday. It was not just a coincidence!

All my Chinese friends were so surprised that we had received our green cards in such a short time. Normally, it would have taken two to three years to obtain one. I owe my thanks to Liza, OCOM and the universe.

The First Qigong Trip to China

One of my ideas to help the Western qigong students deepen their understanding of qigong and the Chinese culture was to organize qigong trips to China. Having many connections with qigong masters, philosophers and Traditional Chinese Medicine (TCM) doctors in China, I knew they would have much to offer the Westerners. Liza agreed with my proposal and in the name of OCOM, I contacted Professor Chen, Fu Yin, the director of the Chinese Academy of Somatic Science. By the end of June, 1994, I had everything well prepared for the 30 people who had signed up for our first qigong trip to China.

When we arrived in Beijing, group members were surprised to see that Beijing was such a modern city. The architecture in the city was a combination of ancient Chinese traditions and modern Western styles. The density of population was another surprise to the group. Thousands of people were walking along the sidewalks in addition to busy lanes of bicycles, buses, and cars moving through the streets.

Our group stayed in a garden-like hotel not far from Beijing's downtown area. Early morning wake-up calls from the front desk got everyone out of bed so we could do qigong in the courtyard of the hotel. After breakfast, we heard lectures on many different subjects given by teachers provided by the Academy of Somatic Science. They talked about ancient Chinese philosophy; Chinese medicine techniques and reports on the scientific research of qigong. We watched a few demonstrations of some rare extrasensory abilities. I stressed that these demonstrations were to prove that every human had these potentials and that they should work to cultivate them.

One special technique shown by a psychic Chinese medicine doctor was to cure a patient on the spot. The patient was carried to the classroom directly from the hospital where he had been bedridden for several weeks. The TCM doctor used his qi to deaden the diseased part of the patient and to adjust his spine using his special techniques. Instantly, the patient could stand up and walk. A woman from the countryside performed a psychic demonstration. She said she was afraid to look at the blue-eyed Americans, but she manifested a pill from thin air. She asked a few people to stand in front of her and tell her what diseases they had. Then she reached out her arm and from the air, grasped pills of differing colors or shapes for the different cases. The pills had a strong scent of Chinese medicine. When asked where she got the pills, she said, "The Buddha gave them to me." Some people saw a flash of light over her outstretched hand, before the pill appeared.

Apart from the spiritual studies, we also visited one of the most remarkable engineering feats of mankind–the Great Wall–considered one of the Seven Wonders of the World. We also toured the Summer Palace, which is one of the loveliest imperial parks and we walked through the Forbidden City where the emperors lived and worked. Later, at the Lama Temple, we observed a huge Buddha statue carved out of a single piece of wood, which was brought to China from India. Each experience was an opportunity to enrich the participants' understanding of the Chinese culture. We also made time for shopping; the most popular purchases were scrolls with Chinese paintings and calligraphy on them, silk products, and peasant handcrafts. Of course, we also feasted on the many varieties of authentic Chinese food that we ate throughout our journey.

The day before our departure from Beijing, we had a farewell party where everybody spoke about the ways in which they had benefited from the trip. Almost every person started their speech in tears. They all said, "The China trip has been a life changing experience." After listening to their stories, all the Chinese teachers praised the American students by saying, "These American qigong students are of a high consciousness."

First Time Homeowner

Early in 1995, I decided that I needed to buy a humble house. The ideal location was neither too far away from my school, nor from the community college where Ping Ping was enrolled. Since the public transportation in Portland was excellent and very convenient, both of us could travel easily by bus as we didn't have a car. The house I found was not new, but had a beautiful yard. The seller of the house was a Chinese professor named Peter Chen, who taught gardening at a local college as well as on television. A prizewinner, his gardens had been featured on a Portland TV program. When the realtor took me on a tour of the property, the beauty of the backyard immediately enchanted me. A typical oriental landscape–it included Chinese peonies of many colors, a rose garden, three Japanese pine trees, some oriental fruit trees and other rare Asian flowers.

Behind the flower gardens at the back of the lot, there were eight raised beds where Peter grew all kinds of vegetables. Ever since my childhood, I have loved gardening. I fell in love with this property. Right away I made an offer and gave a deposit for the house. Later, Peter told me that one of the reasons he wanted to move away was because nearly every day he had visitors, garden-lovers, who came seeking gardening advice for their own yards. He said he didn't care for the attention and decided it best to move away.

When we moved in, we had a house warming party that we coupled with a first-year birthday celebration for my twin grandsons. Sha Sha's whole family drove up from California for the event. More than one hundred guests attended, most of who were from my college. We had prepared lots of Chinese food for our friends. Gifts from the guests, such as potted flowers, hardware pots-and-pans, clothes, pictures and more piled up in the sitting room. Some people sat on the grass, others were on chairs and some stood

Ping Ping, Niu Niu and me in our garden in Portland (1997)

drinking, eating and talking. It was a wonderful party, and almost every one commented on my beautiful garden.

This was the first house that I had owned in my entire life. You can only imagine how happy I was! In China, I had been working for about forty years and never did I have the right, or the money, to buy a house. I was fortunate to have an apartment to live in due to my position at the university, but we were never allowed to purchase a house at that time. The social system would not allow people to buy any kind of property. All the land–houses and apartments in the cities–belonged to the government or other organizations. Chinese people were assigned living space according to their academic or social positions. We were able to rent from our university's organization and the fee was very low, a small portion of our salaries. The best part of this arrangement was that we would never be turned out for any reason from the apartments where we lived.

Later, I would find out that what the prior owner told me was true. After I moved in, there were several calls from strangers saying that they simply wanted to visit my garden. As time went by, less and less people called to visit the yard, even though I still kept the gardens as beautiful as he had, if not more so. Spending at least two hours a day working outdoors, I added even more flowers, plus a grape vine. Changing the landscape to suit my taste a bit, I thoroughly enjoyed being out in the fresh air, whether it was a rainy day or one filled with sunshine. It felt as if I were meditating as I did my gardening each day.

With such positive energy in my yard, I encouraged my qigong students to practice in my backyard. Some students would come to practice qigong early in the morning. This alarmed my neighbor's dog that would bark crazily when he saw the light come on for our practice. So, I spoke to my neighbor and he permitted me to put up a wooden fence so the dog could no longer see us. After it was built, the dog did not disturb our practices any more.

This dog incident reminded me of a true story that happened in Beijing. There was an old man who practiced qigong every morning alongside the river near his home. Whenever he was doing standing meditation with his legs apart, a white goose would come, sit between his legs, and stretch its head forward. Later, somebody took a picture of the unusual postures displayed by the man and the goose, which was published in the local paper. It seemed that animals love qi, too.

As the fruit from my backyard trees ripened, I would ask the students to come to my home and pick some for themselves. Sometimes when they did not come regularly, I would take the fruit on the bus and into the classroom to share with them. I also grew lots of vegetables and would share the fresh bounty with my friends and students. All of them loved my wonderful garden. Over the years of living there, we had many parties at my home. The video of Chinese Soaring Crane Qigong was made in that garden, which means that thousands of qigong students witnessed its beauty; the video has become a wonderful souvenir.

Spiritual Teachers Everywhere

After I moved into my house, I rode the bus to and from the OCOM every day. Very often, I had to wait at the bus stop for a while before it came. One day, while I was standing there, I saw a man in a wheelchair rolling around the bus stop as he picked up cans and bottles from the ground. I thought perhaps he did this to sell them, but I was wrong. Instead he rolled his wheelchair over to the garbage bin and dumped them all into it. As I observed him, I felt ashamed of myself for what I had been thinking. Being an able person, as were the rest of us waiting for the bus, I wondered why I had not thought to do this. There we stood, while he rolled around picking up those cans and bottles. Here I thought he did it for his own monetary gain. What a false assumption! I vowed that I would learn from him; he too served as a spiritual teacher for me.

One evening, after class I attended a farewell party. It was late when I got to the bus stop. I waited for about twenty minutes, but the bus did not show up. Thinking that I must have missed the last bus, I decided to walk home. There were no people and only a few cars drove along the street. After walking past the next two bus stops, I heard the gears of a bus as it pulled up beside me. The middle-aged female driver poked her head out and asked, "Where are you going? Don't you know it's very dangerous to walk alone in the street at night? Get in the bus and I'll take you home." We talked a bit as she drove, and when she reached my house I thanked her a lot for helping me.

Her kindness reminded me of an event in 1987. I was living in Arizona and my sister Yi Xian and her husband came to visit me. One day, we took the bus downtown to shop, but missed the last bus that would take us back to the school. We wanted to hail a taxi, but, there were none around. So, we decided to walk home. Soon after, my sister complained of a terrible pain in her feet; we were only halfway home. We were both hopeful that someone would be kind enough to give us a lift, so we stood by the roadside waving at the passing cars. Soon, a car stopped, the doors opened automatically and we climbed in. We could hardly thank the lady enough. She nodded humbly but said nothing. After we arrived at the campus and she got out of the car, we saw that she only had one leg. I was touched to tears and hugged her tightly. Over the years, I have found there are many kind people in this country. They are all good spiritual teachers, showing me how I can be a better human being.

The Credit Goes to Others

During the years of teaching qigong at OCOM and at other places, I saw that interest in qigong was developing fast. OCOM required a full year of compulsory qigong and still the students requested additional elective classes in qigong for their second and third year of study. The college's administration was very supportive and agreed to set up the teacher-training program. That meant I had many classes of different levels to teach including: Chinese Soaring Crane Qigong, Turtle

Teaching Soaring Crane Qigong in Montana

Longevity Qigong, Chinese Essence Qigong and Super Energy Clapping Hands. As a follow up to the Teacher Training in Soaring Crane Qigong, I even taught the certified Level I instructors Chinese Cosmic Qigong. With the students' increased interest, I added more qigong theories and Chinese ancient philosophies to the curriculum. The students loved their qigong classes and reported that their practice had changed them greatly, both in health and in their spiritual life.

For all those years, I was kept really busy. But, without the extensive support from the college and the assistance I received from the teachers whom I certified, I could not have successfully accomplished my work. The college provided me with a Teaching Assistant (TA) for each class so that I could spend most of my time coaching the students in their forms. Holly Ann Alswell was my first TA; she did a wonderful job and helped me a lot. She not only assisted me with my regular classes, but she also helped me teach the weekend workshops OCOM offered to

312

the general public. Kim Schmidt had studied in Taiwan and helped the students understand more about Chinese cultural experiences. Steven Foster-Wexler proved to be an outstanding teaching assistant for his serious and careful work with each student in the class. Later, Teri Applegate became my permanent teaching assistant in the classroom and at our public workshops. Whenever there was a weekend workshop, she would pick me up at my home and drive me to the college. Not only did she assist in teaching, but she also helped me prepare all of the written materials needed for Soaring Crane Qigong.

Roger Lore who was on the teaching staff at OCOM also came to help me after he had mastered the forms. He was especially valuable with the qigong healing techniques that I taught to the third-year students. Since I was not trained as an acupuncturist, I had to have him put needles into the students' acupoints so that we could transmit qi energy through the needles into their bodies. There were other assistants who also made my workload lighter, such as Carrie Bleiweiss and Tony Murczek. At the weekend workshops in Portland, I was very fortunate, at times, to have more than four certified qigong teachers who worked hard to guarantee the participants a success experience. Among the many were Joyce Spreyer, Teri Applegate, Jo Ann Albrecht, Julie Porter, Kathleen Greene, Shari McBride, and others.

They all volunteered their time while simultaneously learning how to teach. They arrived early to do the preparation for the workshops, which included arranging the chairs, putting up acupoint charts and even bringing fresh flowers. When the students came, the assistants checked the registration book, answered questions, provided special care for the sick people, distributed teaching materials and so on. During the practice, they coached the students and answered their questions with great patience. After the workshop, they cleaned up the room and often left late. I was so grateful for all of them. Without their help, the teaching in Portland would not have been as meaningful. I owe my success to all of them, especially Teri Applegate, who first diligently assisted me and then taught with me for many years before I retired from OCOM.

During those years, I was often invited to teach in different cities throughout many states and even in other countries. So, it seemed like almost every weekend I was teaching, at the college or out-of-town. As I started to teach in one place, I committed to keep traveling there until some of students could be trained to become certified teachers. Only in this manner, could I ensure that qigong would become a popular means to benefit the most people. I did my best to fulfill my mission as I traveled from Portland to the following places: New York, Seattle, Helena, Livingston, Juneau, Chicago, Hawaii, New Mexico, Montrose, Mt. Shasta, even to Montreal, Canada, Paris, France and Ireland. Rarely, was I at home during weekends or vacations. But, it made me so happy to be busy and I had wonderful opportunities to visit all these places and see so many new sights. I truly learned a lot about this country and its people from my travels. Wherever I went, there were always warm-hearted people who took care of me and helped me with my teaching.

After I began teaching in the United States, Hiroko Ishimura who lived in Manhattan, became the first practitioner I certified as a qigong instructor. She taught qigong for many years in New York and always sent her students to me for advanced studies. Recently she returned to her hometown in Japan and is teaching qigong and dance there.

Chu-lan Chiong and Will Brucks worked tirelessly for many years in order for me to teach qigong in Seattle and thus contributed greatly to the qigong community there. During that time, I reconnected with Leigh Dean whom I got to know in New York before I moved to Portland. She cared a lot about my work and gave me constructive suggestions and comments on my teaching. From Seattle, she served as my spiritual sister working quietly to support me.

Phyllis Lefohn drove back and forth between Helena and Portland to learn qigong, and was the first certified qigong teacher in Montana. She taught in Helena, sent her students to Portland for further qigong studies with me and organized many workshops for me to teach in Montana. I made many spiritual friends in the beautiful city of Helena, including Marcie, Carol, Jennifer, Julie, Terri and many others. Whenever I went to Helena, I felt as if I were returning home. All of these friends treated me like an older sister. Jennifer Daly later became one of the foremost qigong teachers in this country. Larry Jones worked very hard in spreading qigong in Livingston, Montana. His students report to me that he is a very responsible teacher.

From our earlier days, in 1988, Master Zhao had certified Ruby Cubano as a Soaring Crane Qigong teacher in Fairbanks, Alaska. She began to teach qigong in 1989 and later, she invited me to teach other qigong forms there. Ruby drove me overnight to see the icebergs and glaciers and her love for me touched my heart deeply. Steve Kong in

Juneau hosted me in his cozy home. His hospitality impressed me so much that I will never forget him for the rest of my life. My dear qigong friend in New York, Michael Oruch, taught Zero Balancing in Chicago. After he talked a lot about me in his classes, a number of his students traveled to Portland to study qigong with me there. Rita Vahling was one of the students and would later bring me to teach at a Catholic church in Juliet, Illinois. I was so happy to be able to teach there and we even had some nuns among the students. They were especially curious about other cultures; in the cafeteria all the nuns smiled at me. Some even asked me questions about qigong including Mary, a nun in her 90's, who was especially nice to me. Rita was the sweetest lady I had ever met in my life and worked very hard to spread qigong in the Chicago area.

Among my qigong students from Portland were Lew and Karen Whitley, who moved to Hawaii's Big Island. They invited me to teach Turtle Longevity Qigong on their property. Karen even got me into a research project for the scientific study of energy modalities like qigong. It was both a meaningful and successful project. I was fulfilling a wish that I had for more medical and scientific interest in researching the powerful effects of qigong.

Many of my OCOM students left Oregon after graduation and moved to other parts of the country. Alain and Jody Herriot went to New Mexico and were faithful to qigong and introduced it to that area. Judith Boice invited me to teach in Colorado. She attracted more and more people to qigong through her hard work and the classes she taught.

Leslie Piper and Bill Vanden Boom spent much time and energy making the video of Soaring Crane Qigong so it would be easier for students to learn the forms. Kris Caldwell established the Tian Tian Qigong School in Seattle and worked very hard to spread qigong there.

An especially exciting adventure came about as Jennifer Daly and her friend, Peter Tadd, arranged for me to teach in Skull, West Cork, Ireland. Susan O'Toole served as the local organizer. She got more than forty people to attend a Soaring Crane Qigong workshop on my first trip to Skull. She continued to encourage me to come and teach advanced levels and finally some of the students were certified as teachers in Europe. Later, Susan and Peter became major European instructors.

So many people have paved the way for me to spread the teaching of qigong; I owe all the credit to them. Without their help, I could not have achieved so much in less than ten years.

Wu Dao Jing She:
Establishing an International Qigong Association

As more and more people learned qigong, a need arose to establish an organization to bring the qigong community together for the study of advanced qigong theories and relevant philosophies. Additionally we wanted to provide the opportunity for the qigong practitioners to share their experiences. After brainstorming with some qigong teachers whom I certified in Portland, we decided to form a non-profit organization.

Professor Charles Wu and I discussed many options in selecting the best Chinese name for this organization. Finally we recommended that it

Practicing Soaring Crane Qigong on Wu Dao retreat (1998)

be called, "Wu Dao Jing She". "Wu Dao" in Chinese means to contemplate the Dao and "Jing She" translates as a hut where a group of people meet, study and work together for a common spiritual goal.

The first meeting of "Wu Dao Jing She" was held at my home on September 13, 1996. Dozens of qigong practitioners gathered together and filled my house with harmonious qi. Happy to see each other, they talked to their hearts' content. After a potluck dinner, we sat in meditation. The new meditation room that I built was not big enough for all the participants; we had people sitting on the living room, kitchen and even the bedroom floor. My house was packed with people, but when the meditation began, silence fell upon every corner of the house. Our qi mingled together and a flow of love penetrated everybody's heart. We were one!

After the meditation, we elected a board of directors. Those chosen were: myself, Kathryn Cooper, Roger Lore, Diane Ma, Michael Nagel, Deborah Oceana, and Charles Wu. The participants all cheered the members of the board.

Another important aspect of our initial meeting was to set out the mission statement: Wu Dao Jing She is a nonprofit educational organization dedicated to the pursuit of spiritual awakening via the study and practice of qigong. Specifically it facilitates the sharing of knowledge and experience among qigong practitioners and brings the benefits of this ancient Chinese art to the awareness of the general public.

The birth of "Wu Dao Jing She" marked a new stage of qigong development in our community, which pleased everyone. After that first meeting, all of the board members began to work enthusiastically. Very

Talking with Teri at Wu Dao retreat (2002)

soon, the membership numbers shot up, more than one hundred qigong practitioners had joined the organization. Our first newsletter was published under the care of the chief editor, and vice-president of Wu Dao Jing She, Professor Charles Wu. Diane Ma assisted him as they printed it out on beautiful pink paper and sent it off in the mail. The newsletter carried wonderful articles, which were written by several members of the organization. It included information about the monthly meetings, study aids on Dao De Jing, and other qigong related activities.

With such a great interest in qigong, I began to lead a daily morning practice in my neighborhood park. Often, more than twenty people came to practice Soaring Crane Qigong under the huge old pine trees. It reminded me of the days when I was practicing qigong with my Chinese friends back in Beijing. Sometimes on the rainy days, we would practice in the meditation room in my home that Guy Bodfish, one of my qigong students at OCOM built. It was a great addition to my home, a home dedicated to qigong practice and used by Wu Dao Jing She.

This new organization was full of life; it was like the blossoming of spring flowers. Motivated by the positive response, the board decided to have an annual qigong retreat for the membership. Our goal was to invite famous qigong masters from China or other spiritual teachers to lead us at the retreats. We all believed that by putting our energies together, "Wu Dao Jing She" would accomplish its mission and lead our qigong practitioners to further develop their spiritual practice.

A Great Experience Well Deserved

With qigong having such a great impact on people's health and spiritual growth, more and more people were drawn to it. One Sunday in the summer of 1997, I was invited to participate in a gathering of spiritual teachers from different countries. It was held in a small town outside of Portland. Over that weekend I had been teaching a qigong workshop, so I arrived much later than most of the other participants.

The purpose of this gathering was to pray for world peace; there were dozens of spiritual teachers meditating when I got there. I knew no one except for my qigong student who had invited me to participate. Their energy field was very strong and I felt a special closeness to these spiritual friends. After meditating, some people said they saw a Blue Star up in the sky shining brightly, but they could not reach it.

A qigong student of mine, who had already taken Level Two of Soaring Crane Qigong, quietly suggested that I help them reach the light. Although I was capable of doing this, I hesitated. This gathering knew nothing of Soaring Crane Qigong, but I decided to break the rules since they were all spiritual teachers who had achieved a high level of consciousness. After I explained about the sitting posture, I led them in chanting the mantra, "Yao, yao, yao, jiu; Jiu, jiu, jiu, yao." Then the whole group meditated for about half an hour. After we finished the meditation, many people said that the light from the Blue Star had shone down upon them. After all, they had been doing spiritual practice for a long time; they deserved this great experience!

Marine, the group's leader was a Canadian who had organized spiritual gatherings for years. She invited me to join them the following spring on the east coast and requested that I teach them qigong. Gladly, I agreed even though I had no idea exactly where it would be held.

In early spring the following year, I flew across country to teach qigong at Marine's gathering near New York. I was very happy to find there were little cabins for us right on the seashore. Nearly forty people were waiting for me to teach them "Chinese Essence Qigong". Our practice site looked out over the ocean and was surrounded by trees that were shooting out new buds. The air there was very fresh; it was a qi-filled environment.

The students faced me and Marine stood in the middle of the first row. While we were doing "Gathering Qi from the Universe to Beam It into Six Acupoints", I noticed tears streaming down her cheeks. While I sensed something was going on, I did not see anything, nor did I interrupt her. After the morning session, on our lunch break, I asked her what had happened during the practice. She told me, "When I was bringing qi from the universe and beaming it into "Shan Zhong", the point in the middle of the chest, three figures appeared in a very thick flow of light between you and me. Facing me, in the middle stood the Buddha, on his left was Jesus Christ, and on his right was an unknown figure. Jesus spoke to me, 'I am glad that you are learning qigong. Qigong is very helpful to the world's people.' He then said to me, 'Just continue your work. Don't worry!' Then they disappeared. I was so moved; I could not hold back my tears."

That this had happened did not surprise me at all. So I asked her if she would like to share this experience with the rest of the group that evening, before the meditation session. She agreed to do so. After listening to her story, all of the spiritual teachers were very touched.

I had been told that Marine had worked very hard for many years to bring spiritual teachers together from different countries in an effort to pray for world peace, and thereby raise people's level of consciousness. However, without a regular income, her life was very difficult. Sometimes her generous friends helped her out financially. She remained clear that organizing spiritual gatherings was her mission, and she never hesitated at carrying on with it. She has since, traveled all over the world. Later I lost contact with her. But, I feel certain that the Saints are sending her support through the many people that help her do her work well. She truly deserved her great spiritual vision!

I Am Impressed with Master Zhang, Yu Lei and His Students

The weekend workshops that I taught at OCOM were open to the general public. However, I personally had to watch for anyone exhibiting signs of mental illness. All of the qigong forms, which I introduced into this country, were contraindicated for those diagnosed with mental disorders. I felt sorry for those who came to my workshops hoping that this exercise would be helpful for their mental health. We had to talk privately so I could advise them to leave the workshop, because I was forbidden to teach them these. Qigong in general is a practice using the mind to guide the qi throughout the body. If the mind is not stable, it may result in serious consequences since the qi could become errant and not under the control of the mind.

For years I had wondered if there were other methods that could help people with mental illness. I pored over the qigong magazines, which I had brought from China. One day, I came across an article about a master who was teaching a form called Chinese Wisdom Qigong. Master Zhang, Yu Lei taught this qigong form to dozens of people with mental illness who were housed at the Beidaihe Sanatorium in Hubei Province. After locating the telephone number of the sanatorium, I tried to contact him. However, he had left for a short visit to his hometown so I was given his home number. Master Zhang answered the phone and said, "How lucky you are! I just opened the door and stepped in. I have been away for seven years and it is the first time I have returned."

I told Master Zhang that I was a qigong instructor in the United States and that I had been looking for a method to help people living with mental illness. He told me that he had been teaching the mentally ill for several years and that the results

Master Zhang, Yu Lei lecturing on China trip (1998)

were wonderful. Expressing a warm welcome, he said I could study with him in China.

Ping Ping and I discussed his openness and decided that on the next China qigong trip we would take the group to visit Master Zhang as part of our program. So in 1998, after studying with several spiritual teachers in Beijing, the group rode the train to the Beidaihe Sanatorium. It was a big institution near the seashore, where hundreds of people came to improve their health. There were Western and Chinese medicine doctors and therapists from other oriental modalities there to provide treatment for the in-patients. Master Zhang's patients stayed in a separate building with a sports field and a garden close by.

Anticipating our arrival, his group of mostly young patients had lined up along the path leading to their building to welcome us. As soon as our group entered the area, they began to sing in English, "Do, Rei, Mi" from the American film "Sound of Music". They sang beautifully, "Let's start at the very beginning, a very good place to start..." Upon hearing this sung in English by mentally ill patients, there were few dry eyes among us visitors. We were so touched by them. They all looked healthy and were well behaved. Master Zhang's two daughters Zhang, Lu and Zhang, Ling assisted their father in the teaching and care of the patients. The students, as Master Zhang called them, were taught Chinese Wisdom Qigong which included rolling on the ground for a long time every day. In this manner, Master Zhang had found that their minds would become quiet, instead of chaotic.

They were also taught a sitting meditation and other remedy qigong forms to develop peaceful minds. I had never had the opportunity of observing people practicing this type of rolling qigong. In most other types of qigong, the practitioners usually do routines while standing, sitting, walking or when lying still. But, Chinese Wisdom Qigong basically involved rolling on the ground. With the central channel at the core, the whole body rolled horizontally on the ground with the spine as its axis turning the whole body over and over. It is well-known that exercising the spine is essential because the spine is the pillar of the body. In Wisdom Qigong, the body is completely relaxed while lying down, and at the same time it is exercised. Thus, Chinese Wisdom Qigong is an "Exercise in Relaxation".

As the body rolls, all the internal organs, the meridians, and the blood vessels are rotated. Internally, the qi flows to every part of the body to benefit blood circulation, aid the digestion, quicken metabolism, adjust the spine, and balance the two hemispheres of the brain.

Outwardly, the skin and joints are massaged. The rolling action actually imitates the rotation of the earth. As the body rolls, the practitioner gathers a lot of earth qi from the ground. As human beings, that is vital to us, for we are also earthlings.

Chinese Wisdom Qigong has worked wonders. Before the focus of his teaching on those with mental illness, Master Zhang had already introduced his type of qigong to thousands of people suffering from all different kinds of disease. Their response was very positive.

Master Zhang shared with our group his experiences working with students that had been diagnosed with mental illness. He said that when the patients first came, violence frequently occurred among them. He found it very difficult to keep them under control. On one occasion, a male patient hit Master Zhang and then pinned him on the ground while trying to dig out his eyeball! Fortunately, Master Zhang was strong enough to stop him. On another occasion, a female patient was so out-of-her-mind that she almost cut off her breast with a knife.

But, after several months of qigong training, these behaviors began to change. In fact, dozens of patients recovered from their illness and returned home. Some even found jobs and were able to live a normal life. More and more people heard about the successes and wanted to enroll in this healing section of the sanatorium. However, Master Zhang and his helpers could take care of only a few patients, so they had to limit the number.

At the time of our visit, there were only twenty-some patients remaining. They lived an orderly life and much of their time was spent

Master Zhang's students (1998)

on qigong practice. In their free time, they played basketball, grew vegetables and learned to swim, sing and dance. Their lives were full of color and vitality. In a big room, Master Zhang lectured our group for long hours about qigong.

All the while at the back of the room, the patients sat on the floor with their legs crossed and their upper bodies straight like young monks and nuns in a temple. All of us were amazed to see them so quiet and disciplined. How could mentally ill people behave like that?

After lunch, all of Master Zhang's students came to talk with us; they expressed their desire to become friends with us. Each of us gave them our addresses and even our telephone numbers in the United States. Some patients gave us gifts that they had made themselves. Following our afternoon session with Master Zhang, there was a basketball game between Zhang's male patients and the men from our China trip. It was a heated match and we got very excited watching them play. No one would have been able to tell who the sick ones were. Moreover, the patients won the game!

A big dinner was served followed by lots of watermelon, which were set out on tables in the courtyard. It had been a hot day and everybody was happy to have the watermelon after dinner. We ate and talked, ate and talked. When evening came, Zhang, Ling announced that there was going to be a singing contest between our two groups. It was a beautiful night with the moon casting a faint golden light upon the ground where we sat. Two spotlights had been set up to light the space where the performers stood. First up was Zhang, Ling who sang to honor her students. She was a good singer and won loud applause from everyone. Then I presented an English song on behalf of our American group. After that, one after another, volunteers came from both groups to sing, to dance, or even to perform martial arts. We cheered each act; we were really happy to have had this talent contest. The entire visit proved to be fruitful and the love we shared with each other warmed everyone's heart.

Master Zhang proved what a great qigong master he is and his two lovely daughters showed their devotion by helping him and his students. I have great respect for all three of them.

Off to France

In the summer of 1999, I made my first trip to France. Invited by a long-time qigong friend Liu, Dong and his sister Liu, He, we arrived in Paris, the first destination of our trip to Europe. Ping Ping accompanied me to serve as my assistant for the qigong workshop I would teach. The event was held in a castle in the suburbs of Paris, an area of quiet in the beautiful countryside. The participants were almost all Western medicine doctors who were very open-minded. They all understood English, which meant there was no problem for them to understand my lectures. I taught them Chinese Essence Qigong, a form that they all came to love.

On a day of leisure, Liu, He and some of the students took me to visit a neighboring castle that was open to the public. It seemed to be a famous old place because the line for admission was very long. While waiting in front of the castle, we joined hands and encircled an old pine tree to absorb some qi. Noticing us, a middle-aged woman came up to us and asked, "Are you energy workers?" All the students pointed to Liu, He and me. With that, the woman motioned for the two of us to step aside with her. Then, she introduced herself as the manager of the castle. She said she needed our help and told us the following story. This castle was more than three hundred years old and it had belonged to a rich Duke. After he married a pretty young lady, they had two children, a boy and a girl. The wife was very happy with her life.

Later, however, her husband fell in love with another young woman and her happy peaceful life was ruined. Not long after this sorrow, another tragedy took place. One day her children were out playing on the castle grounds in the back which were connected to a wild forest. From out of the trees, came a pack of hungry wolves. They killed her two children and dragged their bodies away. It was impossible for this already distressed woman to withstand such a horrible shock. Upon hearing the terrible news, she went crazy and remained out-of-her-mind forever. Every day and every night she cried and screamed and refused any food. Not even a modern psychiatrist would have been able to help her. Later, she was shut away in the castle's big kitchen. But she continued her crying and yelling and even threw all the kitchenware to the floor. Finally, she died in that kitchen. Ever since then there has been no peace in the castle.

For three hundred years, nearly every night, strange noises come from the kitchen. No one has dared live in the castle; it has become known as the ghost-haunted castle. Nobody had been successful at chasing the ghost away, but the manager asked if there was anything we could do to drive her off. After listening to this sad story, I had much compassion for this poor soul. It was her home and I had to wonder why she should be driven away. And to be honest, I did not know how to deal with this kind of thing. It was my guess that Liu, He was thinking the same thing. So, neither of us said a word.

The manager led us to the castle's kitchen. As soon as she opened the heavy door, a chilly flow of yin qi struck me, which made the hair all over my body stand on end. The kitchen was dirty; an abundance of spider webs hung from the walls and in every corner of the room. Pots, pans, ladles and other ancient kitchenware were strewn all over the floor. With dismay, we quickly left the kitchen. We told the manager it was beyond our abilities to stop the night commotion. With that, the manager led us to view the major parts of the castle: the family church, the conference room, the living rooms, the dining room and the bedrooms. Then, we departed in silence. That night I was sleepless; the story of that poor woman kept turning over and over disturbing my mind.

A Journey to Ireland without Visas

After visiting many magnificent places in Paris, Ping Ping and I headed for West Cork, Ireland. Before we left San Francisco, we had not had time to obtain our visas for Ireland, so I thought we would not be allowed to enter the country. But we decided to trust our luck as we went to the Paris airport. When the young man found out that we did not have visas for Ireland, he looked us over carefully. Then he said that he would let us through but warned us not to tell anyone that it was he who had granted us permission. Luckily enough, there were no other passport checkpoints.

We boarded the plane headed for Ireland and arrived in West Cork right on time. When the customs official looked over our passports, he turned every page seeking our visas for Ireland; he failed to find any. I explained that we had sent in our application in San Francisco, but had not received the visas before the departure time so we left without them. The Irish officer smiled kindly and asked me whom we were going to visit. I said that we were going to visit a friend of ours named Susan O'Toole in Skull. "For how many days?" he inquired. Without thinking, I blurted out, "Ten days!" To which the nice officer replied, "Okay. Enjoy your stay!" That was how blessed we were to enter the country of Ireland–without visas!

Susan greeted us warmly and we headed for Skull. Along the way, wild bushes with yellow flowers contrasted beautifully with the vast green pastures. The scene reminded me of the old folk song, "The Green, Green Grass of Home". The melody echoed in my mind amid the residual noise from the plane. After we arrived at Loretta's Bed and Breakfast, we

Waiting for dinner in Cork, Ireland (1999)

were served afternoon English tea. A delicious homemade desert accompanied the hot tea, which was poured from a beautiful round teapot. It was a treat that made us feel right at home.

The following morning, around thirty students came to learn qigong. They were all very quiet and mild-mannered. With the ocean breeze blowing across the lawn, I began to teach them the Five Routines of Soaring Crane Qigong. Jennifer Daly and Ping Ping assisted me. The Irish students were very attentive in class, their faces lit with smiles as they picked up the movements quickly. When the workshop came to the end, everyone performed the routines perfectly. On the second day during the afternoon break, I was resting in a chair in a small room. From the other room, I heard soft voices singing a folk song. Initially, I did not pay much attention. But then all the Irish students quietly walked into my room single file, each carrying a white candle, to formally present gifts to Jennifer, Ping Ping, and me. I was so touched by their gentle formality and their love.

After the workshop, when I thought everyone had left, Susan brought a young lady to me who looked very tired and worried. Susan said that she really needed my help. About half a year earlier, this young lady had accidentally received an electrical shock and her third eye had opened. Every night since then, she saw many souls walking busily throughout her home. She had inherited the house from her grandmother and it was two hundred years old. Based on the clothes they wore, the souls seemed to be from different generations. Busily, they worked in the kitchen and walked up and down the stairs making lots of noise. To make matters worse, one was an old lady who claimed to be her great-grand aunty and she would always invite her to go outside to play. This young lady was so scared she could hardly sleep. As time went by, her health had deteriorated.

Susan asked me if there was some way I could help to close her third eye. I looked at the young lady with sympathy, but I really had no such training. All of a sudden I remembered the method that Master Zhao had used to heal the Yin Yang person in New York. I decided to try the same healing technique on her. Asking her to sit quietly in front of me, I told her to close her eyes. I used my hand to move the qi into her forehead from left to right and from right to left. I then tried to "seal" the third eye by moving my right thumb along Tian Mu , the third eye. I did this several times with my mind focused on closing her third eye. Following the treatment, she got up and left.

The next day, we had the day off so Ping Ping and Jennifer went to town. When they came back, Ping Ping told me that she had met the "third eye" lady on the street. The lady told Ping Ping she had finally had a good night's sleep because she did not see the souls as clearly, just somewhat vaguely. She asked Ping Ping to thank me. I was excited to hear the good news, so I asked Susan to call her and ask her to come back for another treatment. After the second treatment, she did not see the ancient souls in her house anymore. I encouraged her to practice qigong more to raise her vibration frequency, so she could avoid channeling things that were of a lower vibration frequency. She listened to me and recovered her health quickly. When she came to the teacher-training workshop during my fourth visit to Ireland, she looked like a totally different person. Her cheeks were pink, her eyes bright, and she had a happy smile on her face.

Jesus "Appears" Again

A few days before Christmas in 1999, I had a wonderful dream-like vision during the night. In it, I was standing on top of a high mountain near a big open tent when an earthquake began to rock the whole mountain. People from all around rushed inside the tent in terror. At the same time, two men came to the tent and robbed the frightened people of all their jewelry and watches. They did not bother me because I did not wear a watch or jewelry. As I looked at them, I thought, "You are doing a very evil thing at this moment!" As I continued to think, the two men ran out of the tent. Where upon, a tall falling pine tree killed them. How quickly their karma came.

Suddenly, someone shouted, "Look at the sky!" I looked up and saw a huge image of the upper body of Jesus Christ. It was his real likeness only much bigger in size. His long blond hair, his eyebrows, his eyes, his nose, his mouth, and his ears all shone with love. As I looked at Jesus, my whole body and heart filled with the love from Him. I got excited and turned around trying to find my camera, but instead, an idea came to me, "Why should I take a picture? Now, everybody on this planet can see Jesus in the sky." So, I began to shout at the top of my voice, "All peoples in the world wake up! All peoples in the world wake up!" Then the vision disappeared.

However, the vision remained very clear and vivid in my mind. While I could not sleep anymore, I lay in my bed "looking at" the beautiful image until dawn. After I got up, I called my good friend Charles Wu and told him about my spiritual experience of the night before. He was very happy to hear about it and said, "Thank you for telling me. It is the best Christmas present you could give me this year."

I Retire from OCOM

In addition to my regular qigong teaching at OCOM, I continued to teach workshops for the public in the USA and a few other countries. It left me with little time off for weekends or vacations. Often I flew to other cities on Fridays to teach weekend workshops. On Spring Break, I would fly to Europe or Canada to teach. And during school vacation time, I would either take a group of qigong practitioners to visit China or teach more workshops. Life was very busy. And I was very happy and successful in doing my tasks.

Yet in 2000, I began to contemplate retiring from OCOM. Many people did not understand why I would even consider that. When they asked, my answer was that I had been very clear about my mission to spread qigong all over the world. Ever since then, I tried my utmost to accomplish this mission. I knew very well that training English-speaking qigong instructors in a Chinese Medicine school was the best way to fulfill my mission.

It was at this time I began to realize I was too busy. Lacking time, I never had an opportunity to prepare sufficient materials for all the new teachers that I had certified. After observing the methods of some of the certified teachers, I felt strongly that they needed more information and theories for their teaching.

The Chinese tradition for qigong instruction requires that teachers be well informed in qigong theories and relevant Chinese philosophies, not just exhibit accuracy in their forms. I knew that if I could not provide the new instructors with the necessary materials, they would not do as well as they could. I held all the information they needed, however, it was all in Chinese. Since there were not many other qigong teachers who were fluent in both Chinese and English, the job of translating these materials fell to

After my retirement party with bouquet and plaque (2001)

331

me. That meant I needed ample time to translate and compile the information. Should the certified instructors ad lib or explain qigong theory loosely, I worried that the quality of the teaching would suffer in the Western countries. Without knowledgeable teachers, I felt that my mission would not be complete.

Another reason I thought it best to retire was that the genetic high blood pressure that plagued my other family members surfaced a bit in me in my late sixties. With regular qigong practice, it was well managed. But, I was concerned that if I kept doing due to my schedule, I might not stay healthy enough to accomplish my life's task.

Therefore in 2001, I handed in my notice of retirement. President Liza told me that she was sorry I wanted to retire because the qigong program was such a success. However, I told her, "There is an old Chinese saying, retreat while the current is swift." The qigong program was at its prime, and I had two potential qigong instructors to recommend to OCOM from among my many students. Teri Applegate and Roger Lore were both Chinese Medicine doctors and I believed they could do the job very well. So the college accepted my retirement and wished me well.

At the end of the school year in June 2001, I was given an opportunity to deliver my retirement speech during the graduation ceremony. Afterward, as the graduates and attendees cheered for me, I felt overwhelmed. On this occasion, the school presented me with a plaque that read:

> *The Oregon College of Oriental Medicine*
> *Honors*
> *PROFESSOR HUI-XIAN CHEN*
> *For her exemplary commitment and dedication to*
> *the field of qigong and as a professor who has*
> *contributed significantly to our culture with*
> *her expertise, wisdom and compassion.*

My nine years of working at OCOM seemed to have passed quickly; it made me really happy to realize how fruitful the years that I spent there had been. During those years, I made so many good friends with the faculty, staff, and students. The college was truly a good community. Every member of the faculty and staff had contributed their best to nurture the college and the students were diligent in their studies. Every year, graduates would leave the school and then in the fall we would welcome the newcomers. Of course it was very important to me that the college had done so much to support the spread of qigong in this country. Without the administration's support, I could never have taught so many people. So with their assistance, my mission for this lifetime was nearly complete. My gratitude for the college will remain in my heart forever.

Moving on to Complete My Mission

Upon my retirement, I moved to Vacaville, California the residence of both of my daughters, Sha Sha and Ping Ping. Sha Sha and her husband had their hands full with their four cute children, Rena, Jenny, Dann and Eric. Sha Sha had commuted to Oakland to study Chinese Medicine and had then set up a private acupuncture practice in Vacaville. Ping Ping was completing a graduate program in San Francisco, where she majored in Psychology. Having been so far away when I was living in Portland, I was very happy to live close to my children and grandchildren once again.

In Vacaville with my grandchildren on my 76th birthday (2009)

When my grandchildren got out of school, I would spend some time helping them with their lessons, telling them stories, or taking them to the playground. Of course, I felt that the kids were very smart and had great potential. Once, I asked them to discuss the topic, "Which is more important, love or money?" One after another, all of them said that love was more important than money and gave explanations and anecdotes to support their point of view. I was so happy to hear what they had to say. Finally, I asked, "Who can sum up our discussion in a few words?" Eric, the youngest grandson said, "Love is more important than money, because we can use up money, but we can never use up love!" I was astonished at his remark for he was only in the first grade. Sometimes, I led them in a simple sitting meditation or told them spiritual stories; they were very good listeners. I really loved the kids and they truly loved me, too.

Establishing a daily routine was important for my well-being. Basically, after my morning qigong practice, I spent time working in my garden growing vegetables and beautiful flowers. During the remainder of the day, I translated or wrote qigong instruction materials.

Working in my vegetable garden in Vacaville (2009)

Translating all the books and information about the six qigong forms that I had introduced into the West, required a significant amount of work. I had to review all the notes I had taken while studying with the different masters and read all the information from the available books and magazines. Thanks to Teri Applegate, Shari McBride, Phyllis Lefohn, Ping Ping, Roger Lore, Kris Caldwell, Leigh Dean, Leslie Piper, and Bill Vandenboom, whose help was invaluable, I finally finished this huge project. Ever since then, all the necessary materials including books, DVDs and CDs for qigong teaching have been available to assist the certified teachers in spreading qigong.

During my retirement, every now and then, I would receive phone calls from the certified teachers and even their students asking me questions or talking to me about their personal problems. I have always been ready to answer their calls. I felt I was still present in their life and could be of some help to them. I have been very happy to keep in touch with them. It has

Teaching the kids Clapping Hands Qigong (2004)

been really rewarding to know that qigong has entered the life of so many people.

On occasion, I would also teach qigong workshops in Vacaville or in other locations. New friendships formed in Vacaville from among my diligent qigong students. Jan, Joe, Janet, and Pedar have become some of my closest friends. Not only have we practiced qigong together, we have exchanged ideas and experiences. They also come to help me out at home with whatever I need. At other times, we go for outings to see the mountains and to rivers where hundreds of ducks swim in the waters. We have great fun visiting each other's home, or getting together at parties. Janet was a second grade teacher at an elementary school close by my home. After inviting me to teach her pupils "Super Energy Clapping Hands", Janet and I have continued this practice for many years. The kids enjoyed the exercise and Janet found that after practicing, they studied better and showed more self-discipline. Sometimes, I would introduce aspects of the Chinese culture to her students as well.

Adventures in Peru

In winter of 2002, I flew to Germantown, NY to pay a visit to my precious friend Judith Haber. One of the first things she told me was that she was going to move to Peru to help the poor people there and she hoped that I would support her. I told her, that of course I would and I promised to join her there the following year.

In May of 2003, I taught a qigong workshop at the Mother's House in Juliet, Illinois outside of Chicago. From there, I was prepared to fly out to Peru. So, I hugged all of the sisters and said goodbye to everyone, including Rita who had done such a wonderful job of organizing our qigong workshops in that area. Then she drove me to the airport.

Having lived in the countryside of China for several years, I thought I was pretty well prepared for the hardships I might encounter in the days to come in Peru. Judy had her project underway for six months, had given out a lot of money and had expended much effort. When I learned of her selfless deeds, it deeply touched my soul. Wanting to follow her example, I was determined to do a good job as a volunteer. I also thought it would be a good opportunity for me to work in a poor country and through my connection with these poor people to improve my spiritual growth. I knew I had been spoiled by the comfortable life I had enjoyed during all my years in America.

After a long flight to Peru, I spent the first night in Lima. The next morning, I was driven to Humay, where Judy was living. What struck me most on my way there was the endless "sand mountains" along the road. From Lima to my destination, I saw almost no greenery. When I reached Judy, it was already two hours after lunchtime because our car had broken down twice en route. Laughing heartily at our blight, Judy gave me a big hug. Our dear friend, Evelyne, was also there to help Judy. We were so happy to be together again, all staying in the same house.

In line with my regular routine, the next morning I got up early and went to practice qigong at the seashore. At first look, the seashore was beautiful, but the closer I got, I found the beach covered with garbage, such as old bottles, bits of cloth, old shoes, dirty papers, torn boxes, dead crabs, broken seashells and human excrement. It was so bad, I could not find a clean spot for my practice; I had to retreat to the side of the road to do qigong.

Judy's first project was quite an undertaking; it was to dig big fresh-water wells for the Humay villagers. There was only one mountain stream that ran through the village and the water was not clean. Local people drank from the stream and had to depend on that dirty water for their daily use. No wonder so many people were sick. Many people died because they had no money or means to seek medical care or to visit doctors. One woman came to us carrying her very sick child, asking Judy to help pay for the doctor's treatment. Such things happened almost every day. It was clear that to dig wells was essential to providing the most basic of necessities to the local people.

The other project I witnessed was Judy helping the villagers to improve their housing. The living spaces were not really houses by our standard. There were only three earthen walls and the inside was absent fixtures and furniture. Without much structure, there was no roof or door, to say nothing of windows. The earthen floors were littered with rags, or some old, filthy clothes. The people had no stoves or pans. They cooked dried yams in broken clay pots over an open fire. Watching them eat their food with their bare hands, I could not control my tears. Judy sent people to buy food and distributed it among the villagers.

Next, Judy encouraged the villagers to build their own houses for which she provided all the construction materials. I saw family after family build their dwellings, made with a strong roof, a beautiful door, and big glass windows. To furnish the rooms, Judy bought tables and chairs, along with beds and mattresses, plus quilts, blankets and sheets for them. This was such a change for them. One little boy refused to sleep on his new bed because he was afraid that he would fall from it during the night. For every family with school-age students, Judy provided desks with comfortable chairs. The local elementary school was also endowed with computers, desks, chairs and TV's and the teachers were given money to buy supplies for teaching. What tremendous changes in their lives!

Judy and her Peruvian friends gather for her birthday (2003)

Since the villagers had no indoor plumbing, they were accustomed to relieving themselves in the fields, on the seashore, near their living areas, or in the streets. To improve the health conditions, Judy went as far as having public toilets and bathrooms built for the local people. There was no one that took care of the trash, so garbage was scattered everywhere. When the wind was strong, the garbage would be carried throughout the village. Even though the natural scenery was extremely beautiful the place was always dirty. What a pity.

Having never learned Spanish, I could not speak to the Peruvians. The only contribution I could make was to sew clothes for the women and girls. Seniors were given priority so I began by measuring the old women and made dresses out of the material I had brought from California. As I helped each woman put their new dress on, they could not help but shed tears. They told me it was the first time that they had such beautiful dresses to wear. Since I had never learned how to make men's clothes, I was not able to meet their needs, even though they kept asking me to sew for them. I "talked" to them through my gestures. The children loved me and were always around while I was sewing. The villagers assumed that I was a tailor, which made me smile with pleasure. Later, I taught some of the Peruvian women how to sew; they learned fast and did very well. They got so excited when they could sew for themselves. This method of empowering the locals was part of Judy's overall plan.

One day, with the help of the translator, I told the locals that I was going to teach them qigong. The next morning, dozens of people were waiting for me to give them a treatment. I explained to them I was not there to treat their diseases, but to teach them something that if they practice daily would improve their health. The following morning, only twelve people showed up to learn "Turtle Longevity Qigong". I helped them practice every day and they benefited a lot from qigong.

Sometimes, I would go along with Judy as she visited the villagers. Then I came to understand the people's sufferings even more as I learned that people had no land, no house and no money. Most of the men worked one season a year in the cotton fields. The little money they received could only feed their families for a few months out of the year. The rest of the year, there were no jobs available. People were sometimes without food for several days and there were almost no vegetables to be found.

In an effort to lessen the food shortage, Judy took out a ten-year lease for four and a half acres of farmland to serve the 21 families of the village. The soil there was very rich and the weather was agreeable to farming. There, they would learn to grow grains and vegetables. She even hired an agriculture specialist to teach them how to farm and how to raise chickens and rabbits so that they can have a meat supply. Further, she even promised to financially support local high school students to go to college if they would study hard in the School of Agriculture. I introduced the idea to the Peruvians of growing beans, cucumbers and green vegetables all around their houses. The villagers were very happy to improve their life in these simple ways. As they distributed the harvests among themselves, they were all smiles and laughter echoed over the fields that Judy had provided them.

My stay in Humay was only for one month, but I witnessed Judy's love for the Peruvians and their love and respect for her. Whenever Judy's car passed by in the street, the villagers' eyes expressed their gratitude. She would hug the old people in their shabby clothes, and kiss the children just like a grandmother would. I could feel her happiness in aiding the people of Humay. Of course, she had to deal with many difficulties from the governmental officials and the many problems that can arise. A few times when she left town on business, her house was robbed. But, she took it all in stride and understood it was not personal. To me, Judy is a living Buddha. She has always served as a role model for me.

During my time there Judy arranged for me along with Evelyne and three other people to visit a few of the many places of interest. The Inca Ruins called "Tambo Colorado" was the first of my tours. The Incas were believed to have lived about one thousand years ago. We visited the Inca military base where the rooms for the soldiers and officers had walls but no roofs. The corridors and rooms all looked so similar that it seemed as if we were walking in a maze. We could hardly find our way out until we climbed to the top of the ancient base. While touring the grounds I became a bit scared because, for a short time, I lost sight of my friends. The place reminded me very much of Potala in Lhasa, Tibet. It was a magnificent sight!

One Sunday, Judy surprised me by having her translator, Margarita, take me to the sand dunes. In order to prepare myself for this special trip, I armed myself with a big pair of goggles that almost covered my whole face. I looked like a giant frog in human clothing. As we were driven into the desert in a sand dune jeep, I saw layers of sand dunes, both long and wide, that extended for miles and miles. The driver asked me if I liked adventures, to which I shouted, "Yes!" like a little girl.

I figured that meant the adventure had already begun, for I had no clue what would happen next. All of a sudden, he drove up the wall of a sand dune like a circus acrobat scrambling up a long rope. My whole body flopped onto one side until he drove the jeep down onto the flat ground again. In the next moment, the jeep flew up to the top of the next dune only to slide down another steep slope. I had to believe that the driver wanted to get back home alive, too! So if he was fine with this, then I would be fine with it. And again, the jeep went flying up to an even higher peak then dropped down to the bottom like a plane crashing to earth. My heart sank. Even though I was a bit nauseous, I did not want to show it. I knew if I stopped him, there would be no more adventures and I would regret it for the rest of my life. At 70 years old, why would I miss out on an opportunity like this! Then it occurred to me that this was a real adventure, but it might also be my last sand dune adventure this lifetime!

Sand slide in Peru (2003)

The next outing was sand skiing. I thought, why not try it. The driver warned me that if I took my feet off the board, I would be killed. When I began to ski, the board went so fast that I could hardly handle it. Next thing I knew I was tumbling head over heels as we came to a stop at our destination. My mouth, nose and ears were stuffed with sand. But, it was so much fun! The whole trip lasted an hour and a half. When we returned back home and I saw Judy, I kissed her to thank her for offering me such an amazing adventure. Then I hurried off to take a shower. I dumped more than a cupful of sand from my shoes. My ears, nose, face and hair were full of sand. I had never spent so much time cleaning myself in the bathroom before I could shower.

Close to the end of my stay in Humay, Judy asked a Peruvian woman, Viki, to take me to visit the islands where there was a wildlife preserve. Our small boat of 30 tourists went to famous Cadelabro, which was considered the beginning of the Nazca Lines (Nazca mountain range). The tour guide told us that the cactus design we saw etched on the side of the mountains was done in 200 BC. Another local legend said that it had been done by a priest hundreds of years ago to guide the local fishermen safely to shore. Whatever story was true the design was huge and beautiful.

Then we headed to the Ballestas Island, the natural habitat of various marine species. Numerous islands with strange shapes had arches so deep that we could not see the other end of the openings. They looked like deep caves! They were very mysterious and frightening. We saw countless birds, big and small in different sizes and colors, black, gray, white, brown, blue, red. It seemed that we had come to the kingdom of birds and that they were in the middle of a big mating celebration, as many varieties chattered, danced and sang. I had never been to a place so totally occupied by birds.

Mixed in with the birds, there were Humbolt Penguins, Inca Terns and thousands of sea lions, both old and young. While I had observed amazing sights of sea lions lying basking in the sun and roaring by the seashore in Alaska, it was totally different here. Within the groups of sea lions, there were several very big ones–nearly the size of African lions– that sported long hair. I wondered why they were so big and if they might be the mothers of all the young ones. The guide answered my question, "The biggest ones are the fathers of the youngsters. They come back annually to their 'families' and stay with them for only a short time before heading back to sea for another year. You notice that there is only one huge male sea lion in each group." Then I asked, "How many babies does a mother sea lion have in a year?" "Only one!" said the guide, "The mother has to feed the baby, teach it how to fish, and then she abandons it." The animals were peaceful, but the visitors in the boat became "crazy" as everyone was trying to get the best view to take pictures and videotapes! No one had discipline. Some stood on the seats, others climbed onto the back of the seats, and some even stood on the rim of the boat while their companions held on to their legs. As island after island passed by, their excitement grew and grew. Several times, our small boat nearly capsized!

When my one-month stay came to an end and I had to leave, it was hard to say good-byes to the local people. With my own eyes I saw that there were still many people living miserable lives. My heart was heavy because I realized that I had been able to do very little to help with fundamental changes. But, Judy's help was crucial for them. Eventually, as they strive for a better life, the people must learn to depend on themselves for the needed change.

Once I returned to Portland, I talked a lot about my trip with my qigong students. Encouraged by them, I wrote a booklet based on my diary and titled it, *30 Days In Humay, Peru*. I had 200 copies printed, which my students eagerly purchased. As a result, I was able to donate a good deal of money to the Peruvian cause.

Wisdom-and-Peace Wellness Center
Is Born in 2003

My retirement life was busy and happy. But Ping Ping and I always felt a call to establish an organization that would give many people access to qigong. We also wanted to find a convenient way for me to continue to give guidance to the certified teachers who lived all over the country. We decided if it were to be done, we would have to create it ourselves.

Ping Ping worked very hard establishing a qigong center in Vacaville, California. While still in graduate school, she designed the website, did the registration and other communication work. As I was inexperienced in business, I was unable to contribute much to the planning, developing, and administration of the center. In 2003, our new organization: "Wisdom- and-Peace Wellness Center" was legally established. We selected the name by combining my name with Ping Ping's. My first name translates as 'wisdom" and Ping Ping's name translates as "peace." When news of this center was announced in our qigong community, letters came from many qigong teachers expressing their warm greetings and best wishes for the success of our newborn wellness center.

Shortly after launching the wellness center, I was invited to a conference titled, "Cancer as a Turning Point" where I was asked to be a presenter. It was a great opportunity to introduce qigong to a wider audience given my personal history with cancer. After this event, we drew significant interest in qigong as a healing method. We received many questions concerning qigong in general, qigong workshops and our qigong trip to China. Our answers were prompt and detailed.

Leading Qigong trip to China (2008)

Another reason to establish the center was to support certified teachers and the unique challenges they encountered in their own teaching. A lot of qigong stories from different teachers came to me through the center. The positive feedback and experiences shared with me have served to reinforce my dedication to spreading qigong.

Our China trips have been the most demanding part of the center's work. Since the establishment of "Wisdom-and-Peace Wellness Center", we have successfully led multiple Qigong Trips to China. The major purpose of taking qigong practitioners to China is to further studies in qigong theories and ancient Chinese philosophy. Our schedule typically includes a week in Beijing, initially focusing on qigong studies. We invite well-known philosophers and qigong masters to enrich our knowledge of qigong, open our minds and raise our conscious level with their lectures. It is my privilege to translate for these speakers. During the remainder of the trip, we visit Beijing's ancient and most famous sights and then travel throughout China to tour other historic places as well. Each year, those who go on our China Trips tell me how much they have benefited from their time in China. Many say that it has been a life-changing journey. For me the lectures given by the masters are like torchlight brightening up my spiritual path.

Training Advanced Qigong Teachers & Qigong Lineage Holders

In order to carry on teaching the qigong forms that I have introduced to this country, it was absolutely necessary to train some advanced teachers to carry on the qigong lineage. After discussing this matter with some of the masters, we decided to choose some of the certified qigong teachers in this country to be trained as advanced teachers and lineage holders who would then be qualified to train and certify future teachers. This was of the utmost importance to me. In China, qigong has proven throughout thousands of years of history to be one of the most effective ways to improve the health and quicken the spiritual growth of humankind. Now America would have a system for passing on the wisdom and knowledge of qigong.

In 2002, after discussions with a leading group of the form in China, Teri Applegate was honored as the lineage holder of Chinese Soaring Crane Qigong in the United States. For many years when we were both at OCOM, Teri had been assisting me in teaching different levels of the form. Later, she taught the form herself, both to the OCOM students and to the general public. Having been inspired by my cancer survival through qigong, Teri started qigong programs for cancer patients at both of Portland's Providence hospitals. The response to her teaching was very positive. Not only did Teri perform the form well, but her knowledge of Chinese medicine theories and relevant philosophies had also reached a high level.

In 2008, Susan O'Toole was authorized as the first lineage holder of Chinese Soaring Crane Qigong in Europe. Also an acupuncturist, Susan continued to introduce the form to many Europeans, after she had been certified as a Level I teacher. She had studied its theories and philosophy very well and worked very hard to spread qigong awareness in Ireland and other European countries. Susan maintained a practice group at her home in Ireland for many years where her qigong teaching benefited many people.

Another form that I brought to the United States was Chinese Essence Qigong. Through my contact with Professor Chen, Fu Yin, I was authorized to train lineage holders after I moved to Vacaville. In 2006, I chose experienced certified teachers of Chinese Essence Qigong to complete the studies of theories for lineage-holder training: Jo Ann Albrecht, Teri Applegate, Judith Boice, Jennifer Daly, John Motley, Susan O'Toole and my daughter, Ping Ping. They were all very happy to be able to carry on this wonderful form and accepted responsibility to train teachers and lineage holders in the future.

Anything that benefits mankind should be inherited by the younger generations regardless of nationality. This is how culture and civilization develops. From my perspective, nothing belongs to any one individual. Qigong is a gift from the universe and it has such wonderful effects on mankind, physically, mentally and spiritually. Most of the world's people have not come to understand it yet, but I believe qigong will thrive in the years to come. We need to have more qigong teachers and lineage holders, so I hope all the qigong practitioners work diligently in their practice and their studies of the theories and philosophy. It is with confidence that I look to the future with many good teachers emerging in the qigong community to carry out the task of spreading qigong all over the world.

Lessons I Have Learned

I was blessed to have had the opportunity to study with more than ten very skilled well-known Chinese qigong masters. I believe this was all due to an arrangement by the universe. I was also fortunate to have made many friends in the qigong communities of China and of other countries. Truly, without their teaching and help, I could not have learned so much or achieved all that I have. I owe all credit to them.

During those years, I also experienced many spiritual tests and learned well from my mistakes. I also learned from mistakes made by some of the masters, as well as my qigong friends. These lessons have served to teach and nourish me along my spiritual path.

In the past, I was very naïve. I used to think that all my masters and teachers were perfect. I would obey whatever they told me to do and would believe in whatever they said. As I worked with them more closely, I found that sometimes their behavior did not match what they taught. One master cared too much about money and was sometimes dishonest. Once, when he was asked to treat a female student who had a paralyzed arm, he accepted her request even though he knew he did not have the power to heal her. During the treatments, he reached out his hand to gather qi from the universe and sent it to the patient's arm, making the patient's paralyzed arm move up and down. The patient, of course, was very happy. Actually he was using qi to move her arm, but the movement was only temporary. It was a trick. He charged the student for each treatment, but she did not improve. I knew that the master did not have the power to heal her paralysis, so I asked him why he pretended that he could. He said, "So what? We are leaving here soon anyway!" I was very upset by his attitude. Both in China and abroad, wherever he went to teach, he always suspected that the organizers who sponsored him were underpaying him. Eventually, nobody was willing to sponsor him. Once he said to me, "I know that you think I love money too much." I replied honestly, "Yes, I do." But, he did not change, despite being conscious of his own weakness. He did not show any signs of change, so many of his disciples, including myself, finally left him.

Another master had helped me spiritually a great deal when we were in China. But, when I accompanied him to America, he disappointed me. He was a married man, but he tried to persuade me to marry him and stay in America forever. He said, "Now that we are in the United States, we are completely free!" I flatly refused him. Then, he shifted his focus to a woman from Taiwan. That attempt also ended in failure. It was very hard for me to work with him for the rest of our trip. Finally, when I saw him off at the airport in New York, he did not even say good-bye to me. I did not care; I knew refusing him had been the right thing to do.

One day another one of my teachers told me that he was totally enlightened. I believed that he had reached a certain level of enlightenment, but not complete enlightenment. He went on to say that over three nights he had been shown the whole history of the universe projected on to the sky as if it were a movie screen and he now knew the source of all life. I thought it was a good thing for him to have received such a great gift from the universe, but, he never shared anything that I understood to be true. What I did notice, though, was that his ego finally consumed him. One day, he told me that he was Jesus Christ living in the present world. He claimed that every 2000 years only one person in the world could achieve total enlightenment. He said to me, "I am like Chairman Mao and you are like Premier Zhou, En Lai. You can assist me in my work!" I said, "I don't think so." I thought this was a big spiritual test for him and I was very sorry that he could not pass it. In one of his lectures, he even said to the audience, "As you climb up from the foot of the mountain with great difficulty, I am now at the top of the mountain looking down upon you." In his lectures, his huge ego was exposed and his behavior pushed many students away.

The fact is, that all the above-mentioned teachers were very good and very humble when they first began to teach. They brought great benefits to the public and helped to raise people's level of consciousness. We honored them for their hard work for their many accomplishments. In the qigong community, they had truly played important roles in developing a course for all of us. But, as they became more and more famous, they failed to remain spiritually disciplined. Their egos grew large and they did not behave well. They were pursuing money, fame, material comforts, even sex. When these things trap someone, they are blinded and go down the wrong path. The loss is great, both to them and to the public.

Among the better lessons that I have learned, were those from my qigong friends who had been very sick and had cultivated great healing powers through qigong practice. Some of them had even quit their original jobs to become professional healers. They helped many people improve their health. Yet, as they became well known and pursued their healing work, they failed to give enough attention to their own health. They did not practice enough qigong to rejuvenate themselves after healing others. As a result, they got sick again and some even died.

For instance, there was a Soaring Crane Qigong practitioner, Xiao Liu, who had suffered from late stage stomach cancer when he was in the navy. After he learned qigong, he practiced diligently. Within a short period of time, his latent potentials were cultivated, especially his healing powers, throughout the qigong community, he became very famous for his healing power, and many sick people sought him out for healing treatments. Later, he accepted the opportunity to work in Shenzhen, where people paid him very well. Soon he became very rich and began to pursue a luxurious lifestyle. In general, he was a good man. But once he became enchanted by money, he overworked himself and did not get enough rest. On one occasion, I suggested that he charge less for his healing, but he would not listen. Later, he did not spend enough time practicing qigong and his stomach cancer returned. He regretted that he had used too much of his qi in healing others and realized his mistakes only after he got sick. When he came back to Beijing for surgery, it was too late. Six months later, he died at the age of 28. What a pity!

It was true that qigong healings did have a great effect on some illnesses, but it was unwise for people to depend only on the healers to improve their health. Healers should also encourage patients to learn qigong themselves. For it is the practice of qigong itself that provides the best path to eliminate diseases and to maintain health.

Qigong is not only for health, but also for the development of the practitioner's spirituality. Healers cannot do that for their patients. Since I have learned so many lessons from my teachers and friends, I would never give treatments except in an emergency situation where immediate measures have to be taken. I know well that I am not young anymore and that I have already survived late stage breast cancer. I know that I have to focus on my own health. Once, I was encouraged to open a qigong clinic of my own, but I chose not to because I knew clearly that my mission was to teach qigong.

Over the past years, I have also learned not to pursue extrasensory powers. For a period of time after my diligent practice, I developed some extrasensory powers. I felt that I had a gift and got excited at the thought that one day I would become famous. It pumped up my curiosity, vanity

350

and ego. Later, I was grateful to all my teachers who criticized me for showing off my powers; they got me back on the right path. They reminded me that, *"To pursue Dao is the real goal of qigong practice!"*

Later, when I studied Buddhist and Daoist philosophies, I came to realize that all extrasensory powers are like the branches of a big tree. If too much energy is given to grow the branches, the tree itself will become distorted. Instead, we should focus on how to grow the trunk of the tree, so that it can be of great use, unlike the branches that are used for firewood. To grow the trunk is to pursue Dao and to achieve enlightenment. When a person wants only to pursue extrasensory powers, that person might fall into a negative trap and end up in danger.

Such was the case with one man I knew in Beijing who went to a teacher to have his third eye opened. The teacher did open his third eye, but he did not teach the man how to close it on his own. Actually, the teacher did not know how. At the very beginning, the man was excited that he was able to see many things that other people could not see. Not long after that the teacher, having collecting a lot of money from those seeking extrasensory powers, left Beijing. Later he was nowhere to be found. After a while, the man began to suffer, as his third eye would open against his will. He told me that at times when he was having dinner, all of his family members would become skeletons who were using chopsticks and eating out of bowls. What a horrible scene to witness! On other occasions when he was outdoors, those walking past him in the street appeared to be skeletons. He worried a lot and tried in vain, to close his third eye. His health suffered and he could not work anymore. He feared he would suffer the rest of his life.

Another important lesson that I gained from others' experience was that no one should ever alter the qigong forms that they practice. It is important that a qigong master, who either inherits from an ancestor or a master or channels it directly from the universe, must maintain that qigong form. The form must have been proven to be effective through many years of practice by thousands of practitioners. A certified teacher should be the only trainer and those without certification should never teach qigong.

More than 25 years ago, when I was teaching qigong in Arizona, a man from Hong Kong was teaching Chinese Soaring Crane Qigong in Chicago. He claimed that he was a disciple of the form's originator and got forty American students to join his class. After a month of his teaching, nearly all his students had developed headaches, other pain and qi stagnation in their bodies. Once the students began talking about their problems, the teacher found an excuse to abandon them and to return to Hong Kong. His students were suffering, but no one in Chicago could do anything to help. One of those students found out that I was teaching Soaring Crane Qigong in Arizona and she paid me a visit to tell me about the problems in her class.

After listening to her story, I wanted to find out what had caused their symptoms, so I asked her to perform the Five Routines. I noted many mistakes with her movements. When I quizzed her, she said she had done the routines exactly the way her teacher had taught them. I was shocked at how wildly the teacher had changed the forms. Knowing that there are altogether 108 movements in the Five Routines, I would estimate that nearly half of them were changed or distorted. I then instructed this student to call her fellow classmates and tell them all to stop practicing as soon as possible, to avoid even more suffering. I went on to explain to her that I did not believe that their teacher had learned the form from Master Zhao, to say nothing of being his disciple. I personally knew all of his disciples in China and I had never heard of this person. The next day, this woman came to me and reported each student in the class had paid $400 to the teacher. What a loss, but they had to give it up! My reply to her was, "Which is more important, money or health?" Later, I learned that they had listened to me, so I felt relieved.

Throughout my years of teaching qigong, I was very strict with my students and always encouraged them to study the theories and philosophy along with the form. In order to pass on the correct methods to the generations to come, all of us must have the right attitude towards qigong. By never changing the forms or by never freely mixing one form with another or inventing something new when you are not ready, it will keep qigong in its purest state. Qigong is not something to play around with, as the qi is very powerful. Qigong should only be practiced with diligence and accuracy. Qigong is a kind of sign language we can use to communicate with the universe; qigong is the science of self-realization!

From all that I have related, you can see that to progress on a spiritual path is not easy. We have to go through many tests, even from our own teachers. We should remain humble all the time, learning from others how to develop ourselves as much as possible. Yet, when we find anything wrong with others, even our own teachers, we should speak the truth! We need to be aware that we are our own masters.

"Return of the Matrilineal Society"

On our China trip during the summer of 2005, our highly respected spiritual teacher, Professor Yu, Xiao Fei, gave us a lecture titled "The Return of the Matrilineal Society". This talk had an especially great impact on me, as well as many other people. Professor Yu talked of a more compassionate way of living together in our societies; he believed we could change by leaving the more patriarchal mentality of possessing and warring

Professor Yu, Xiao Fei lecturing (2005)

behind us. He told us there were predictions that this transformation would begin by the year 2012, as the feminine energy increased globally.

Now, I would like to share with you some important points of his lecture in 2005:

The essential premise of Chinese culture is the balance of Yin and Yang. The Chinese people look at the world and their overall history in the same manner, as transference between Yin and Yang. Human beings from 3,000-5,000 years ago lived a matrilineal way of life, which was more Yin. Over the more recent 3,000 years, a patrilineal society was increasingly established. Since that time, the patrilineal culture has been the major trend of most societies. During this long historical period, the defects and shortcomings of patrilineal culture have been witnessed. It is important to note that the Chinese people do not think that the society will stay in either matrilineal culture or patrilineal culture forever. Instead, they will continually cycle, from one to another

In ancient China, predictions were made that the 21st century would be the turning period from a predominant patrilineal society, to a stronger matrilineal culture. With such changes underway, countries like China and India have much to contribute to the world because they have inherited cultural information from their matrilineal societies of 3,000 years ago. In the Chinese culture, it has been the Daoist philosophy that has carried the matrilineal culture. Even though matrilineal culture passed on like a hidden current, sometimes even distorted or suppressed, it has survived throughout history. One of the greatest Daoist philosophers in ancient China was Lao Zi, who claimed that what he inherited and promoted was the matrilineal culture of 2,500 years before him. His famous writing "Dao De Jing" basically was in praise of matrilineal culture.

The same has held true in India's long history. India, China's neighboring country is a huge territory that is densely populated. In recent years, India has been developing very fast. Historically, there has been a close relationship and much cultural exchange between these two countries. Sakymuni was one of the greatest religious leaders in ancient India. He founded the Buddhist philosophies that became very popular in India at that time. The basic teachings of Sakymuni are representative of a matrilineal culture and Buddhism. Later, as the matrilineal culture found it difficult to survive in India, Buddhism was introduced to China and it has spread throughout the whole world. Both China and India have a lot to offer for the returning matrilineal culture. The politicians and philosophers of China and India have come to realize that these two countries are going to play very important roles in the future development of the world. Other indigenous cultures have passed on their more matrilineal philosophical and spiritual practices, such as with Native Americans and some African tribes. From their ancient teachings, many contributions can be passed down generations to aid the contemporary world in significant ways.

One of the things that will happen during this change is the collapse of existing marriage systems. In the ancient matrilineal society, women were the major force of the society, holding decisive roles in public matters within the community. Communal marriage was a common practice at that time. Elder women of the community served as the leaders. With the establishment of patrilineal society about

3,000 years ago, marriage became more systematic. Along with it, a key concept was that of "ownership" of property. A man was allowed to marry one or more women and he legally possessed his wife or wives. This gave rise to private ownership, from which the concept of whole societies originated. In order to possess more, one country would invade another country; it all started from the patrilineal marriage system.

Lately, it has become more and more evident that a large number of young women from all over the world, are reluctant to marry. More so, for the women who enjoy high social standing and make sufficient money to support themselves and their families. Women have proven their leadership abilities and many hold high positions in society. In increasing numbers of countries throughout the world, there are women who have even been elected as legislators, premiers, even as presidents. This phenomenon will continue to grow and expand as time passes by.

In order to keep harmony between people, religions and nations, it is important that we embrace tolerance, a key concept in the matrilineal culture. It has proven very difficult to reverse the practice of being intolerant. Be it individuals or entire countries, much trouble arises because of intolerance. In this century, we must learn to be more accepting and open to different ways of being. If we learn and accept this, we can have a peaceful and happy life. Otherwise, life will be difficult for us.

In the West, many deeply religious people think that we should only believe in one God. When they visit China and see many statues of all sorts of gods in the temples, they think our religion is very backward. It is said that in India, there are more statues of gods or goddesses than the actual population. In general, Asians are more tolerant, owing to their cultural influences. We would never say that if you do not believe in my god, you are evil. Some religions are exclusive in their teachings; this must change. Otherwise, the conflict will give rise to more and more disasters throughout the world. What we can do now is to teach people about the matrilineal concepts.

Chinese medicine, which respects nature will become more popular with a return to matrilineal culture. Nature has provided sufficient nutrients for us. Man-made supplements may not be necessary and may even give rise to disease. For instance, many people take vitamins, which are extracts from nature's plants or fruits. Chinese medicine believes that to take food in its natural form is the best form of nutrition. Instead of taking chemical compositions, the Chinese medicine doctors use herbs, because they are natural. They can be easily made into tea, pills, or granules. Herbs function differently than chemical compounds, rarely causing side effects. Westerners are skeptical of Chinese medicine, but they are willing to have surgeries and take chemicals in the form of pills. Herbal formulas are basically for tonifying (enriching the qi and blood) or for releasing diseases. The original taste of the herbs is important, because each taste has its own functions. For instance, if the patient has heart heat, he might take herbs with a bitter taste to reduce the heat. Sweet flavor is used to build up the digestion, but there is no need to eat sugar for that. A sweet tasting herb in its natural form has the power required.

Chinese medicine has the goal of bringing one's whole being in to harmony or balance. In the four different seasons, a good Chinese medicine doctor will prescribe differently for the same disease. In order to maintain good health, one should also keep the body in balance. In summer, the qi and blood come to the surface from deeper within the body. It is very easy to have diarrhea if one eats too much raw or cold food. A remedy would be to eat warm food. On the contrary, in winter when the weather is very cold, the qi and blood go deep inside the body, therefore it is warm inside and it is okay to take in something cold for balance. To live in harmony with the universe, is the key to good health.

Another matrilineal concept is the principle that we term "win/win". Conversely, the patrilineal practice has been to win at the expense of others—even by force if need be. Nowadays, we promote the idea of "win/win" in business so that the result benefits both parties. When it comes to natural resources, we should also gradually remove them from nature, instead of hording them. When we take wood from the forest, trees need to be planted as replacement. We should always seek to achieve balance in all that we do and be gentle with our Earth. Imbalance will bring about nature's destruction. We must learn to forego immediate reward and think to the future. This, too, is a matrilineal concept. The most basic principle of a matrilineal culture is to live in harmony with everything.

As we turn to more matrilineal ways of living, qigong will become more and more popular. The first consideration in qigong practice is to give. But, we are programmed with the idea of possessing. For growth in our spiritual practice, we need to give and to contribute. Without changing the need for possessing, there can be no achievement made in qigong practice. With an increasing matriarchal mindset, more people will have their intuition cultivated, especially women. This is not prejudice against men, but women tend to be more intuitive. With the dominance of patrilineal thinking in the past, the reliance on intuition decreased and people became more hypocritical. That is why Lao Zi said, 'We must return to our origin and to our innocence. We should return to the state of infancy.' With the return of intuition, more and more people will be attracted to qigong.

Both, in our daily life and in our qigong practice, we should absorb the essence of both the sun and the moon. The moon has a great influence on people. People should learn to absorb qi from both the heavens and the earth. Many Chinese qigong practitioners wear cotton-soled shoes so that they absorb more earth qi. Earth qi is more important to prolong one's life span. People typically pay attention to the physical form and ignore the unseen part of a human being. There are actually three layers of life in a person, the physical body (including the intellectual mind), the qi body and the spirit. The physical body is the shallowest layer, to which people pay a lot of attention. They do physical exercise and eat good food to nourish themselves. Daoist philosophers said that if there is any problem in the physical body, the root must be in a much *deeper layer. For instance, when you find a tumor or cancer in the physical body, it is a manifestation of a problem from another level of life, long before the present finding. Actually many years before any disease is found in the physical body, there have been changes at a deeper level of your life. Chinese medicine doctors diagnose diseases at a deeper level. For example, if a person feels tired and there are no other obvious symptoms other than a very dry tongue in the morning upon waking, it might mean the person's kidney qi or yin is insufficient. The Chinese medicine doctor would tonify the kidney qi or yin of this patient. It is important to take care of the symptoms and not wait until a disease shows up on the physical level.*

In terms of the physical body, the most important part is the spine; its state determines the state of health. Adjusting and exercising the spine in many qigong forms is a very important way to take care of the spine. The qi shows the actual state of a person's health, yet qi has no form. Qi circulates in the meridians carrying the blood throughout the body. Qi and consciousness are closely related. Perhaps you have wondered how the meridian system was discovered. Li, Shi Zen, a great Chinese doctor from ancient China, said that the meridian system could be seen only through one's intuition. In the future, it will be a very common phenomenon for people to be more intuitive.

In every living thing, there is a qi layer to life. When you prepare your food, use the freshest source. Fresh fruit or vegetables cannot be substituted by taking vitamins, for they have lost the qi of the original plants. Qigong practitioners should know to use only fresh foods or fruit so as to get more qi from them. People living in the countryside are able to pick up the freshest food more than city dwellers and their health is generally better. Of course, it would be much better if everyone could eat organic food. Should you need to take tonics, it would be better to take something that grows high in the mountains in very cold weather, such as cordyceps[22]. When you cook soup, you only need to put in a tiny bit and it is very beneficial to your

---

[22] A species of fungus called *dong chong xia cao*

health. Both qigong practice and Chinese medicine are for the second layer of life, the qi layer.

People actually should be living up to 120 years old. According to the recorded Daoist teachings, many Daoist practitioners lived to be 145 and up to 175 years old in ancient China. There is another deeper layer of life, which does not pertain to Chinese medicine or ordinary qigong. To pursue the Dao is to work on this layer of life, the highest spiritual practice. As qigong practitioners, we are on our way to that level. Chinese people term it qi but the written character is different than that of qi. On the top of the character is "Nothing" and "Heart" lies below. The character's meaning is to use your heart to contemplate the emptiness. People cannot feel this "Qi". For once you have attained the Dao you are enlightened. In contrast, the qi in the meridians can be felt during qigong practice or an acupuncture treatment. Qigong can benefit our health and prolong our life, to the point that we are not using up the yuán qì we were given at conception. The reality is, most people die before they use up their yuán qì[23]. They get sick frequently, or have a serious accident or disease, and die. Qigong and Chinese medicine can help people properly manage the use of their yuán qì.

But, to pursue the Dao is another thing. The practitioner's aim should be to attain the Dao and get enlightened. Throughout the world, there have been many spiritual practitioners who attained the Dao and thus, enlightenment. There were many reported in ancient times and there are still some today. In Beijing twenty years ago, there was a building where more than fifteen families lived. Down in the basement, there lived an old tailor who had no family. His work was good and he charged people very little. The people in the neighborhood liked him a lot. During one Spring Festival, every family in the building invited this kind old man to be their guest for dinner on the eve of the Spring Festival. He promised every family that he would be there. The next day as people were out talking,

---

[23] "Innate" or "pre-natal" qi as distinguish from acquired qi that a person may develop during their lifetime

they all mentioned that this old man had had dinner with them. All fifteen families had him at the same time! They were all surprised by this phenomenon and rushed to the basement to talk to him. But, they only found a big lock on the outside of his door. He was gone!

The old tailor must have been an immortal that had attained the Dao and was able to materialize in physical form. This is the highest level of the Chinese spiritual practice. Also in India, there are many immortals that have attained enlightenment. Many have left this world, but some are still here taking care of the world. It is said that they will come to teach us once we are qualified to be taught. I believe that we will have such opportunities if we prepare ourselves well. Especially, in light of the return of the matrilineal culture, more people will be ready to receive their teachings.

Life Seems to Start All Over Again

After finishing writing this book, I went back to China for a visit in April, 2012. For a long time, I had wished I could go back to Guizhou when I could still sit for a long train ride. So I did. When I got to Guiyang railway station, my sixth sister's third daughter, Chen, Ling and her husband, Wang, Hua Rong came to meet me. The city had changed so much that I could not find any trace of the old town. There were tall buildings lining the sides of the busy streets with high mountains surrounding the city. My 91 year-old brother-in-law, Chen, Qi Shen and his other three daughters and their families welcomed me with great enthusiasm. They took me to the famous Huangguoshu Waterfall, the biggest waterfall in Asia, to Miaozhai, the biggest Miao stockade village deep in the high mountains, and to many other places of interest. Wherever I went, I often saw many Miao people wearing their beautiful traditional costumes and carrying bamboo baskets full of fresh vegetables for the markets. It reminded me of the local fairs I used to go to when I was a child. The smiling round faces of the Miao women brought back the image of the Miao woman who carried me back home from the mountains after I had lost my way running away from home. As I was looking at the mysterious high mountains in the clouds, memories of childhood kept appearing in my mind. Beautiful authentic Miao folk songs echoing in the air between the mountains carried me back to the Miao Moon Festival Wedding Ceremony I had attended. The music from the broadcast was not from the thrilling voices of the young boys and girls standing on top of the mountains expressing their love for one another, but it still touched my heart. I could not help entering a local music store and buying a CD of Miao folk songs. When we came across a square where visitors could rent Miao costumes and have pictures taken, my brother-in-law put on a "Miao Chief" robe and posed for us. I had never seen him so active and so funny before. My grandnephew, Hai Hai gave me a surprise birthday party at the very luxurious restaurant run by him and his partners. What a wonderful time I had with my sister's family in Guiyang!

In front of the Jiaxing Trinity Hospital (2012)
Sister-in-law, me, 4th sister and 5th brother

After returning to Hangzhou, I began preparing for our biggest family reunion. About 60 family members including four generations of the Chen family gathered together first in our hometown, Jiaxing and then in Hangzhou. The age range was from two years old to 92. We came from Guiyang, Xi'an, Zhengzhou, Jiaxing, Hangzhou, Beijing, Taiwan and the United States of America. Two of the older people had not met one another for over sixty years. You could imagine how happy they were to meet again in their nineties. It was the first time for some younger family members to participate in our family reunion. The four days together gave us sufficient time to share our life stories. We chatted to our hearts' content and became more familiar with one another. We sang and danced like schoolboys and schoolgirls. The reunion and our birthday celebration were full of harmony and happiness. The family paid a special visit to the new "Jiaxing Trinity Hospital" that had expanded on the hospital that my parents had built. The leaders of the new hospital welcomed us with a reception. They praised our parents highly for establishing the hospital. Wu, Fang, the director said, "Dr. Chen, Shao En and his wife Lin, Guo Rei founded this hospital 80 years ago. It has served thousands of people. Its contribution to the city of Jiaxing is greatly appreciated by the people and the government. They were role models for us to follow. Their loving hearts touched many generations. We are going to celebrate the 80th anniversary of the Trinity Hospital in October this year."

Four generation family reunion - Hangzhou (2012)

The family reunion ended successfully. Everybody was happy and found it hard to separate. Li, Yuan, my grandnephew, spoke for all of us when he said to the whole family, "I belong to the fourth generation of this family and I teach at the Xi'an University. Before the family reunion, I only had some vague ideas about my family history. The four days' reunion enriched me with the knowledge about our older generations. They were all hard working people and made excellent contributions to society. I am very much touched by their loving spirit. I hope all of us younger generations learn from them and catch up with them!" His short speech won lots of applause. We, of the older generations wish for them to live up to our expectations.

We parted in Hangzhou on the last day of May. My second daughter Ping Ping, her husband Eric, my nephew You You, his wife Feng Lan and I took a bullet train to Beijing. It took us only 6 hours to get to our destination! I still remember that 60 years before it took me 36 hours to get to Beijing from Suzhou by train. How time flies and how fast technology has advanced!

As I had planned, on June 2, all my close friends in Beijing were invited to my birthday dinner party at a restaurant. More than 30 guests showed up. I began my welcome speech saying, "I have been wishing for many years to have this opportunity to express my most hearty thanks to you all, my benefactors! I would rather call this dinner party a party of gratitude than a birthday party. I should say that without your help, I would not have been able to live to see this day. As you all know 30 years ago I nearly died of late stage cancer. It is you who reached out with your helping hands and made it possible for me to get through this difficult stage of life. At that time, I wanted so much to come back to UIBE from Dalian, but the leaders of the Dalian institute would not let me go. After my cancer surgery, President Sun, Wei Yan comforted me by saying, 'Only focus on the recovery of your health and do not worry about anything else.' Mr. Miao, Jun Qing, the head of the Personnel Department of UIBE, said to me at that time, ' I will get you back from Dalian one way or another even though you are sick today. If you die tomorrow, we will hold a memorial gathering for you.' On hearing this, I burst into tears." I also told the touching stories about how my old schoolmate Gu, Ze Qing and my sister-in-law Li, Zhi Lan and her husband Hao, Zhong Zheng had hosted me when I could hardly walk ten steps in a row. Xiao Ming, now already in his forties, was the little nephew who accompanied me to the qigong practice site on cold winter

Dinner party in Beijing with lifelong friends (2012)

mornings. I pointed at him saying, "Look, what a successful man he is now and how happy their families are today. Everything that goes around comes around." I also reported what I had done abroad and how much help and support I had received from my friends both at home and abroad. When I was telling these stories, some listeners were shedding tears. I also encouraged all my friends to practice qigong as it had benefited me greatly for the past 30 years, both physically and spiritually.

Everybody present was very happy and we laughed and talked while enjoying the delicious meal. After dinner, Master Ma, Cheng Kai stood up and offered to teach Super Energy Clapping Hands. His loud voice and his Guinness-record clapping thundered through the restaurant as he was chanting, "Chao Chang Neng Liang ...". The whole group joined him enthusiastically. The party of gratitude ended in excitement!

The rest of my time in Beijing was spent mainly with qigong masters and qigong friends discussing the big changes in the world. We were excited to meet again. We all felt lucky to have been living at this time of history to experience the evolution of our mother earth, the ascending energy, the shift of consciousness of humankind and to welcome the coming "heaven-on-earth" in the new millennium. Thanks to the constant qigong practice for years, we were able to understand what the big changes would mean to the world and how these changes would help other people prepare for the new epoch. We encouraged one another to prepare ourselves to cope with the coming high vibration frequencies and to help as many people as possible in times of difficulty.

As many know, a polar shift has been going on. There have been many drastic events coming up almost everywhere in the world. Some people say that it will be the end of the world. I disagree. I do not believe this. But, we can call it "the end of the old world" as we know it. To be prepared physically is necessary in terms of going through the transitional phase, but it is the change of consciousness and our spiritual attitude that will be the real challenge. We must be positive in our thinking, talking and acting. In times of difficulties, we all benefit from supportive groups of good, close, loving friends who generate positive and loving energy. This is a time for the members of the planetary family to bring forth their best nature and share their love and care for one another.

According to the Maya calendar, there are 25,900 years in a cycle. The Maya calendar forecasts the end of the present cycle is December 21, 2012. As the current cycle reaches its final phase, the Earth will draw closer to the light region of the galaxy. Earth is progressing toward a higher orbital frequency. The return of the light at this time in history is having intense effects on our consciousness and growing spiritual awakening. As the light vibration continues to increase, people will gain health, understanding, wisdom, and spirituality. So, it is important that we use this historical moment well, and pay close attention to the transformative value of prayer, meditation, qigong, body work, all forms of physical and emotional clearing and being of service in order to heal ourselves.

We qigong practitioners should know that qigong has been a heavenly gift to open our minds and to connect us to the universe and to bring us closer to the Dao. Through qigong practice we receive the light from the universe to heal ourselves not merely on the physical level, but more importantly, to purify our minds and souls so that we become clear about the true meaning of life, which is to serve mankind and raise our conscious level.

My visit to China has greatly recharged me with positive energy. I feel that life seems to start all over again. There is no past, no present and no future. When is the ending of life? There is no ending. Even though I am 80 years old in terms of earthly age, I have just begun to see a glimpse of the universe and to know the true meaning of life. My deadly disease brought me to the practice of Qigong and that has paved the way to my good health, stable emotions and spiritual freedom. I am grateful to the universe for putting me through a life of hardships, wars, political pressures and diseases. I survived all these tests! I feel blessed I am here to welcome the new "heaven-on-earth" millennium. My heart is full of joy that my dream world is coming. I love to see people's lives filled with happiness, harmony and love. It is my hope that all my dear readers take time to pursue a spiritual practice. You will be blessed by the universe all your life. Life truly is always smiling!

Acknowledgement

In the end, I would like to express my sincere thanks to my siblings, especially my fourth sister Yi Xian who helped me grow in a healthy way. To all my teachers who brought me onto the spiritual path, the universe thanks you and I thank you. To Teri Applegate, who assisted me for many years at OCOM, who did the initial editing for this book and still works tirelessly teaching qigong to cancer patients, I bless you for coming into my life, and staying. To my son-in-law, Eric Orr, Ping Ping's husband, who navigated the electronic publishing of this book, you are always in my heart. To my daughter Ping Ping I owe an extra debt of gratitude for making time in her busy life to beautifully format all my previous books, for assisting me in all aspects of my qigong career, for planning all our qigong tours to China, and for creating with me the Wisdom and Peace Wellness Center. And, finally, I would like to express my special thanks to my spiritual sister, Leigh Dean, who made the paperback edition of this book possible.

38235967R00224

Made in the USA
Middletown, DE
06 March 2019